Political Negotiation

Political Negotiation

A Handbook

Jane Mansbridge and Cathie Jo Martin
Editors

BROOKINGS INSTITUTION PRESS
Washington, D.C.

Library of Congress Cataloging-in-Publication data

Political negotiation : a handbook / Jane Mansbridge and Cathie Jo Martin, editors.
    pages   cm
  Includes bibliographical references and index.
  ISBN 978-0-8157-2729-3 (pbk. : alk. paper) — ISBN 978-0-8157-2730-9 (epub) — ISBN 978-0-8157-2731-6 (pdf) 1. Political planning—United States. 2. United States—Politics and government—Decisionmaking. 3. Decisionmaking—Political aspects—United States. 4. Polarization (Social sciences)—Political aspects—United States. 5. Political culture— United States. I. Mansbridge, Jane J., editor. II. Martin, Cathie J., editor.
  JK468.P64P657 2015
  302.30973—dc23   2015019159

9 8 7 6 5 4 3 2 1

Typeset in Sabon

Composition by Westchester Publishing Services

Contents

Acknowledgments

This volume expands on and revises a report published in 2013 by the American Political Science Association, "Negotiating Agreement in Politics." The APSA report drew from all major subfields in the discipline of political science. The report could not fully cover the rich insights of those subfields; for example, given our mandate to reflect on the US situation, we emphasized the comparative politics of advanced countries rather than studies of developing countries. Moreover, we could not represent all theoretical traditions, such as rational choice and historical institutionalism. Yet we aimed to be as comprehensive as possible and are deeply grateful to the participants in the five working groups of the APSA Task Force, who were willing to think beyond the confines of their subfields. We particularly thank Kimberly Mealy, Michael Brintnall, and Steven Smith at APSA for their dedication and help in this project. Chase Foster provided exemplary research assistance, while Bruce Jackan and Juanne Zhao of the Ash Center for Democratic Governance and Innovation at the Harvard Kennedy School were extremely helpful in the early stages. We are grateful to many institutions and their supportive staff for making this project possible. We thank the Ash Center for supporting the Cognitive Bias Working Group, the U.S. Working Group, and part of the European Working Group; the Centre for the Study of Democratic Institutions at the University of British Columbia for supporting the Normative Working Group; the Weatherhead Center for International Affairs at Harvard University for supporting the International Relations Working Group; and APSA for supporting part of the European Working Group as well as a meeting of representatives of all working groups at the 2013 Midwest Political Science Association annual meeting. In particular we thank APSA for publishing the original report and Liane Piñero-Kluge for her commitment, effort, and goodwill in the publication process. As always, Cathie Jo Martin thanks her husband and children—Jim, Julian, and Jack Milkey—for their love and choice one-liners about the art of politics.

Introduction

This book begins a long-overdue discussion of the institutional conditions that facilitate successful political negotiation within nations. Starting with an analysis of the cognitive mistakes the human brain is likely to make in negotiating situations, it draws from the experiences of national legislatures, including U.S. Congress, and from sixty-five years of study in international relations. It concludes that at least five conditions facilitate successful political negotiation:

1. the capacity to link issues and make trades on issues on which different parties place differing values
2. the capacity to agree on basic facts
3. the capacity for each party to reveal relevant information to the others
4. the capacity to forge informal and ongoing personal relationships
5. the capacity to negotiate in private

Subjecting these conditions to scrutiny in the light of democratic ideals, we also conclude that in the right contexts all of the conditions pass democratic tests.

Our investigation opens with the puzzling breakdown in U.S. Congress today. The United States used to be viewed as a land of broad consensus and pragmatic politics, in which sharp ideological differences were largely absent. Today politics is dominated by intense party polarization and limited agreement among elected representatives on even basic facts about policy problems and solutions. Americans pride themselves on their community spirit, civic engagement, and dynamic society. Today, however, our national political institutions often stifle the popular desire for policy innovations and political reforms. The separation of powers helps explain why Congress has a difficult time taking action. Yet many countries with equally severe institutional hurdles to simple majoritarian rule still engage in political negotiations that yield results reflecting the interests and values of broad majorities.

What has happened? In the United States, Congress faces greater structural obstacles to decisionmaking today than it has at any time in the past century. What can be done? Political negotiation is part of the answer. Yet political negotiation, although often essential to democratic rule, is not easy. The human brain makes mistakes that stymie even good-faith efforts to compromise. The institutions we design can either magnify or correct these mistakes. Using evidence from both the recent failures of U.S. politicians to forge political pacts and success stories from the United States, Europe, and international relations, this book offers practical advice on how political parties with diverse interests can often (although certainly not always) overcome their disagreements to negotiate win-win solutions.

The Human Brain

Although many attempted negotiations fail because the interests of the parties are fundamentally incompatible, this book focuses on "tractable" situations, in which outcomes exist that could make all parties to a negotiation better off than they are now. We use the term *negotiation myopia* to describe one or both sides' inability to see these potential gains. This myopia produces two kinds of cognitive mistakes that are especially common in failed negotiations. *Fixed-pie bias* typically blinds participants to possible gains from a negotiation; almost half the time they do not see the potential compatibility of their interests. *Self-serving bias* also often produces impasse even when both parties could gain from a deal. The scholarship in commercial negotiation and cognitive psychology, which is easily transferable to political negotiation, identifies these and other cognitive and emotional barriers to successful negotiation and also suggests practices to combat those barriers.

Structural Obstacles to Negotiation in U.S. Congress

The parties in Congress are more polarized now than at any time since 1906. The causes include the realignment of the two major political parties after President Johnson signed the 1964 Civil Rights Act, the closely matched electoral strength of the two parties since 1980, and the combination of growing income inequality with the growing importance of fundraising in politics. Recent studies indicate that neither nonpartisan redistricting nor open primaries is likely to help much. Campaign-finance reform could probably reduce polarization, but significant reform in this realm is unlikely in the near future.

Overcoming Negotiation Myopia

Even in conditions of polarization, however, procedural arrangements for resolving political strife—called here the *rules of collective political engagement*—can reduce myopia and augment the potential for deliberative negotiation. These arrangements include the careful incorporation of technical expertise, repeated interactions between participants, penalty defaults if a negotiation fails, and the ability to speak freely in off-the-record private meetings. Countries that incorporate these arrangements into their political institutions can often achieve cooperation and compromise in the normal practice of politics. Even without such ongoing institutions to facilitate cooperation, countries can adopt these rules on an ad hoc basis to produce more successful negotiations on specific issues.

Facilitating Negotiation in Congress

Institutions matter. Political actors need to negotiate in the United States more than in Great Britain, for example, because the U.S. Constitution, with its separation of powers and its checks and balances, generates many veto points that keep simple majorities from ruling. Because of all these veto points, members of Congress must negotiate at least partial agreement not only within their parties but also across party lines within each house, between the two houses, and with the president. A close look at Congress reveals which practices facilitate negotiated agreements in this setting. Repeated interactions across party lines, private spaces for deliberation, and what we call *penalty defaults* all facilitate agreement. Congress also has the capacity to bring several issues or facets of an issue into a negotiation so that the participants can trade items that are low priority for one of them but high priority for the other (*integrative negotiation*). Currently, however, the parties in Congress are less willing than parties in other advanced industrial countries to rely on nonpartisan technical expertise.

Is Negotiation "Democratic"?

In most democracies, negotiation is as important as majority rule. Yet many citizens and democratic thinkers are inevitably suspicious of deals made behind closed doors. *Deliberative negotiation* describes the kind of political negotiation most likely to produce agreements that encompass the interests and values of broad majorities while remaining compatible with democratic ideals. Subjecting the rules of collective political engagement to democratic scrutiny identifies the conditions in which closed-door arenas for discussion, long incumbencies, and various forms of side payments can be compatible with democratic ideals. These conditions include low levels of corruption, warranted constituent trust, citizens authorizing the negotiation process in advance, and retrospective transparency in rationale.

Lessons from International Negotiation

In political science, international relations is the only field that has studied negotiation in depth. Drawing from the experiences of negotiations among nations, international relations provides a body of wisdom that can help improve political negotiation more broadly. Yet lessons from this field are rarely adapted to domestic political venues for either studying or inspiring practice. Some of the many lessons learned are compatible with the rules of collective political engagement derived from studies of Congress and of European nations. They include the following:

—Link issues in which each party gains on matters of high priority and sacrifices on matters of low priority.

—Engage in joint fact-finding or rely on nonpartisan expertise for the factual basis of negotiations.

—Reveal information to others on your preferences and on the facts you have regarding the topic of negotiation. Actively request information from the other side on their preferences and their knowledge of the facts.

—Negotiate behind closed doors.

Conclusion

The lessons learned for political negotiation from various sources—psychology experiments, commercial negotiations, studies of U.S. Congress and other legislatures in democratic countries, and international relations—are remarkably consistent. They show that when polarization and negotiation myopia pose major problems, deliberative negotiation is a good solution. In deliberative negotiation, the parties share information, link issues, and engage in joint problem solving. In that way they can both discover and create possibilities of which they were unaware before the process began. They can also use their collective intelligence constructively, for the good of both parties, of the citizens, and of the country. This book explores these possibilities in-depth, drawing on research from all the major fields in political science.

"Politics *is* negotiation," quipped Tom Edsall after a meeting of one of the expert groups convened for this book, whose members for the first time systematically analyzed the structure, incentives, and conditions of success for political negotiation. Political negotiation is indeed central to national, state, and city democratic politics. Domestic political negotiation also differs from both international political negotiation and business negotiation in important respects. Political negotiation involves public or common goods more frequently than does commercial negotiation. It also has a higher percentage of "mission-driven" (internally motivated) actors. The political arena often has a greater capacity than the commercial one to link a wide variety of unrelated issues. Many negotiators in the political arena depend for reelection on voters, interest groups, and other nonstate actors. The likelihood of ongoing interaction among the actors in domestic political negotiation is higher than in most commercial or international negotiation. Yet the overall field of political negotiation has rarely been studied, and political negotiation on domestic issues is largely uncharted territory. This book introduces that field and provides an initial exploration of that territory.

The Genesis and Evolution of This Book

The analyses that follow in this volume are the result of an extraordinary iterative collaboration of some of the best thinkers in negotiation theory, cognitive psychology, American government studies, European comparative government, normative democratic theory, and international relations. Groups organized around these themes met together for a weekend (or in one case more often) and worked by e-mail on their subsequent drafts. The different groups varied in the members' degree of involvement after the initial meeting, but in every group the lead authors produced a first draft of the chapter, got feedback from the other members of the group, and took responsibility for the final product. The process would never have been possible without the vehicle of a presidential task force of the American Political Science Association and the support of that association, whose presidential task forces are designed to bring to the public the best of what political science knows on a subject of political importance.

CHAPTER ONE

Negotiating Political Agreements

CATHIE JO MARTIN

The recent gridlock in U.S. Congress may well be a metaphor for the erosion of cooperation in contemporary political life. We Americans often value cooperation at the community level, but our national public space is dominated by endless bickering and stalemate, and our national political institutions seem to betray our best intentions. Many other advanced, industrial democracies do a better job at locating pragmatic solutions to pressing policy problems through political negotiation, using the very norms of cooperation that we teach our children and often practice in our communities. These nations manage the tussles and traumas of politics with a level of grace, efficiency, and effectiveness that today seems absent from the American political process, and they avoid the extreme deadlock that often paralyzes contemporary American politics. The "high-noon" brinkmanship between our Democrats and Republicans is fundamentally at odds with the quieter mechanisms for policymaking in Northern Europe, and our politics of stalemate sharply contrasts with their politics of cooperation. One wonders, then, why America—one of the most economically and socially vibrant countries in the world—has become relatively impotent in the political realm.

This book explores the problems of political negotiation, by which we mean the political practice in which individuals—usually acting in institutions on behalf of others—make and respond to claims, arguments, and proposals with the aim of reaching mutually acceptable binding agreements. We begin by considering the particular obstacles to political negotiation in the United States and the ways that Congress currently addresses these obstacles. Drawing from writings in experimental psychology, we identify forms of what we call *negotiation myopia*—that is, the mistakes made by the human brain in processing information and calculating collective political interests. We summarize how the institutions and procedural *rules of collective political engagement* help overcome negotiation myopia, and we highlight European and international examples of institutions that create dramatically different incentives for cooperation among political actors, interest groups, and citizens. We offer suggestions for how policymakers might overcome institutional constraints against negotiating agreement in politics.

In great part, the institutional obstacles to political negotiation in the United States are well known: a strong separation of powers between the presidency and Congress (with branches often controlled by different parties) and the structure of two-party competition (particularly when these parties are polarized and relatively equally matched) produce few incentives for political cooperation between the warring sides. By contrast, politicians in countries with multiple major parties must practice cross-party cooperation to gain and hold power, and the governments of those countries often have close linkages between the executive prime ministers and their legislative parliaments. Our two major parties in the United States have no such incentives. Win or lose is the name of the game, and constant conflict, changes in government, and frequent policy reversals make for an unstable policy and business climate.

U.S. institutions for organizing private interests do little to further successful political outcomes. For example, American firms are adept at demanding narrow regulatory concessions that pertain to their own industries, and Congress is bombarded with demands from every nook and cranny of the business community. Yet employers and unions have weak associations to help them meet collective political goals; consequently, they have difficulty expressing collective interests. They do not trust government, but they also cannot trust their collective selves.

It would be naive to think that all conflicts may be negotiated, and this is particularly true for the current American Congress (see chapters 2 and 3). Legislators may derive greater benefits from blocking deals than from making a good-faith effort for mutual accommodation. In their reluctance to negotiate a mutually acceptable compromise, they may be driven by their well-heeled funders, by electoral and partisan priorities, or by deep ideological divisions. Even political agreement does not ensure democratic or just solutions to policy problems: deals may benefit those at the negotiation table but may adversely affect those whose interests are not represented (for example, the future generations, the marginally employed, and the nonvoters). When reformers confront parties that prioritize electoral gain above substantive solutions to economic and social problems, and deep-seated ideological divisions result in stalemate and blindness to the fortunes of future generations, then political struggle rather than negotiation may well be the better recourse for altering the status quo.

Yet, despite the institutional odds against it, political negotiation sometimes works in the United States and elsewhere. This book analyzes how these episodes of success may occur. These unexpected successes in political negotiation often happen when participants adopt the rules of collective political engagement that routinely enable higher levels of cooperation in other advanced democracies. For example, procedural arrangements that incorporate a formal role for *nonpartisan, technical expertise* in policy deliberations in advance of specific legislative proposals may facilitate a collective "meeting of the minds." *Repeated interactions* among participants establish informal punishments for deception and bloated claims at the same time that those interactions nurture norms of trustworthy behavior. Dire consequences for inaction (or *penalty defaults*) help prevent stonewalling behavior. Allowing negotiations to take place in *private settings* encourages pondering rather than posturing.

We argue that adopting many of these rules of engagement may facilitate *deliberative negotiation*, in which participants search for fair compromises and often recognize the positive-sum possibilities that are otherwise frequently overwhelmed by zero-sum conflicts. Of course, deliberative negotiation is possible only in situations in which some potential common ground or zone of possible agreement exists and participants have a genuine desire to achieve a deal. But practices of deliberative negotiation have been central to American democracy since the construction of our nation. We think that it is time to return to the basics. Thus, this book reviews the institutional disincentives for cooperation and rewards for conflict and also suggests best practices in the art of collective politics.

Negotiation Myopia

Individuals often fail to agree to resolutions that would leave everyone better off in part because the human brain falls prey to negotiation myopia, a constellation of cognitive, emotional, and strategic mistakes that stand in the way of achieving agreement and mutual gains. Two major forms of cognitive myopia—*fixed-pie bias* and *self-serving bias*—impede successful negotiation. A successful negotiation may either simply settle on some point in the zone of possible agreement among the parties or, more expansively, produce an agreement that captures all the joint gains that can be discovered or created in the situation. Fixed-pie bias prevents participants from seeing and exploiting all possible joint gains and sometimes prevents any agreement at all. Self-serving bias makes the parties to the negotiation overestimate their likelihood of winning, thereby standing in the way of actually making an agreement. Emotions also may block successful negotiation; the emotional barrier of anger particularly interferes with the production of collective agreement. In addition, myopia relevant to our sense of timing—such as uncertainty and difficulties considering second- and third-order effects—may distort or diminish our incentives for long-term thinking because few want to make short-term investments in exchange for risky, long-term rewards (Jacobs 2011, p. 52). Global warming is a classic example of time myopia: citizens are asked to make changes in their lives and automobile manufacturers are called on to invest in emissions-reducing technology that will have an impact on climate change twenty years hence.

Strategic hardball tactics also can stand in the way of concluding successful negotiations. Such tactics particularly come into play when parties seek to maximize personal interests over broader, collective ones or to use blocking mechanisms for political advantage. As the chapter on the causes and consequences of polarization in the United States explains, such tactics bring the most benefits when the parties in Congress are almost equally matched: if the minority party can possibly gain the majority in the next Congress, it has strong political motivations to prevent policy successes that will result in electoral advantages for the current majority party. In any negotiation, participants may rationally reject a resolution that benefits them in the short run if they believe that forgoing immediate gains will set them up for an even bigger future victory. This is no less true of Congress. At a significant point in the Clinton-era negotiation over health reform, for example, Republican strategists determined that their best chances for a surge in public support at the next election lay in simply killing the Clinton health-reform bill. Thus, they urged legislators to reject any alternative bipartisan measure. The tactic was highly successful in the short run. Along with many other developments, however, it helped poison future relationships, undermining the potential for long-run joint gains.

Deliberative Negotiation

Under certain conditions, negotiation myopia may be overcome with institutional rules of collective engagement that enable deliberative negotiation, by allowing participants to rise above their internecine squabbles and focus on value-creating accords. By *deliberative negotiation*, we mean negotiation characterized by mutual justification, respect, and the search for fair terms of interaction and outcomes. This kind of negotiation lies between pure deliberation, in which the parties develop a collective understanding of the problems confronting them and seek to articulate a common good, and pure bargaining. It may include fully integrative negotiation, partially integrative negotiation, and fair compromises.

In *fully integrative negotiation,* the parties find a creative way to approach the problem that provides both with what they actually want and neither party loses. More often, in what we call *partially integrative negotiation,* the parties find or bring in a host of issues on which they place different priorities so that they can trade on those items that are high priority for one and low priority for the other. As Binder and Lee point out in chapter 3 on deal making in Congress, this kind of negotiation is more possible in Congress than in the commercial or legal world because Congress will usually be looking to resolve numerous issues at any one time. Linking those issues in a productive way is thus easier than when complementary issues must be sought out and actively brought into the discussion. Finally, deliberative negotiation includes the search for *fair compromises*. As with the search for integrative solutions, such a search is best conducted by members who know and respect one another and who appreciate as well the different and often conflicting interests that each represents.

Integrative, partially integrative, and fair compromise negotiations differ from pure-bargaining situations in which opponents strive to obtain the maximum number of concessions from one another. In pure bargains, the parties make distributive, zero-sum exchanges with particularistic payoffs, aiming solely for the greatest strategic advantage.

The issues of justice and the long term are also more relevant in deliberative negotiation. In a just deliberative negotiation, the parties at the table strive to incorporate as much as possible the interests of those not represented, including future generations. From a practical perspective, deliberative negotiations are also more likely to consider the longer-term ramifications of the agreements reached.

Rules of Collective Political Engagement and Conditions for Deliberative Negotiation

Lessons from the practice of political negotiation reveal some of the conditions under which negotiation myopia may be overcome and "pie-expanding" deals with joint gains may be obtained. We suggest that bargaining processes—whether in the sphere of private conflict resolution or national policymaking—are structured by *rules of collective political engagement*. These rules of the game stipulate specific procedural arrangements that set the terms of negotiation and define acceptable sources of information, patterns of interaction among participants, consequences for inaction, and autonomy of the bargaining partners. Choices of these specific procedural arrangements influence individuals' conceptualizations of problems, their emotions about cooperation, and their incentives to take action. When a zone of potential agreement exists, the adoption of specific rules for collective engagement may overcome the various forms of negotiation myopia—and even shape the conditions for integrative negotiation.

First, participants must agree to acceptable sources of information. In some cases, the various sides rely on their own partisan facts; however, in other cases, the negotiation setting builds in an explicit role for *nonpartisan third parties* or *technical expertise*. These external experts may help participants overcome the forms of myopia related to perspective taking and incomplete information, mitigate self-serving biases in the perception of facts, foster a shared understanding of policy problems in more neutral terms, build shared conceptions of justice, diminish ideological left-right cleavages, and enable creative "cognitive leaps." Countries have different rules about acceptable sources of information relevant to national political accords: these characteristic "knowledge regimes" and modes of discourse shape their production of policy ideas (Blyth 2002; Campbell and Pedersen 2014; Schmidt 2002). Some nations and international governing bodies use fact-finding bodies, peer review, and performance benchmarking against agreed indicators; these tools can help define problems and solutions in relatively neutral, mutually acceptable terms. Nonpartisan fact-finding bodies help correct self-serving biases in the facts, act as interpreters of truth, and contribute to all parties developing common conceptions of justice (Sabel and Zeitlin 2010). All these features enhance the opportunities for deliberative negotiation.

Second, a bargaining situation includes implicit decisions about patterns of interaction among participants; in particular, the decision to incorporate *repeated interactions* among parties may help overcome myopia-inducing short-term and zero-sum calculations. The fear of each party that others will not cooperate (for example, in the prisoner's dilemma game) creates incentives for short-term, self-interested choices. Bringing participants together in repeated engagements facilitates future punishments for uncooperative behavior and, consequently, fosters trust and commitment. It also cultivates shared perceptions of both the facts and the bargaining dynamics of the situation (Axelrod 1997; Hardin 1982; North 1990; Olson 1965). Particularly when negotiators are engaged in long-standing processes of cooperation, repeated interactions help them take the longer view and grasp one another's perspectives. Recognizing that repeated interaction in the legislative realm often requires long incumbencies, chapter 5, on deliberative negotiation, specifies criteria for judging when relatively uncontested elections in any district might represent the will of the voters and when this might reflect failures in democracy.

Third, decisions must be made about the consequences for nonaction in a negotiation process. Setting *penalty defaults* may move negotiators toward action, overcome blocking coalitions, and improve the chances for agreement (Ayres and Gertner 1989; Carpenter 2001; Sabel and Zeitlin 2010; Weaver 1987). By setting a penalty default, we mean creating a situation such that if the negotiating parties do not come to agreement by a certain time, a penalty that all parties want to avoid will become the default. In some cases, of course, procedural rules stipulating deadlines, exclusion from the table, and other action-forcing rules may simply overcome stalemate without moving participants toward pie-expanding deals. If judges are setting the penalty defaults, the accompanying expansion of judicial oversight may trespass on the legitimate policymaking prerogatives of democratic legislature (Ferejohn 2002). These are important trade-offs to consider. When courts threaten a penalty default if the negotiating parties do not agree on an alternative, the courts may be able to craft a default that promotes the broader public interest. The Los Angeles groundwater basis negotiations that provided the foundations for Elinor Ostrom's (1990) "bottom-up" theory of governing the commons were held under the California Supreme Court's threat of a penalty default. We call such a judicial move, or legislative moves in the same direction, the imposition of a *public-interest penalty default*.

Finally, decisions must be made about the degree of autonomy and privacy accorded to negotiators. In general, privacy boosts negotiators' capacities to bargain effectively by producing some autonomy from influences that try to shift the focus away from the core objects of negotiation or that insist on hard-line positions opposed to compromise. Chapter 5, on deliberative negotiation, points out that legislative transcripts have revealed more expressions of mutual understanding in closed-door versus public legislative settings. The chapter takes up the normative trade-offs associated with privacy and specifies criteria for judging when the closed-door interactions required for effective negotiation might be most democratically acceptable.

Institutions and Rules for Collective Political Engagement: The Cross-National Perspective

Rules of collective political engagement are embedded in governing institutions and structure the deliberative practices and patterns of democratic struggle that contribute to diverse policy outcomes. Advanced postindustrial democracies face broadly similar challenges yet demonstrate different responses to exogenous threats. In some countries, the rules of engagement embedded in governmental institutions, as well as in the more transitory procedural arrangements in specific policy areas, help overcome negotiation myopia and facilitate deliberative negotiation. Moreover, because these rules of collective political engagement have an impact on actors' strategic calculations of preference, they also influence the types of coalitions available to policy reform and the strategies for political struggle. In these countries, the strategic and psychological impacts of the governing institutions and their embedded rules of collective engagement may facilitate the development of social and economic reforms that benefit a broad cross section of interests. Other countries, such as the United States, have institutions that tend to produce distributive bargaining with zero-sum and short-term gains or even stalemate and inaction. The United States is in such a situation today. This section considers the institutions and rules of engagement that give some countries both the *need* for more encompassing political pacts and the *capacities* to produce them.

Before considering how rules of engagement may aid in negotiation, we note that not all political systems require negotiation. In the much-celebrated Westminster model—a parliamentary system with two-party competition and majoritarian rule—the ruling party (arguably representing a majority of the people) may legitimately claim a mandate to impose the will of the people without having to negotiate with the minority (Cox and McCubbins 1997; Linz 1990; Shugart and Carey 1992). Because the majority party simply implements its platform in Westminster model countries, extensive negotiation is unnecessary.

A presidential system, such as that in the United States, that separately elects two legislative houses and a president makes simple majoritarian rule more difficult to achieve. The separation of powers between Congress and the presidency creates greater hurdles to achieving political deals than a parliamentary system does. The independent election of both houses of the legislature and the executive decreases the chance that the same political party will control all branches; distributing responsibilities for policymaking between separately elected branches gives politicians in the two branches the means to wage institutional warfare on one another. The institutional warfare found in a presidential system may result in gridlock, dual government policies, and unilateral action. President Nixon engaged in this kind of institutional warfare when he tried to impound duly appropriated funding for certain social welfare programs, and the Reagan administration tangled in this way with the Democratic-controlled House when the two branches formulated separate foreign policies on Nicaragua (Cox and McCubbins 1997; Ginsberg and Shefter 2002; Kiewiet and McCubbins 1991). In short, except in extraordinary circumstances in which the same political party has control of the presidency, the Senate, and the House, the separation of powers in the U.S. system usually requires negotiation.

The Westminster model of majoritarian rule is also not an option for most European countries, and these "consensus-model" nations require significant multiparty negotiation to form governments and to develop policy reforms (Lijphart 2012). Most of these countries encounter crucial obstacles to the imposition of majoritarian rule because they have proportional-representation electoral rules, which allocate legislative seats to parties according to their share of the vote. Multiple parties vie for power and a single party seldom captures government; therefore, coalition governments are the norm. Politicians must engage in substantial negotiation simply to win political power, and ministries are often controlled by separate parties. Opposing parties may call for a vote of no confidence and bring down the government at any time.

Confronted with multiple interests vying for power, the consensus-model countries have developed a governing style that embraces political negotiation rather than simple majority rule. Political leaders seek to bring as many factions as possible into the governing coalition in order to retain power; even when governments fall, their successors are likely to include parties from the former regime. The potential weaknesses of these governments contribute to their ultimate strengths because the brokered deals in multiparty systems—although perhaps more time-consuming to create—are more stable than those in two-party systems, in which the ruling party may be voted out of office in the next election and the incoming party may dramatically change the policy (Downs [1957] 2001).

With power distributed across competing parties, one wonders how these countries have managed to produce a consensus governing style for negotiating political agreement. We suggest that many of these multiparty countries have the capacities as well as the need for consensual governing because their institutions incorporate rules of collective engagement that help overcome negotiation myopia and facilitate deliberative negotiation. This facilitation appears most vividly in the core institutions that structure citizens' interactions with their political leaders—that is, the party systems and the organizations for the representation of major economic interests.

First, proportional representation party (PR) systems, compared with majoritarian systems, enhance capacities for deliberative negotiation by incorporating rules of collective engagement that overcome many forms of negotiation myopia. Proportional parties represent distinctive groups of voters, endorse well-defined policy programs, and appeal to constituents on the basis of these ideological platforms. Therefore they are typically less likely to compete for the median voter than parties in majoritarian systems. In contrast, U.S. parties were characterized historically as "patronage parties," meaning that politicians appealed to constituents with material benefits rather than ideas (Burnham 1970; Cusack, Iversen, and Soskice 2007; Kitschelt 1999).

In contrast to the majoritarian patronage parties found in the United States, proportional parties are more likely to nurture *technical expertise* in their units for policy development because they make appeals to voters based on their policy programs. But because these democracies require high levels of multipartisan cooperation, they have developed a technique to smooth over partisan divisions by using nonpartisan commissions to develop ideological consensus on key policy issues. Representatives of proportional parties are also more likely than those of majoritarian parties to engage in repeated interactions with one another because, in proportional multiparty systems (with rare majority rule), the parties must cooperate to form a governing coalition and to enact legislation.

Second, institutions for organizing core economic interests are much stronger in countries that require a consensual governing style—a distinction that is captured by the concepts of "pluralism" and "corporatism." Majoritarian countries usually develop pluralist systems of interest representation that do not restrict the number of representative interest groups and that have no singular representative of business. These pluralist groups engage in policymaking solely through their lobbying of individual legislators. In sharp contrast, countries with a consensual governing style have evolved corporatist systems of industrial relations, in which nonoverlapping, functionally differentiated organizations represent the main economic actors. Thus, a company would be represented politically and in collective-bargaining channels by an industry association, and industry groups would be organized into an encompassing "umbrella" organization with special privileges to represent broad business interests. The groups representing business would formally negotiate with the parallel associations representing labor to make public policy so that much of what is done by politicians in the United States is done by organized private sector actors. Business and labor formulate policy regulations through collective bargains that extend across the economy and through tripartite commissions (composed of business, labor, and government representatives) convened under the auspices of government ministries.

As with proportional party systems, corporatist industrial relations systems incorporate rules to overcome negotiation myopia. These institutions rely on a formal role for technical expertise because the forums that bring business, labor, and the state together to consider policy problems develop such expertise and nurture shared understandings of problems and solutions. Repeated interactions are an important feature of both collective-bargaining processes and participation in the tripartite commissions, and they help build trust among the social partners. In macro-corporatist industrial relations channels, a *public-interest penalty default* appears in the state's threat to intervene if the social partners do not reach agreement (Anthonsen and Lindvall 2009; Hicks and Kenworthy 1998; Martin 2000; Martin and Swank 2004, 2012; Rothstein 1996; Streeck 1992; Trampusch 2007; Visser and Hemerijck 1997).

The impacts of rules of collective engagement embedded in governing institutions have effects not only on negotiation myopia; they also have significant effects on strategic calculations of interests, possibilities for coalition building, and patterns of democratic struggle. For example, the German industrial relations system incorporates extensive repeated interactions among business and labor representatives in industry-level collective bargaining, and this produces mutually beneficial deals for their employers and workers. But compared with the Nordic countries, there are fewer opportunities in Germany for peak associations representing the social partners to participate in policymaking forums at the national level (for example, in commissions with nonpartisan technical experts and tripartite commissions under the auspices of ministries). This reduces the scope of repeated interactions and reliance on shared expertise in Germany and changes the nature of the consequent deals. Whereas Scandinavian countries tend to produce broadly solidaristic public policies that address the interests of the long-term unemployed and marginal workers, Germany often produces "dualist" policies that benefit core employers and workers but do little for labor-market outsiders (Martin and Swank 2012). Moreover, in the German system of subsidiarity, in which policymaking is expected to be conducted at the lowest level possible, the national state cannot easily threaten penalty defaults. In Scandinavia, by contrast, threats of state intervention provide significant incentives for the macro-corporate bodies to take policy action.

The different institutions and rules of collective political engagement also provide the building blocks for diverse varieties of capitalism (Hall and Soskice 2001). In coordinated market economies, institutions and rules are conducive to inclusive negotiations by relying on technical expertise, repeated interactions, and penalty defaults to move negotiators toward consensual outcomes. These processes constitute the cell structure of cooperation in industrial relations forums, vocational training programs, proportional party negotiations, and other important domains. Alternatively, liberal market economies have fewer opportunities for repeated engagement among organized representatives of business and labor, because anonymous markets facilitate economic exchange. Penalty defaults also become less necessary when the "invisible hand" is expected to provide market discipline. In addition, liberal political philosophy tends to minimize the use of technical expertise in decisionmaking processes, by delegating most policymaking to the political legislative realm as well as expecting the pluralist aggregation of self-interests to add up to a collective interest.

For these reasons, the choice of a specific set of rules of collective political engagement has facilitated deliberative negotiation within the consensus-model countries. The result is many policy successes, often with restrained political conflict. The crucial role for nonpartisan technical expertise is illustrated by the use of royal commissions in Sweden, such as the expert task force on climate change in the 1970s, which set the stage for early clean-air legislation. Although the resulting Swedish legislation was less extensive than the parallel legislation in the United States, its impact was far more substantial because the legitimacy established through the expert investigation made for easy implementation and extensive compliance (Lundqvist 1980). Denmark used repeated interactions in private meetings to develop sweeping active-labor-market reforms that were then ratified wholesale by the parliament. The Labor Market Commission (or the Zeuthen Udvalg) convened representatives from the major labor-market associations, parties, and ministries to propose solutions for extensive long-term unemployment. The resulting proposal drew inspiration from ideas on both the right and the left, thereby combining extensive investments in training with more restricted access to passive social assistance (Martin and Swank 2004, 2012).

In contrast, the United States relies far less on the rules of engagement that foster deliberative negotiation. Americans rely less frequently on panels of technical experts, such as government-sponsored bipartisan task forces, to study policy problems in advance of the legislative cycle and to slowly build shared perceptions of social and economic challenges. Instead, legislators derive much of their information from partisan think tanks. In recent years, political parties have developed dueling facts and contested narratives about policy problems, and they are quick to challenge one another's motives and data. This divergence in accepted truths has given rise to websites such as FactCheck.org, which reported in 2012: "A fog of misinformation has settled on the fiscal cliff, as both House Speaker John Boehner and Treasury Secretary Timothy Geithner have traded conflicting, misleading and false statements in recent days on the president's deficit-reduction plan" (FactCheck.org, "Dueling Fiscal Cliff Deceptions," www.factcheck.org/2012/12/dueling-fiscal-cliff-deceptions/). Repeated interactions in private meetings among opposing parties or stakeholders have never been a feature of the American political economy because collective bargaining is both limited and largely focused on economic rather than political issues (Gottschalk 2000). The opportunities for exchange among political parties have diminished significantly with the recent ideological polarization of Congress. U.S. Congress has also had mixed success with penalty defaults, perhaps because politics trumps substantive goals. It would be difficult to argue, for example, that across-the-board cuts in many programs in the U.S. "sequester" of March 2013 derived from careful public policy. But that sequester was designed explicitly to provide an unacceptable penalty that would force negotiation.

Rules of Collective Engagement and Negotiating Agreements in International Relations

In chapter 7, Odell and Tingley suggest that when a zone of potential agreement exists, the same procedural arrangements that facilitate domestic political agreements in European countries also contribute to successful deals in international negotiations. Of course, raw power, conflicting interests, and zero-sum territorial disputes motivate many international conflicts, and the decision to negotiate is neither wise nor even moral when the other side has ambitions for humiliation or annihilation. No one believes that Roosevelt and Churchill could have negotiated a win-win deal with Stalin at Yalta if they had had better negotiation skills. But in cases that have the potential for mutual gain and realistic grounds for trust, rules of engagement may help political actors achieve gains that exceed their anticipation rewards from unilateral action.

International settings, however, often magnify the problems of negotiation myopia because it is harder to take the perspective of others outside one's own culture. As we move beyond our own hearths, tribes, and nation-states, our capacities for understanding are increasingly strained by cultural and linguistic misunderstandings. Thus, when Americans and Japanese engage in cross-cultural negotiations, they obtain fewer joint gains than when members of either country negotiate with their compatriots (Brett and Okumura 1998).

Problems of long-term uncertainty and credible commitments related to time myopia also become more pressing in international affairs, where no supranational world-governing body can make assurances that today's promises will be honored by tomorrow's political elites. Deals that satisfy a broad scope of interests may be more difficult to achieve when the collective identity of community or nation-state is transcended. In these cases, actors often are inclined to view choices in terms of minimizing their losses rather than maximizing their gains. Yet the rules of engagement that we discuss in this book (incorporating the use of technical expertise, repeated interactions, private meetings, and penalty defaults) may facilitate negotiated settlements even in the more difficult terrain of international relations. First, a reliance on *nonpartisan technical expertise* is often helpful in international settings, particularly in framing the issues at the problem diagnosis stage. In some situations, international actors have developed shared perspectives after outside experts—perceived by all to be nonpartisan and unbiased—offer insights into multifaceted problems. The use of an external third-party mediator (for example, the United Nations) or a single negotiating text also helps deemphasize the purely political considerations in a conflict. For example, the use of nonpartisan technical expertise was immensely important in developing the Law of the Sea Convention, which created rules for regulating the mining of critical metals in the deep ocean floor. Both first and third world countries were split over the rights to seabed resources and the issue of private companies' present and future payments for the use of this common heritage. The impasse was overcome by a computer model developed by scientists at the Massachusetts Institute of Technology, which offered a value-free vehicle for resolving exceedingly complicated questions in the payment scheme (Antrim and Sebenius 1992).

Second, *repeated interactions* facilitate negotiated settlements in international relations. Establishing a platform for negotiation is vital to negotiating success among international units because this sets opportunities for repeated interactions that build trust and shared understandings among diverse interests. These forums work well with efforts to balance interests and issues with contrasting distributional effects so that participants with diverse interests might have available to them a large pool of issues on which to compromise. Informal meetings with no official records allow exploratory discussions to determine whether a zone of agreement exists and possibly to develop the broad outlines of a settlement. Third, deadlines and penalty defaults are also important for forcing action in international agreements because negotiators tend to withhold concessions until the last possible moment.

Institutions and Rules of Collective Political Engagement: U.S. Congress Revisited

Political negotiations in other institutional settings shed light on the special problems of political agreement within the American Congress. The United States differs from the two dominant modes of rule found in other countries. With multiple veto points, it lacks the institutional motivations and capacities to exercise majoritarian rule, as in the classic Westminster system. With a severely polarized party system and weak interest groups, it has neither the structural political incentives nor the societal capacities to adopt the consensual governing style found in the proportional parliamentary systems of northern Europe. Negotiation certainly cannot offer a ubiquitous palliative to the deep wells of political conflict caused by American institutions, and the rules of engagement that inspire negotiation elsewhere may even have perverse effects. Moreover, an environment of austerity may well reinforce a mentality of zero-sum competition over shrinking resources.

The structure of American political institutions requires, but discourages, deliberative negotiation. Power sharing among branches of government and the supermajorities needed to overcome the presidential veto, along with Senate filibuster, make it more difficult for a single party "to form a government" and complicate the exercise of majoritarian rule found elsewhere in Westminster settings. That the branches are so frequently controlled by different parties further complicates the attribution of blame that elsewhere inspires compromise (see chapter 2 of this volume; McCarty, Poole, and Rosenthal 2006).

Incentives for negotiation are also shaped by the structure of party competition. Two-party systems produce fewer incentives for negotiation than proportional multiparty systems because each party seeks an electoral majority and neither has an incentive to compromise to create a governing coalition. Moreover, the relationship between political representatives and their constituencies is more attenuated in the United States than it is in Europe. Politics is always a two-level game; however, European programmatic parties have fairly stable and homogeneous constituencies that largely ascribe to the parties' broad ideological views on key questions of governance: the role of government, the nature of social problems, and the prescriptions for economic growth. In contrast, the two major parties in the United

States are umbrella organizations, with often-conflicting memberships, organized around ambiguous policy platforms, and motivated
both to compete for the illusive median voter and satisfy the narrow
policy goals of core funders. Consequently, the parties in the United
States can seldom claim a clear-cut mandate for action, as Newt
Gingrich discovered in 1992 when he unsuccessfully sought to implement his "Contract with America" (Downs [1957] 2001; Page
and Jacobs 2009). Individual legislators must defend their policy positions to their constituents, even while party leaders seek to gratify
key groups in the party coalition and to preserve the party brand.

Campaign financing also creates disincentives for integrative negotiations. Political campaigns are longer and far more costly in the
United States than in most other advanced countries. According to
the Campaign Finance Institute, the cost of winning a House seat was
$1.5 million in 2010, a 200 percent increase in real dollars from 1984
(Campaign Finance Institute, www.cfinst.org/data/pdf/VitalStats_t1
.pdf). Campaign spending has increased in many countries with television advertising, but elections in the United States are particularly costly.
For example, total spending on U.S. national elections topped $6 billion
in 2012, compared with $91 million in 2010 in the United Kingdom
(CNN, "International Campaign Finance: How do Countries Compare?," www.cnn.com/2012/01/24/world/global-campaign-finance/).

In the "old days," the structure of political action committee (PAC)
financing encouraged the quid pro quo exchange of concessions associated with distributive bargaining; before the rise of strongly polarized parties, concessions to important PAC constituents were often a
medium of exchange in striking deals. Unlike individual contributors,
corporate and interest group PACs have rather narrowly focused policy goals that mainly pertain to their industrial interests or issue areas.
PAC contributors are largely motivated to secure access to legislators
rather than to influence broad ideological choices. Yet individual campaign contributions have increased from less than half to almost three
fourths of the total campaign pool, and individual contributors and
super PACs (also on the rise) are more ideologically motivated than
their corporate counterparts and less likely to favor compromise (see
chapter 2 of this volume; McCarty, Poole, and Rosenthal 2006).

A tremendous upswing in party polarization, associated with this
rise of individual campaign contributors, has diminished opportuni-

ties for bipartisan cooperation on both distributive and integrative negotiations, as Barber and McCarty vividly describe in chapter 2. Partisan differences in roll-call voting have increased dramatically since 1980, as have differences on policy issues among the elites in the two parties. The move of Southern Democrats into the Republican Party prompted some of this change; however, northern parties also became more ideologically consistent, at least at the elite level. Party polarization reflects the growing impact on party platforms of ideologically driven individual donors and specific interests and, more broadly, rising economic inequality. More polarized parties and elites are not likely to want to negotiate.

The growing strength and structural changes in American parties have further diminished opportunities for political bargains, as Binder and Lee show in chapter 3. Bargains were easier before the rise of strong, more ideological, disciplined national parties in the 1990s because earlier legislators were largely free agents. They could engage in distributive deal making to secure special concessions for their home constituencies, and "Christmas Tree bills" often contained "baubles" for swing voters. Party polarization and party discipline reduce the number of special concessions to individual voters and make these kinds of distributive bargains more difficult to attain. Party leaders now have greater capacities to protect their political brands, and the ideological polarization of the parties has increased the political threshold for entering into negotiation. It is true, as Binder and Lee point out, that bipartisanship is easier when there are clear majority and minority parties because the members of the minority need to make deals with the majority to get action on their projects and favors for their constituents. Moreover, when both sides recognize a mandate for action, strong leadership can increase the potential for interparty negotiation and integrative outcomes. In recent elections, however, the parties have won or lost with narrow vote margins, and the anticipation of winning the next election makes it strategically rational for the minority leadership to organize to block the policy ambitions of the majority party.

The U.S. configuration of organized interests further constricts the likelihood for integrative negotiations. Success in negotiating political agreements is greatest when politicians perceive a mandate for legislative action; however, in a pluralist system, interest groups are fragmented and seldom speak with one voice. Certainly, interest groups sometimes form electoral and policy coalitions to demonstrate their broad support for a candidate or issue, and these may have a significant impact on electoral and policy outcomes (Box-Steffensmeier, Christenson, and Hitt 2013; Kingdon 1984; Schlozman and Tierney 1986). Yet the organizational structure and rules of American trade associations make it difficult for employers and workers to pursue their self-defined, long-term collective goals. Majorities of business managers in the United States, for example, have been shown to support many governmental social and economic policies, but their organizations are too weak to support these initiatives or to issue a clear mandate for legislative action. Even the big umbrella business associations—for example, the Chamber of Commerce, the National Association of Manufacturers (NAM), and the Business Roundtable—fail to articulate broad policy positions when a majority of their members support such positions. These groups compete with one another for members, which makes them act more like sales organizations than decisionmaking bodies, and they have great difficulty ignoring minority objections and taking strong stands. This lowest-common-denominator politics, or the "art of offending no one," leaves the big-business community in a kind of political limbo, better at rejecting regulations that offend their narrow self-interests than endorsing policies that further their long-term collective concerns. Business managers recognize that their political associations fail to address their long-term concerns. In a March 1983 *Businessweek* poll, two-thirds of the executives sampled judged the representation of business views to be only poor or fair. The formal organizations that represent business received the worst evaluations from this group: only 30 percent found NAM to be highly effective; the Business Roundtable rated only 33 percent, and the Chamber of Commerce only 17 percent (Martin 2000).

Under these difficult institutional conditions for action, when do American legislators recognize a mandate to negotiate political agreements and under what conditions do integrative negotiations transpire? Binder and Lee (chapter 3) point out that the capacity is there. Congress has a broad reach across many policies—in Barney Frank's humorous words, "the ankle bone is connected to the shoulder bone"—and the capacity to bring many issues into the deal expands the potential for integrative negotiations. The political dynamics might also change with procedural rules that introduced a higher reliance on technical expertise, repeated interactions among core stakeholders, and penalty defaults to spur action.

The rules of collective political engagement discussed here may periodically foster negotiations around broad agreements in the U.S. setting. First, negotiations seem more likely when participants go through the labor intensive process of gathering information from a wide range of sources about the causes and dimensions of a policy problem. A formal role for nonpartisan technical expertise, as such, is more limited in the United States than in other countries; for example, the Government Accounting Office and Congressional Budget Office have a limited impact on congressional deal making today. Yet this relative scarcity of truly nonpartisan technical experts may be partially offset by a process of thorough research in which perceptions of the issues become more nuanced and complex (see chapter 3).

Second, successful political negotiations are more likely to occur when legislators are able to create forums for repeated interactions on the topic at hand, preferably far from the public eye. The rising influence of party caucuses and the declining importance of standing committees have scaled back opportunities for ongoing bipartisan negotiations on specific issues. In addition, "sunshine laws"—designed to make political processes more transparent and accountable—have diminished legislators' capacities to engage in free-flowing dialogue in private spaces about a range of possible solutions. Congress has partially redressed these problems with the development of ad hoc bipartisan policy "gangs"; these forums for private, bipartisan dialogue allow bipartisan leaders to free-associate about possible options. Thus, the Senate bipartisan "Gang of Eight" met repeatedly during the summer of 2013 to negotiate a compromise over immigration reform. The proposed deal would have combined priorities on reform into a single package and disallowed amendments in committee or on the Senate floor.

Repeated interactions are also important for actors in the private sphere to develop shared perceptions of policy problems and solutions, which then may help build public support for congressional action. For example, Martin (2000) found in a study of sixty randomly selected Fortune 200 companies in the 1990s that engagement in group dialogues with other social actors was a significant determinant of firms' positions on national health reform. One respondent explained: "This has been an incredible process: to go through the process of people walking through the door who are obviously going to have conflict. Doctors talking to businessmen. Twenty to forty people sitting down together and staying focused on a complex issue for a long time. One thing that made it work is that they decided to take the sacred cows and leave them at home."

Finally, deadlines and penalty defaults may bolster congressional chances for negotiated successes, in the same way that these processes bring politicians to cooperate in other countries. Politicians of both parties seem most inspired to negotiate when they fear losing the blame game. The two sides may "circle the wagons" to jointly make difficult choices for which neither wants to be held responsible (Weaver 1987). Thus, Newt Gingrich learned important lessons from the Republican-led government shutdown in the 1990s, and, thereafter, congressional Republicans cooperated closely with Bill Clinton to produce expansive policy reforms with a strategy referred to as "triangulation." Blame avoidance also motivated Senate Republicans during the efforts to pass immigration reform in 2013: some senators viewed the electoral costs of blocking immigration as too high and therefore worked with Democrats to try, although ultimately unsuccessfully, to negotiate an integrative solution (see chapter 3).

Penalty defaults that are not constructed in the public interest, however, can do considerable harm and do not always work, especially when the political costs to party negotiation are perceived as greater than the rewards for substantive deals (see chapter 3). The efforts of Tea Party Republicans in the House to prevent the implementation of Obamacare and the subsequent government shutdown in fall 2013 nearly caused a default on government debt and a major financial crisis. This episode can only be explained by legislators' perceptions that their political interests, rooted in the strongly conservative positions of their constituents, justified such a stance.

Contributions of this Volume

We hope with this scholarship to draw the attention of political actors to what the discipline of political science can tell us about negotiation. We want to identify promising future avenues of research, to reflect on the weaknesses and strengths of the U.S. political system, and to offer practical lessons for the art of politics.

First, we synthesize and draw connections among investigations of negotiation by scholars in political science and across the social and behavioral sciences. Scholars are conducting parallel investigations on the micro and macro conditions for success in political negotiation, however, few prior works cross these disciplinary and subfield boundaries.

Second, we invite future research on the institutional influences on preferences and political strategies. In assessing the impacts of diverse institutional structures and rules on individuals' perceptions and incentives for negotiation, we seek to open up interpretations of political interests to the rich perception of human motivation found, for example, in the work of students of voting behavior and consumers' preferences. The institutions and rules for collective political engagement are crucial to explaining the cross-national differences in preferences held by both elites and citizens for governmental, social, and economic interventions. These institutions and rules for political engagement have impacts on governments' capacities to build coalitions of broad majorities, to negotiate social pacts, and to cope with the challenges of the postindustrial economy (Martin and Swank 2012).

Third, we invite scholars to explore the relationship between patterns of political negotiation among elites and citizens' attitudes toward government. Politics is a multilevel game, and the relationship between principals and their agents is not always clearly defined. It would be useful to have a fuller understanding of how political deal making among elites influences citizens' perceptions of public policy and the legitimacy of the state. One danger of negotiation is that it will include only the small number of people at the table, excluding those that the negotiators are mandated to represent. Another danger is that the negotiation itself will exclude important affected parties. Moreover, constituencies themselves can be myopic, asking their representative agents to "fight to the mat" for narrow gains.

Yet knowledge of the dynamics of negotiation and the success of integrative negotiations in politics may also bring citizens to believe more in the legitimacy of their governments and the efficacy of public policies. American institutions and rules contribute to a parsimonious collective political sphere in the United States compared with some European countries. In Denmark, for example, society (*samfund*) is reified, nurtured, and protected, and the location for the "social"—that is, the public sector—commands widespread support. Genuine negotiated exchanges among our leaders in the United States may help us construct collective social identities and change our perceptions of ourselves vis-à-vis the larger society. Citizens may learn from elites that politics is not only about struggle over resources; it is also about the search for value-creating opportunities and social solidarity. Such understandings may, in the long run, bring citizens to view political discourse in more positive terms. We Americans preach cooperation and sharing to our children, but in the political sphere, we have forgotten the lessons of our childhood. As a nation, we have come to a pull-together or pull-apart moment.

Note: The author wishes to thank Jane Mansbridge, Frances Lee, Sarah Binder, Dino Christensen, and Doug Kriner for invaluable comments on this chapter.

References

Anthonsen, Mette, and Johannes Lindvall. 2009. "Party Competition and the Resilience of Corporatism." *Government and Opposition* 44 (2): 167–87.

Antrim, Lance N., and James K. Sebenius. 1992. "Formal Individual Mediation and the Negotiators' Dilemma: Tommy Koh at the Law of the Sea Conference." In *Mediation in International Relations: Multiple Approaches to Conflict Management,* ed. Jacob Bercovitch and Jeffrey Z. Rubin. New York: St. Martin's Press.

Axelrod, Robert M. 1997. *The Complexity of Cooperation: Agent-Based Models of Competition and Collaboration.* Princeton University Press.

Ayres, Ian, and Robert Gertner. 1989. "Filling Gaps in Incomplete Contracts: An Economic Theory of Default Rules." *Yale Law Journal* 99:87–130.

Blyth, Mark. 2002. *Great Transformations: Economic Ideas and Institutional Change in the Twentieth Century.* Oxford University Press.

Box-Steffensmeier, Janet M., Dino P. Christenson, and Matthew Hitt. 2013. "Quality over Quantity: Amici Influence and Judicial Decision Making." *American Political Science Review* 107 (3): 1–15.

Brett, Jeanne M., and Tetsushi Okumura. 1998. "Inter- and Intracultural Negotiation: U.S. and Japanese Negotiators." *Academy of Management Journal* 41 (5): 495–510.

Burnham, Walter Dean. 1970. *Critical Elections and the Mainsprings of American Politics.* New York: W. W. Norton.

Campbell, John, and Ove Kaj Pedersen. 2014. *The National Origins of Policy Ideas: Knowledge Regimes in the United States, France, Germany, and Denmark.* Princeton: Princeton University Press.

Carpenter, Daniel P. 2001. *The Forging of Bureaucratic Autonomy: Reputations, Networks, and Policy Innovation in Executive Agencies, 1862–1928.* Princeton University Press.

Cox, Gary W., and Mathew D. McCubbins. 1997. "Political Structure and Economic Policy: The Institutional Determinants of Policy Outcomes." Social Science Research Network. http://ssrn.com/ abstract=1009999.

Cusack, Thomas R., Torben Iversen, and David Soskice. 2007. "Economic Interests and the Origins of Electoral Systems." *American Political Science Review* 101 (3): 373–91.

Downs, Anthony. [1957] 2001. "An Economic Theory of Democracy." In *Democracy: A Reader,* ed. Ricardo Blaug and John Schwarzmantel. Columbia University Press.

Ferejohn, John. 2002. "Judicializing Politics, Politicizing Law." *Law and Contemporary Problems* 65 (3): 41–68.

Ginsberg, Benjamin, and Martin Shefter. 2002. *Politics by Other Means: Politicians, Prosecutors, and the Press from Watergate to Whitewater.* 3rd ed. New York: W. W. Norton.

Gottschalk, Marie. 2000. *The Shadow Welfare State: Labor, Business, and the Politics of Health Care in the United States.* Ithaca, NY: ILR Press.

Hall, Peter, and David Soskice, eds. 2001. *Varieties of Capitalism: The Institutional Foundations of Comparative Advantage.* Oxford University Press.

Hardin, Russell. 1982. *Collective Action.* Johns Hopkins University Press.

Hicks, Alexander, and Lane Kenworthy. 1998. "Cooperation and Political Economic Performance in Affluent Democratic Capitalism 1." *American Journal of Sociology* 103 (6): 1631–72.

Jacobs, Alan M. 2011. *Governing for the Long Term: Democracy and the Politics of Investment.* Cambridge University Press.

Kiewiet, D. Roderick, and Mathew D. McCubbins. 1991. *The Logic of Delegation: Congressional Parties and the Appropriations Process.* University of Chicago Press.

Kingdon, John. 1984. *Agendas, Alternatives, and Public Policies.* New York: Longman Publishing Group.

Kitschelt, Herbert, ed. 1999. *Post-Communist Party Systems: Competition, Representation, and Inter-Party Cooperation.* Cambridge University Press.

Lijphart, Arend. 2012. *Patterns of Democracy: Government Forms and Performance in Thirty-Six Countries.* Yale University Press.

Linz, Juan J. 1990. "The Perils of Presidentialism." *Journal of Democracy* 1:51–69.

Lundqvist, J. Lennart. 1980. *The Hare and the Tortoise: Clean Air Policies in the United States and Sweden.* University of Michigan Press.

Martin, Cathie Jo. 2000. *Stuck in Neutral: Business and the Politics of Human Capital Investment Policy.* Princeton University Press.

Martin, Cathie Jo, and Duane Swank. 2004. "Does the Organization of Capital Matter?" *American Political Science Review* 98 (4): 593–611.

———. 2012. *The Political Construction of Business Interests: Coordination, Growth, and Equality.* Cambridge University Press.

McCarty, Nolan M., Keith T. Poole, and Howard Rosenthal. 2006. *Polarized America: The Dance of Ideology and Unequal Riches.* MIT Press.

North, Douglass C. 1990. *Institutions, Institutional Change and Economic Performance.* Cambridge University Press.

Olson, Mancur. 1965. *The Logic of Collective Action: Public Goods and the Theory of Groups.* New York: Schocken Books.

Ostrom, Elinor. 1990. *Governing the Commons: The Evolution of Institutions for Collective Action.* Cambridge University Press.

Page, Benjamin I., and Lawrence R. Jacobs. 2009. *Class War?: What Americans Really Think about Economic Inequality.* University of Chicago Press.

Rothstein, Bo. 1996. "Political Institutions: An Overview." In *A New Handbook for Political Science*, ed. R. E. Goodin and H.-D. Klingemann. Oxford University Press.

Sabel, Charles F., and Jonathan Zeitlin. 2010. "Learning from Difference: The New Architecture of Experimentalist Governance in the EU." In *Experimentalist Governance in the European Union: Towards a New Architecture*, ed. Charles F. Sabel and Jonathan Zeitlin. Oxford University Press.

Schlozman, Kay Lehman, and John Tierney. 1986. *Organized Interests and American Democracy.* New York: Harper and Row.

Schmidt, Vivian. 2002. *The Futures of European Capitalism.* Oxford University Press.

Shugart, Matthew Soberg, and John M. Carey. 1992. *Presidents and Assemblies: Constitutional Design and Electoral Dynamics.* Cambridge University Press.

Streeck, Wolfgang. 1992. *Social Institutions and Economic Performance: Studies of Industrial Relations in Advanced Capitalist Economies.* London: Sage.

Trampusch, Christine. 2007. "Industrial Relations as a Source of Social Policy: A Typology of the Institutional Conditions for Industrial Agreements on Social Benefits." *Social Policy & Administration* 41 (3): 251–70.

Visser, Jelle, and Anton Hemerijck. 1997. *A Dutch Miracle: Job Growth, Welfare Reform and Corporatism in the Netherlands.* Amsterdam University Press.

Weaver, R. Kent. 1987. *The Politics of Blame Avoidance.* Brookings Institution.

STALEMATE IN THE UNITED STATES

Causes and Consequences of Polarization

MICHAEL BARBER AND
NOLAN MCCARTY

Rarely these days does a news cycle pass without new stories of political dysfunction in Washington, D.C. New reports of stalemates, fiscal cliffs, and failed grand bargains have begun to erode the public confidence in the ability of our representative institutions to govern effectively. In May 2013, only one American in six approved of the way Congress has handled its job.[1] Sadly, that level of support was a major improvement from the previous summer, when wrangling over the usually routine matter of raising the debt ceiling drove congressional approval down to 10 percent.

The most common diagnoses of Washington's ailments center on the emergence of excessive partisanship and deep ideological divisions among political elites and officeholders. In short, "polarization" is to blame. Consequently, the reform-minded have taken up the mantle of reducing polarization or mitigating its effects. In recent years, proposals for electoral reform to change electoral districting, primary elections, and campaign finance have been presented as panaceas. Other reformers have focused on changing legislative procedures such as those related to the filibuster, appropriations, and confirmation

---

1. See www.gallup.com/poll/162362/americans-down-congress-own-representative .aspx.

process to limit the opportunities for polarization to undermine government.

Although there has been intense public discussion about the causes of polarization, its consequences, and possible cures, social science research has only recently begun to help shape those discussions. The intent of this chapter is to provide a more evidence-based foundation for these debates.

Preliminaries

The academic study on partisanship and polarization is based on a combination of qualitative and quantitative research. Noteworthy qualitative accounts, which often combine historical research and participant observation, include Rohde (1991), Sinclair (2006), Hacker and Pierson (2006), and Mann and Ornstein (2012).

The starting point for many quantitative studies of polarization is the robust observation of rising partisan differences in roll-call voting behavior in Congress. The bipartisan coalitions of the 1950s and 1960s have given way to the party-line voting of the twenty-first century. Although these trends are apparent in simple descriptive statistics about partisan divisions on roll calls, political scientists have developed more refined measures of partisan voting differences. A variety of techniques uses data on roll-call voting to estimate the positions of individual legislators on a set of scales.[2] The primary scale—the one that explains most of the variation in legislator voting—generally captures partisan conflict. At the individual-legislator level, positions on these scales reflect a mix of ideological positioning and constituency interest as well as party loyalty and discipline. Political scientists continue to debate the exact weights of these factors. Some scholars argue that the scores primarily capture ideological differences (for example, Poole 2007), whereas others interpret them as measures of partisanship (for example, Lee 2009). Without taking a position on this debate, we refer to the primary roll-voting scale as the *party-conflict*

---

2. See Poole and Rosenthal (1997); Groseclose, Levitt, and Snyder (1999); Clinton, Jackman, and Rivers (2004).

dimension.[3] However, consistent with common usage, we may also label positions on the scale as *liberal, moderate,* or *conservative*.

All these techniques for estimating the party-conflict dimension produce similar findings with respect to polarization. Consequently, we focus on the DW-NOMINATE measures developed by McCarty, Poole, and Rosenthal (1997). Generally, these scores range from −1 to +1 and are scaled so that the highest scores are those of conservative Republicans and the lowest are those of liberal Democrats.

Given the estimated positions of legislators on this scale, we can measure partisan polarization by computing the difference in means (or medians) across the political parties, where a larger gap indicates a greater level of polarization. Figure 2-1 presents the difference in party means on the party-conflict scale from 1879 through 2011.

From the 1930s until the mid-1970s, these measures of polarization were quite low. Not only were differences between the typical Democratic and Republican legislators small but there also were significant numbers of conservative Democrats and liberal Republicans. Since the 1970s, however, there has been a steady and steep increase in the polarization of both the House and Senate. Other measures of party conflict confirm the trend of increasing polarization in the past forty years.[4]

Although conventional wisdom often asserts that polarization resulted from the changing behavior of both parties (that is, with Democrats moving to the left and Republicans to the right), the evidence shows that the behavioral changes are far from symmetric and are largely driven by changes in the positioning of the Republican Party.[5]

3. It is important, however, to distinguish these scores from party loyalty. Some members who have extreme positions on these scales are not always loyal partisans (for example, "Tea Party" Republicans).

4. Although figure 2-1 shows a steady movement by the average Republican, the Republican caucus in Congress has not become more homogeneous in the same time period. The standard deviation of Republican ideal points has remained around 0.15 since the 1950s. Democrats, conversely, have become much more homogeneous in the same period with the disappearance of conservative Southern Democrats.

5. For a discussion of methodological issues underlying this claim, see Hare et al. (2012).

Figure 2-1. *Average Distance between Positions across Parties.* The y-axis shows the difference in mean positions between the two parties in both the House of Representatives and Senate from 1879 to 2011 using the DW-NOMINATE measures. Congress is more polarized than it has been in over 125 years.

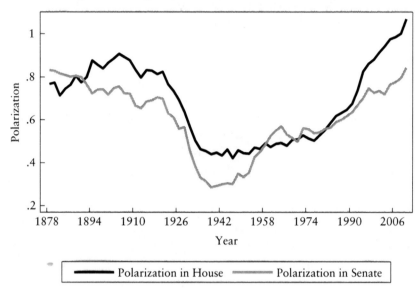

Figure 2-2 plots the average positions of the parties by region. In the past forty years, the most discernible trend has been the marked movement of the Republican Party to the right (for qualitative evidence, see Hacker and Pierson 2006; Mann and Ornstein 2012). It is important to note that the changes in the Republican Party have affected both its Southern and non-Southern members. The movement of the Democratic Party to the left on economic issues in the past fifty years is confined to its Southern members—reflecting the increased influence of African American voters in the South. However, it is important that the implied asymmetry may pertain only to the issues (primarily economic) that dominate the congressional agenda. It may well be the case that on some social issues (for example, gay marriage), polarization is the result of Democrats moving to the left.

Another important aspect of the increase in party polarization is the pronounced reduction in the dimensionality of political conflict. Many issues that were once distinct from the party-conflict dimension have been absorbed into it. Poole and Rosenthal (1997) and McCarty, Poole, and Rosenthal (1997) both noted that congressional

Figure 2-2. *Mean Party-Conflict Score by Party and Region.* The y-axis shows the mean position of each party by region. In this plot, the South is defined as Alabama, Arkansas, Florida, Georgia, Kentucky, Louisiana, Mississippi, North Carolina, Oklahoma, South Carolina, Tennessee, Texas, and Virginia. There were no Southern Republican Senators between 1913 and 1960 and only two before that.

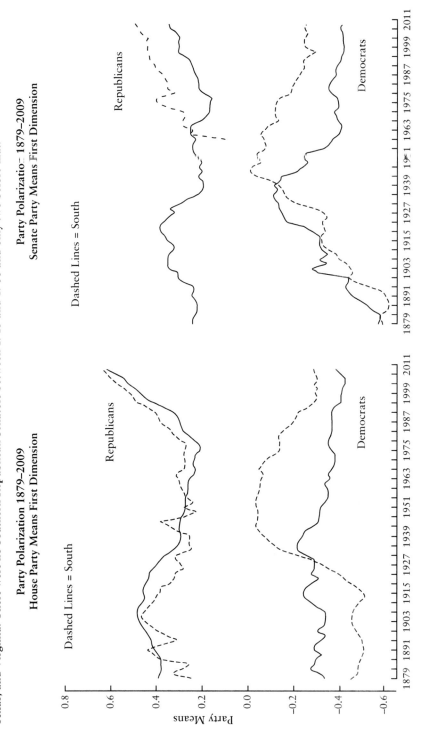

voting can be increasingly accounted for by a single dimension that distinguishes the parties. This situation directly contrasts with that of the mid-twentieth century, when the parties divided internally on a variety of issues primarily related to race and region. Figure 2-3 quantifies these changes, showing the percentage of individual roll-call vote decisions in the House that can be correctly classified by one- and two-dimensional models.[6] The two-dimensional spatial model accounts for most individual voting decisions since the late nineteenth century. Classification success was highest at the turn of the twentieth century, exceeding 90 percent. However, the predictive success of the two-dimensional model fell during most of the twentieth century, only to rebound to the 90 percent level in recent years.[7]

Increasingly, most of the work is being done by the party-conflict dimension. In the period from 1940 to 1960, adding a second dimension to account for intraparty divisions on race and civil rights led to a substantial improvement to fit. A second dimension often explained an additional 3 percent to 6 percent of the voting decisions in the House. However, in recent years, the second dimension adds no additional explanatory value. In the 112th Congress, the second dimension explains only an additional 1,800 votes of the almost 600,000 cast by House members.

Although polarization and the reduction in dimensionality tend to coincide, there is no necessary logical connection between the two trends. One possibility is that partisan polarization might occur simultaneously across any number of distinct dimensions. For example, parties could polarize on distinct economic and social dimensions. However, this would imply varying intraparty disagreements on the different dimensions. To the contrary, the evidence points to similar intraparty cleavages on almost all issues. For example, the most antitax Republican legislators are generally the most pro-life, pro-

6. When legislators cast a vote in the way that is predicted by their estimated position on the scales, we say their vote is "correctly classified." Therefore, the figure simply plots the total number of correctly classified votes divided by the total number of votes in a given congressional session. Patterns for the Senate are similar.

7. The high rates of classification success that we observe do not result simply because most votes in Congress are lopsided votes, where members say, "Hurrah." On the contrary, Congress continues to have mostly divisive votes, with average winning majorities between 60 percent and 70 percent.

Figure 2-3. *The Classification Success of One- and Two-Dimensional DW-NOMINATE Models in the U.S. House.* The solid line plots the proportion of House roll-call voting choice correctly predicted by a single dimension. The dashed line shows the proportion predicted when a second dimension is added. During the 1950s, a second dimension that captured intraparty divisions on race improved the prediction rate from 3 percent to 6 percent per congressional term. In recent years, the improvement has been considerably less than 0.5 percent.

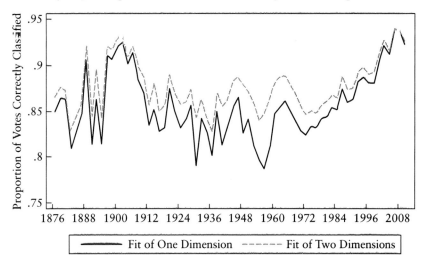

gun, and anti–marriage equality. Similarly, the Democrats most likely to support a minimum-wage hike are those most supportive of abortion rights and gay marriage. Using the terminology of Converse (1964), *issue constraint* at the congressional level has expanded dramatically.

A second logical alternative is that polarization might coincide with the displacement of the primary dimension of partisan conflict by another issue dimension, consistent with the theory of realignments put forward by Schattschneider (1960), Burnham (1970), Sundquist (1983), and others. Such a situation also seems inconsistent with the data on roll-call voting. As McCarty, Poole, and Rosenthal (2006) documented, the partisan division on economic issues has remained the primary dimension of conflict, and other issues—such as social, cultural, and religious issues—have been absorbed into it.

Although there is a broad scholarly consensus that Congress is more polarized than any time in the recent past, there is considerably less agreement on the causes of such polarization. Numerous arguments have been offered to explain the observed increase in polarization, and these causes can be divided into two broad categories: (1) explanations based on changes to the external environment of Congress, and (2) those based on changes to the internal environment. The external explanations provide arguments about how shifts in the social, economic, and electoral environments have altered the electoral incentives for elected officials to pursue moderation or bipartisanship. The internal explanations focus on how the formal and informal institutions of Congress have evolved in ways that exacerbate partisan conflict (or generate the appearance of such an increase). Although we think it is productive to divide the literature along external-internal lines, it is important to note that explanations are not mutually exclusive. Indeed, many of the internal explanations presume a shift in the external environment that stimulates revisions of legislature rules, procedures, and strategies.

In the following sections, we review the current literature on each of these suggested causes and evaluate the evidence for and against each argument.

External Explanations

We begin with arguments about how changes to the external and electoral environment of Congress have increased the incentives for ideological polarization and partisanship.

A Polarized Electorate

Perhaps the simplest explanation for an increasingly polarized Congress is one grounded in the relationship between members of Congress and their constituents. If voters are polarized, reelection-motivated legislators would be induced to represent the political ideologies of their constituents, resulting in a polarized Congress. Evidence of voter-induced polarization is elusive, however.

Empirical support for the voter polarization story requires evidence for two specific trends. First, it requires that voters be increasingly attached to political parties on an ideological basis. Liberal voters should increasingly support the Democratic Party and conservative voters should increasingly support the Republican Party. This process has been labeled *partisan sorting*. Second, the hypothesis requires that voters must be increasingly polarized in their policy preferences or ideological identification. Extreme views must be more common so that the distribution of voter preferences becomes more bimodal.

There is considerable evidence for the first trend—voters have become better sorted ideologically into the party system. Layman and Carsey (2002) and Levendusky (2009) found that over time, voters have increasingly held political views that consistently align with the parties' policy positions. Using data from the National Election Study, Layman and Carsey (2002) found evidence for a pattern of *conflict extension*, in which differences in the policy preferences of partisans have grown in economic as well as social and racial domains. Their results, updated through 2004, are presented in figure 2-4.

The trends presented in figure 2-4 are consistent with the finding that fewer voters today than in the past hold a mix of Democratic and Republican positions. As the parties become more coherent in their policy positions, voters sort themselves accordingly. This may well account for the finding of Bartels (2000) that partisan identification is a better predictor of voting behavior. Also, because the terms *Republican* and *Democrat* now represent increasingly distinct clusters of policy positions, citizens who identify with one party expect the other party's identifiers to hold dramatically different political views. Consequently, party identifiers report that they dislike one another more than they did a generation ago (Shaw 2012) and state that they would be less likely to feel "comfortable" with their child marrying someone who identifies with the opposite party than was the case in the 1960s (Iyengar, Sood, and Lelkes 2012).

Fiorina (2013) argues that the patterns described herein reflect party sorting and not polarization in voters' policy positions. A lively debate has emerged about the mechanisms underlying the better sorting of voters into parties. Sorting may improve for two distinct reasons. First, voters may shift their allegiance to the party that takes their policy position. Alternatively, voters may adjust their policy views to match those of the party with which they identify. Levendusky (2009) found evidence for both mechanisms but determined that position switching is more common than party switching. Carsey and Layman (2006) also found that party switching does occur, but that it is lim-

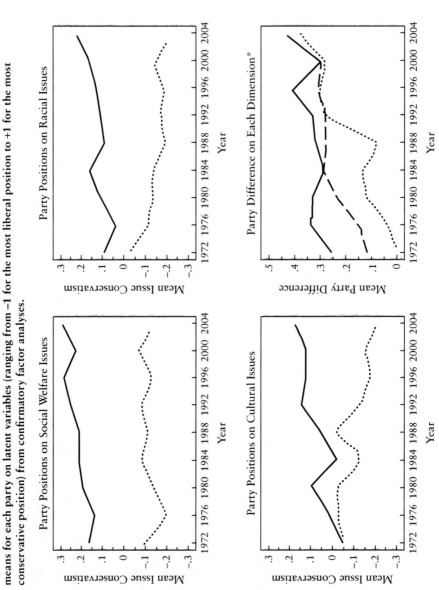

Figure 2-4. *Mass Party Polarization on Three Issue Dimensions, 1972–2004.* Party positions are the estimated means for each party on latent variables (ranging from –1 for the most liberal position to +1 for the most conservative position) from confirmatory factor analyses.

Source: 1972–2004 National Election Studies.
*Party difference is the Republican mean minus the Democratic mean.

ited to those voters who have a salient position on one issue and are aware of the partisan differences surrounding it. However, Lenz (2012) finds little evidence favoring the party-switching mechanism. Ultimately, however, both processes are facilitated by greater polarization of partisan elites, suggesting that the trends in figure 2-4 may be the consequence of elite polarization rather than the cause.[8]

Whereas few scholars doubt that substantial voter sorting has occurred, the evidence for voter policy polarization is less clear. The emerging consensus is that most voters have been and remain overwhelmingly moderate in their policy positions (Ansolabehere, Rodden, and Snyder 2006; Bafumi and Herron 2010; Fiorina and Abrams 2008; Fiorina, Abrams, and Pope 2005; Levendusky, Pope, and Jackman 2008). In studies that produce estimates of voter-issue positions that are comparable to legislator positions, representatives were found to take positions that are considerably more extreme than those of their constituents (Bafumi and Herron 2010; Clinton 2006).

Figure 2-5 illustrates the main finding of Bafumi and Herron (2010). In the 109th Congress, almost every senator was more extreme than the median voter of his or her state was. The ideological distance between representative and constituent may well have increased, but some distance seems to have existed since the introduction of our earliest measurements. As early as 1960, McClosky and his colleagues found that delegates to the party conventions took positions that were more extreme than those of the voters identifying with each party.[9] Recently, Abramowitz (2010) found a more bimodal distribution of preferences among those voters most likely to participate in politics compared with the average party identifier, with further polarization still among party activists and donors.[10] The phenomenon of the more and more active being more and more extreme probably results in part from self-selection, with those having intense feelings being more

8. McCarty, Poole, and Rosenthal (2006) and Gelman (2009) also found that voters have become better sorted into parties by income over time. The question of whether partisan voters are more sorted by geography is controversial (see Bishop 2009; Klinkner 2004).

9. See McClosky, Hoffman, and O'Hara (1960).

10. Based on surveys of convention delegates, Layman et al. (2010) found evidence consistent with activists taking more extreme positions over time.

Figure 2-5. *Senators and Median Constituents.* The x-axis shows the median ideology of the median voter M as well as the median partisan D and R on the same policy scale as sitting senators (indicated by circles for Democrats and squares for Republicans) in each state. In almost every state, senators are more extreme than voters and partisans in their state.

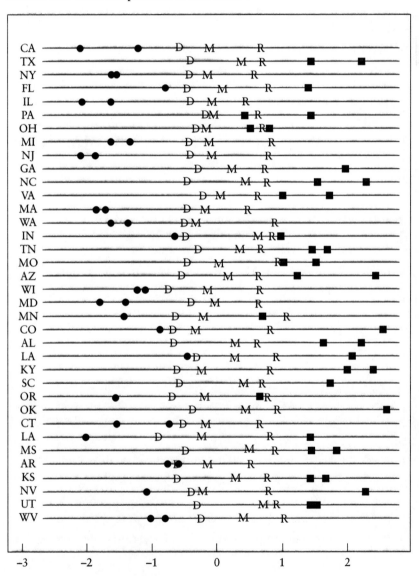

Source: Figure 2 in Bafumi and Herron (2010).

willing to spend time and money on politics, and in part from the dynamic of group polarization (Sunstein 2002), in which people who talk with one another in relatively homogeneous groups end up taking more extreme positions than the party's median members do. Regarding moderate voters, some have chosen middle-of-the-road positions for substantive policy reasons. Others, however, are uninformed, unengaged, or apathetic, checking off the middle position on surveys because of a lack of an opinion.

Although the lack of evidence of voter polarization casts doubt on the simple link between voter and elite polarization, a dynamic version may hold more promise. As voters sort in response to elite polarization, the incentives for parties to take positions that appeal to supporters of the other party will diminish. This leads to greater partisan polarization and greater incentives for voters to sort. Although this mechanism is not ruled out by existing evidence, it has not yet been subjected to formal tests.

Southern Realignment

Although Americans still appear to remain overwhelmingly moderate, there is no denying that dramatic changes have occurred in terms of policy sorting between the parties. The realignment of the South from a solidly Democratic region to one dominated by Republicans is the starkest example of the sorting of ideology and partisanship.

Figure 2-6 places the Southern realignment in the context of the national story of polarization. The left-hand panel shows that since the 1970s, there has been a dramatic increase in the number of Republicans representing Southern districts in the House of Representatives. As these Republicans replace more moderate Democrats, we see two effects. First, the median Southern Democrat becomes more liberal. By the early 2000s, most of these Democrats were representing majority-minority districts. At the same time, the new Southern Republicans were becoming increasingly conservative. However, the right-hand panel in the figure shows that the conservative path of Southern Republicans is mirrored in non-Southern districts. Thus, to blame polarization completely on the disappearance of conservative Democrats would be to ignore the conservative trajectory of non-Southern Republicans. The movement in the median ideology of

Figure 2-6. *Median Position of Parties and Caucus Size.* The y-axis shows the median position on the party-conflict scale. The colored band around each line shows the relative size of the party caucus. Republicans now hold many more seats in the South than forty years ago, but Southern and non-Southern Republicans alike have taken increasingly conservative positions.

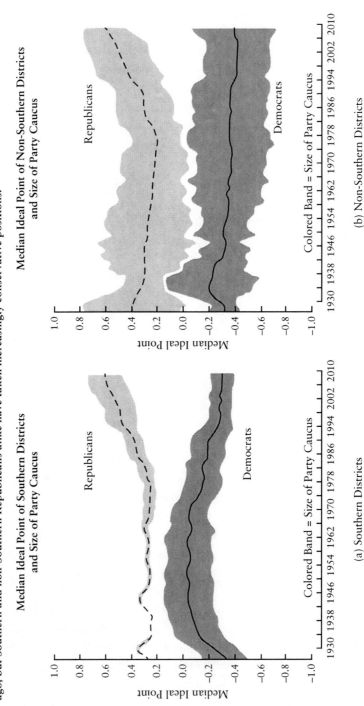

Democrats, however, can be nearly accounted for by the replacement of moderate Southern Democrats with Republicans.

Whereas much attention has been focused on the effects of the Southern realignment for the emergence of a conservative Republican party in the South, the post–Voting Rights Act increase in the descriptive representation of African Americans and Latinos in the House also had a discernible effect on polarization. Although the representatives of those groups are hardly monolithic, they are overrepresented in the liberal wing of the Democratic Party; any leftward movement of the Democrats can be accounted for by the increase in the number of African American and Latino representatives.[11]

Gerrymandering

Scholars have long suggested that allowing state legislatures to draw congressional districts may lead to overwhelmingly partisan and safe districts that free candidates from the need to compete for votes at the political center (Carson et al. 2007; Theriault 2008a; Tufte 1973). However, the evidence in support of gerrymandering as a cause of polarization is not strong. First, we consider the Senate and those states in which there is only one congressional district. In these cases, gerrymandering is impossible because the district must conform to the state boundaries. Yet in the Senate and in at-large congressional districts, we observe increasing polarization (McCarty, Poole, and Rosenthal 2006). Furthermore, McCarty, Poole, and Rosenthal (2009) generated random districts and determined the expected partisanship of representatives from these hypothetical districts given the demographic characteristics of the simulated district. The result was that the simulated legislatures generated by randomly creating districts are almost as polarized as the current Congress is. This finding holds

11. McCarty, Poole, and Rosenthal (2006) found that African American and Latino House members have more liberal DW-NOMINATE scores, even after controlling for party and the ethnic and racial composition of their districts. However, roll-call-based measures of the positions of minority legislators may understate those members' contribution to increasing the diversity of interests represented in Congress. The difference between white and minority legislators is larger on other legislative activities, such as oversight, bill cosponsorship, and advocacy (Canon 1999; Tate 2003; Minta 2009; Minta and Sinclair-Chapman 2013; Wallace 2012).

because polarization relates more to the difference in how Republicans and Democrats represent moderate districts than the increase in the number of extreme partisan districts. Therefore, an attempt to undo partisan gerrymandering with moderate, competitive districts still leads to a polarized legislature because of the difference between rather than within the parties.

Figure 2-7 illustrates this argument. The plot shows the ideal points of members of the 111th House of Representatives and the 2008 Democratic percentage of the presidential vote in that district. Scholars frequently use presidential vote shares as a proxy for district ideology because the vote shares allow for a unified measure of political preferences across the country at any one point in time. Thus, a district with a larger Democratic vote share is interpreted to have more liberal constituents than a district that has a smaller Democratic vote share. Members of Congress from the same party vote quite similarly, even though they represent districts with vastly different political preferences. This difference is illustrated by the regression lines drawn in the figure for each party. Democrats who represent districts that split almost evenly in the presidential vote are not significantly more conservative than Democrats representing districts that overwhelmingly supported Obama in 2008. However, there is a dramatic difference in how representatives of the opposing parties represent districts with identical presidential vote shares. This figure does not support the argument that gerrymandering is producing districts that contain heavy partisan majorities, thereby leading to extreme representatives. Rather, more of the observed polarization can be explained by the differences between the parties in relatively moderate and competitive districts.

Primary Elections

Given the extent to which voters are now ideologically sorted into political parties, some observers suggest that only conservatives can win Republican primaries and only liberals can win Democratic primaries.[12] This suggested feature of contemporary politics has led

12. Note, however, that, as figure 2-7 shows, there are many Democrats who represent districts that won less than 50 percent of the Democratic vote share in the 2008 presidential election and have quite moderate ideal points.

Figure 2-7. *Representative Position on the Party Scale and Presidential Vote Share.* The x-axis shows the partisanship of the congressional district as measured by the Democratic percentage of the 2008 presidential vote. The y-axis is the representative's DW-NOMINATE score for the 111th House of Representatives. There are major differences in the way Republicans and Democrats represent similar districts. These differences account for a larger share of the aggregate party difference than the differences in the types of districts that Democrats and Republicans represent.

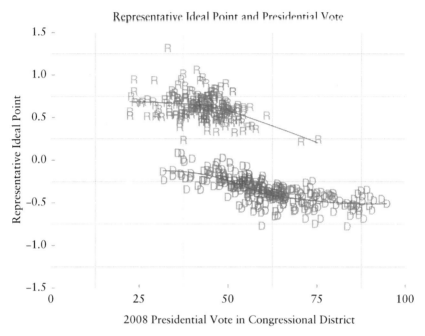

reformers to focus on whether the rules governing participation in primaries might be altered to make it possible for more moderate candidates to win nominations. The standard recommendation is to move from closed partisan primaries to open primaries, which would allow the participation of independents. The state of California has recently gone one step further with the nonpartisan "top-two" primary, in which voters of both parties cast ballots for candidates of either party and the top two vote getters move to the general election.

Based on the historical record, it is implausible that partisan primaries are a major cause of polarization. Polarization increased during the past forty years despite the opening up of primaries to nonpartisans (McCarty, Poole, and Rosenthal 2006). The narrower question of whether open or nonpartisan primaries would reduce contemporary levels of polarization continues to be an active area of research, but the evidence to date provides sparse support for the argument that opening primaries to nonpartisans would reduce polarization.

A few studies have found evidence for a polarizing effect of partisan primaries. Kaufmann, Gimpel, and Hoffman (2003) found that presidential primary voters in states with open primaries hold political ideologies similar to the general electorate, whereas in states with closed primaries, the two electorates are more ideologically distinct. Gerber and Morton (1998) found that the positions of legislators nominated in open primaries hew more closely to district preferences, whereas Brady, Han, and Pope (2007) found that legislators who hew closely to the general-election electorate suffer an electoral penalty in primaries.

However, most of the research suggests that the effects of moving to open-primary systems are modest at best. Hirano et al. (2010) studied the history of primary elections for the U.S. Senate. Their findings cast significant doubt on the role of primary-election institutions in polarization. First, the introduction of primaries had no effect on polarization in the Senate. Second, despite the common belief that participation in primaries has been decreasing, they found that primary turnout has always been quite low. Thus, it is doubtful that changes in primary participation can explain the polarizing trends of the past three decades. Third, they find no econometric evidence that either low primary turnout or low primary competition leads to the polarization of senators. Using a panel of state legislative elections, Masket et al. (2013) investigated the effects of changing primary systems and found little evidence that such switches affect polarization. Similarly, Bullock and Clinton (2011) investigated the effects of California's short-lived move from a closed primary to a blanket primary, in which any registered voter can participate. They found that the change did lead to more moderate candidates in competitive districts but that these effects were not observed in districts that were dominated by either of the parties. This result suggests that the recent change in California to a top-two primary may affect districts that are not firmly controlled by one or the other party.

Economic Inequality

McCarty, Poole, and Rosenthal (2006) demonstrated a close correlation between economic inequality and polarization in the United States.[13] Figure 2-8 shows that economic inequality and polarization have tracked together in the past fifty years. Moreover, unlike most other hypotheses about polarization, the inequality hypothesis can explain the decline of polarization during the first half of the twentieth century, as economic inequality fell dramatically in that period (Piketty and Saez 2003). McCarty, Poole, and Rosenthal (2006) argued that inequality and polarization are linked by a dynamic relationship (or "dance") in which the increased inequality generated by rising top incomes produces electoral support for conservative economic policies and facilitates a movement to the right by Republicans. The resulting polarization then has a dampening effect on the policy response to increased inequality, which in turn facilitates greater inequality and polarization.

In support of the hypothesis that the distribution of income has affected polarization, McCarty, Poole, and Rosenthal (2006) demonstrated that voting behavior and partisan identification increasingly correlate with income (see also Gelman 2009) and that the ideal points of legislators are increasingly correlated with average district income. They then show (see following discussion) that polarization may have exacerbated inequality as a result of its negative effects on social policy. Although the 2006 McCarty, Poole, and Rosenthal study is limited by the fact that the correlation between inequality and polarization may be spurious in the U.S. time-series data, Garand (2010) found strong evidence that state-level inequality exacerbates constituency polarization within states and predicts the extremity of Senate voting behavior. Furthermore, recent work by Bartels (2008) and Gilens (2012) showed that policy reflects the preferences of the wealthy more often than the desires of those on the bottom rungs of the economic ladder.

Money in Politics

Another common argument is that polarization is directly linked to the system of private campaign finance used in U.S. elections. Such

13. See also Brewer, Mariani, and Stonecash (2002).

Figure 2-8. *Polarization and Income Inequality.* The y-axis shows the difference in median positions for the two parties and the Gini coefficient in the United States. The Gini coefficient is a measure of income inequality that ranges between 0 (perfect income equality) and 1 (one person controls 100 percent of the nation's income).

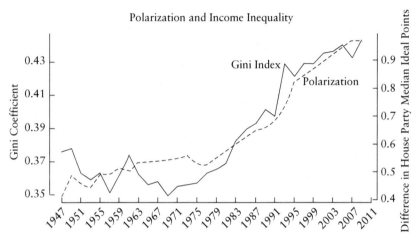

arguments are generally premised on the idea that politicians pursue extreme policy objectives on behalf of their special-interest funders (Lessig 2011).

However, political science research suggests that any connections between campaign finance and polarization may be more subtle and complex than the conventional wisdom. Most research suggests that there is a weak connection between campaign spending and election outcomes (Jacobson 1990) or between sources of campaign funding and roll-call-voting behavior (Ansolabehere, de Figueiredo, and Snyder 2003).

Conversely, the data suggest that fundraising in congressional campaigns has increased in importance, as evidenced by the steady rise in the sheer amount of money required to run for office. Since 1990, the average amount of money spent in U.S. House elections has nearly doubled in real terms. Whereas the amount of money raised in campaigns is important, the sources of funding may be more consequential for polarization. Consider the difference between the two largest sources of money for congressional candidates: contributions from individuals and contributions from political action committees (PACs). Scholars have long argued that although PACs may seek specific policy outcomes, these goals are often narrowly focused such that PACs are less concerned with the overall ideology or party of politicians and more interested in having access to members of Congress (Bonica 2013; Hall and Wayman 1990; McCarty, Poole, and Rosenthal 2006; Smith 1995).

Individual donors, however, are believed to behave quite differently. The literature on the ideology of individual donors is less developed than research into PAC contribution behavior, but recent studies suggest that individual contributors are more extreme than individual noncontributors (Bafumi and Herron 2010; Barber 2013; Stone and Simas 2010). Furthermore, recent work estimating the ideological positions of contributors suggests that individuals are more ideologically extreme than PACs and other interest groups (Barber 2013; Bonica 2013). Given the differences between PAC and individual contribution behavior, an increasing reliance of candidates on ideologically extreme individual donors might force candidates to move toward the ideological poles to raise money (Baron 1994; Ensley 2009; Moon 2004). We may also see a rise in more ideologically motivated PACs, a phenomenon that deserves further investigation.

Figure 2-9 provides evidence of an increasing reliance on individual donors. Since 1980, the average share of a candidate's fundraising portfolio comprising individual contributions has increased from less than half to nearly three quarters. At the same time, the share of individual contributions coming from out-of-district donors, which are believed to be more ideologically motivated, has increased as well (Gimpel, Lee, and Kaminski 2006; Gimpel, Lee, and Pearson-Merkowitz 2008). Together, these data suggest that there may be a direct connection between the rise in individual contributions and polarization in American politics.

However, more research is needed to convincingly link individual contributions and polarization. Although individual contributions and polarization may be increasing at the same time, this does not immediately suggest a causal relationship. Looking at the U.S. states may provide a way to better identify the relationship. Variation in contribution limits among the states has led to differing abilities for candidates to raise money from individuals, PACs, parties, and other sources (Barber 2013). Using this variation in contribution limits across time and place may provide a more conclusive view into the relationship

Figure 2-9. *Average Candidate Fundraising Portfolio.* In the left-hand panel, the y-axis shows the average percentage of congressional candidates' fundraising that comes from individual donors, PACs, and party contributions. In the right-hand panel, the y-axis shows the average percentage of individual donations that come from donors who reside inside and outside the candidate's district.

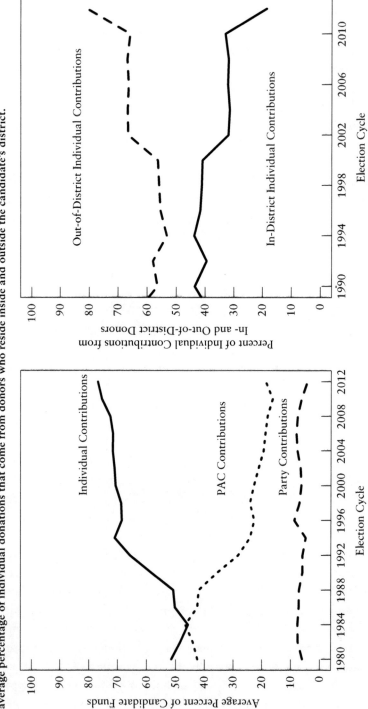

between the increasing money flowing into politics and increasing polarization.

Media Environment

Changes in the media environment of politics may also have had an important role in polarization. Many observers note that American journalism changed markedly following Watergate in a manner that may have contributed to a more confrontational style of politics. The introduction of cameras into the House chamber and the broadcasting of its proceedings on C-SPAN gave the minority Republicans, led by Newt Gingrich, a powerful new weapon against the majority party (Zelizer 2006). Others argue that the proliferation of media outlets through cable television and the Internet has created an additional impetus for polarization. Recently, Prior (2007) found that partisan voters increasingly self-select into news outlets that confirm their basic partisan and ideological biases (that is, Republicans watch Fox News and Democrats watch MSNBC). Such narrowcasting was not absent in media-viewing patterns forty years ago, but it was not nearly as extensive. One effect of this change is that elected officials have less space to deviate from their party orthodoxy for fear of being called out by party activists. Another effect is that relatively extreme activists have a platform to push forward partisan talking points to a subset of the public, contributing to societal polarization.

As troubling is the finding that independents increasingly prefer *Seinfeld* reruns to any news outlet. Prior (2007) called the effect of the alternative news-less media "polarization without persuasion" and suggested that the media's effect on polarization is mostly the result of nonideological Americans avoiding inadvertent news exposure through the availability of cable entertainment, whereas in the past, network television offered no alternative except the news for several hours every evening. When the only option on television was the evening news, Prior suggested, nonpolitical Americans were exposed to political information through the news and mobilized to vote in greater numbers than they would have otherwise. He suggested that this effect is more important than partisan media by pointing to the fact that polarization and cable penetration are correlated beginning in the 1970s, long before Fox News, MSNBC, or any other partisan cable

news stations existed. Others examined how the decline of newspapers, which have experienced thousands of layoffs in recent years
and dramatically reduced their coverage, may also be a contributing
factor. Snyder and Stromberg (2010) found that members of Congress
who represent districts that are congruent with newspaper markets
compile less ideological and partisan voting records.

The reemergence of a more partisan media may also contribute to
polarization. A literature attempting to measure partisan media
bias and its effects on voters has developed in the past several years.
Whereas debate rages as to whether the American media has an overall liberal or conservative bias, there is substantial evidence that media
outlets vary in terms of their ideological and partisan orientations (for
example, see Gentzkow and Shapiro 2006; Groseclose and Milyo
2005), and the slant of coverage appears to affect voter evaluations
and decisions (for example, see DellaVigna and Kaplan 2007; Gerber,
Karlan, and Bergan 2009; Hopkins and Ladd 2014). Of course, the
ideological diversity of the media may be the result of polarization and
not the cause. For example, Gentzkow and Shapiro (2006) found that
the partisan slant of a newspaper is determined in large part by the
partisanship of its local community.[14]

Internal Explanations

Scholars have also offered many explanations of the increase in the
appearance of polarization and partisanship based on the incentives,
procedures, and institutions that are internal to Congress.

Rule Changes

Several scholars have suggested that one of the major causes of the
increase in measured polarization is due to changes in the rules and
procedures of Congress. One argument is that the observation of rising polarization is an artifact of changes in the House regarding how
votes were recorded in the Committee of the Whole (Theriault 2008b).

14. They also provide evidence against a reverse causal relationship between
newspaper slant and local partisanship.

These procedural changes made it easier for amendments to be proposed when considering legislation. These new amendments were often unrelated to the bill at hand, and they were added primarily to force the opposition party to cast unpopular votes to move on with considering the main piece of legislation (Roberts and Smith 2003). This simple change in the rules led to a dramatic increase in the number of party-line recorded votes and therefore led to an increase in measured polarization for indices that use roll-call voting, such as the DW-NOMINATE scores discussed previously (Roberts 2007).

Although this procedural change may have the effect of exaggerating partisan differences, it leaves many questions regarding polarization unanswered. First, the argument is centered on the House of Representatives. Polarization, as we have seen, increased in both the House and the Senate, despite no similar procedural change in the Senate. Second, polarization has increased gradually in the past four decades. It seems unlikely that a onetime rules change would produce such a long-term trend. Third, despite a wide variety of rules for agenda setting and recording roll-call votes operating in the American states, the level of polarization in the U.S. House is not atypical of that found in state legislatures (Shor and McCarty 2011).

Majority-Party Agenda Control

A second institutional argument focuses on the agenda-setting power of the majority party in the House (for example, see Aldrich 1995; Cox and McCubbins 2005; Rohde 1991). Scholars have theorized that leaders of the majority party have been increasingly able to use their control over the legislative agenda to build distinctive party brands and prevent intraparty divisions. This leadership behavior, in turn, generates more party-line votes and a larger level of observed polarization. Like the rules-based explanations, these explanations struggle to explain the rising level of polarization in the Senate. Moreover, McCarty, Poole, and Rosenthal (2006) demonstrated that measures of polarization are robust to the changes in the legislative agenda that might be induced by enhanced agenda control.

Party Pressures

An additional institutional argument for rising polarization is that party leaders in the House and the Senate have become increasingly powerful and, as such, can apply greater pressure on members to vote along party lines. Theories of party government (for example, see Aldrich 1995; Rohde 1991) suggest that party leaders can apply strong pressures on their members to vote the way the party desires. Former and current members have indicated their impression that these pressures have increased over the years (for example, see Edwards 2012). In developing this idea, Theriault (2008b) traced the roles of speaker and majority leader, showing that these offices have increased their institutional reach in the past thirty years. He argued that party leaders coax members to vote along party lines by offering rewards to members (for example, committee memberships in exchange for votes with the party's agenda).

Although the plausibility of increased party pressure is strong, there are major methodological challenges in establishing the magnitude and trends of such pressures. Snyder and Groseclose (2000) attempted to distinguish the influences of parties from other factors, such as ideological preferences on roll-call voting. If we could reliably measure the effect of party pressure on members' voting behavior, we would be able to apportion the effects of partisanship on polarization from changes in ideology, constituency, and so forth. Unfortunately, the effects of party can be recovered only under strong assumptions. For example, Snyder and Groseclose assumed that members are free from party pressure on lopsided votes; therefore, a comparison between positions on lopsided and close votes can reveal the effects of party pressure. They found that, indeed, there are policy areas in which party pressure is more common, but they did not find a steady increase in partisan pressure commensurate with the increase in polarization observed during the past forty years. McCarty, Poole, and Rosenthal (2001) criticized Snyder and Groseclose's methodology. Using an alternative methodology, they found declining party pressure in the contemporary Congress. However, methodological difficulties prevented a consensus on this question.[15]

---

15. Using a different methodology, Cox and Poole (2002) provided evidence similar to McCarty, Poole, and Rosenthal (2001) but interpreted it in a way

Teamsmanship

Lee (2009) argued that the trends in figures 2-1 and 2-2 reflect not only an ideological divergence but also Congress members' increasing efforts to favorably differentiate their own party from the opposition as the two parties become more closely competitive in seeking control of national institutions. She argued that whenever the parties become closer in the electoral support they can garner, such that the conditions are right for a reversal of partisan fortunes in the next election, each party has a strategic incentive to engage in strategies of confrontation to highlight partisan differences and to deny the other party legislative victories. Tight competition gives members incentives to act together with fellow partisans, and a norm of "teamsmanship" has emerged, with members' individual interests becoming increasingly linked to the fate of their parties. Teamsmanship not only deepens existing ideological divisions; it also creates conflict on issues in which legitimate ideological differences are absent. Partisan divisions on nonideological issues, Lee showed, have grown in tandem with the divisions on ideological issues. If Lee's reasoning on the strategic incentives deriving from party competition for institutional control is correct, we should see congressional polarization for as long as both political parties remain roughly equal in their electoral appeal nationwide.

Lee's teamsmanship perspective is related to the literature on strategic disagreement (Gilmour 1995; Groseclose and McCarty 2001). Strategic disagreement describes a situation in which a president, a party, or another political actor refuses compromise in an attempt to gain an electoral advantage by transferring the blame for the stalemate to the other side. Such behavior often results in the appearance of a level of polarization that exceeds the actual policy differences between the parties.

---

more favorable to the finding of party discipline. However, even their interpretation does not support the hypothesis that increased party pressures are associated with polarization.

The Breakdown of Bipartisan Norms

Many personal accounts of former members of Congress link polarization to changes in the social fabric of Capitol Hill, making it more difficult to forge cross-partisan relationships (for a journalistic account, see Eilperin 2007). In the past several decades, members of Congress have increasingly not relocated their families to Washington and therefore spend far less time in Washington and more time in their home districts. This lack of time in Washington has made it more difficult to form the personal relationships that would foster bipartisan trust and civility. Other reasons advanced for the decreasing number of interpersonal contacts across party lines include the ever-increasing workload for members of Congress, deriving in part from the need to spend considerable time fundraising. Although the social fabric hypothesis is compelling, it has not been subjected to systematic empirical tests.[16]

Consequences of Polarization

Although *polarization* generally has a negative connotation in our political discourse, it has a number of potential virtues. In the 1950s, another task force of the American Political Science Association criticized the American party system of the time for not offering significantly different policy choices to the voters. This lack of choice denied American voters any meaningful influence over public policy. Completely centrist and undifferentiated parties would be incapable of representing the diversity of interests of contemporary American society. Undoubtedly, whatever part of the current polarization has been caused by the greater representation of formerly unheard voices has benefits outweighed by any potential costs.[17] However, party polarization has negative consequences to the extent that the parties primarily repre-

16. A possible exception is Masket (2008), who found that randomized seating assignments in the California Assembly produced greater similarities in voting by members who shared desks.

17. Those who feel nostalgia for the bipartisanship of the 1950s must recognize that it came at the cost of the exclusion of African Americans and other groups from the political process.

sent extreme policy views or impede the negotiated compromises required by democratic politics in heterogeneous societies.

As discussed previously, the evidence overwhelmingly supports the proposition that members of Congress are far more polarized than the public at large. As Bafumi and Herron (2010) showed, it is likely that legislators are taking positions that are even more extreme than the voters from their parties in their states and districts. Therefore, although polarization may expand the choices on the political menu, the parties are far from satisfying the palate of most voters. Thus, the effects of polarization on accountability and representation are ambiguous, at best.

Theoretical Perspectives on Polarization and Policymaking

A polarized party system need not have deleterious effects on policymaking. Consider an idealized, purely majoritarian legislature. Imagine that we can represent policy alternatives on a single left-right spectrum and that every legislator has an ideal policy on this spectrum. In such a setting, the median-voter theorem predicts that policy would correspond to the preferences of the median legislator. The distribution of legislative preferences may become very polarized; however, if the median preference is unaffected, the outcome is the same. Although the majoritarian theory is an important benchmark, the real-world deviations from this ideal suggest that polarization should have serious consequences for policymaking.

The first limitation of the majoritarian benchmark is the neglected role of legislative parties and their leaders in the policy process. Many scholars argue that legislators have strong electoral incentives to delegate substantial powers to partisan leaders, to shape the legislative agenda as well as to discipline wayward members (for example, see Aldrich and Rohde 2010; Cox and McCubbins 2005). To the extent that parties can successfully pursue such strategies, policymaking becomes the interaction of parties.

With strong parties and leaders, the effects of polarization are mixed. American political scientists have long suggested that more cohesive, distinct, and programmatic political parties would offer a corrective to the failures of policymaking in the United States. Enamored with the party-responsibility model of Westminster-style parliaments, they argue that a system where a cohesive majority party governs encumbered only by the need to win elections would provide more accountability and rationality in policymaking.

These benefits of polarization are offset, however, when control of the executive and legislative branches is split among cohesive parties; political polarization has occurred in an era in which divided governments occur with increasing frequency. Before World War II, there was no positive association between divided government and polarization, but the two phenomena have occurred together frequently since then.

In situations of divided government with cohesive parties, party theories predict that policymaking represents bilateral bargaining between the parties. The predicted consequences of polarization in this environment are not benign. Increased policy differences shrink the set of compromises that both parties are willing to entertain. Increased policy differences also have a second effect of exacerbating the incentives to engage in brinkmanship in bargaining and negotiation, thereby endangering even the feasible compromises. Low dimensionality compounds the problem of polarization by foreclosing solutions negotiated across distinct policy dimensions. Thus, polarization and low dimensionality lead to more gridlock and less policy innovation during periods of divided government. Polarization might lead to more policy innovation during unified governments because of increased party responsibility. The U.S. system, however, is unlikely to generate consistently unified governments.

The second feature of the American system that generates real policy consequences from polarization is the plethora of supermajoritarian institutions and veto points. Institutions such as the presidential veto and the Senate filibuster inhibit majority rule and allow polarization to hinder policymaking. In the presence of these supermajoritarian institutions, policymaking is driven not by the median legislator but rather by the preferences of the more extreme legislators, whose support is pivotal in overcoming vetoes and filibusters.

To illustrate how supermajoritarianism produces gridlocked policy, we suppose again that all policy alternatives and legislator ideal points can be represented as points on a spectrum from left to right, such as the liberal-conservative scale. Consider, for example, the effects of the Senate's rules for debate and cloture. Under its current rules, debate on most legislation cannot be terminated without a vote on cloture that must be supported by three-fifths of those senators elected and sworn. Thus, if all one hundred senators vote according to their ideal points, the senators located at the forty-first and the sixtieth most leftward positions must support any new legislation because no coalition can contain three-fifths of the votes without including them. Therefore, any policy located between these pivotal senators cannot be altered or it is otherwise gridlocked. Prior to procedural reforms in 1975, the requirement for cloture was a two-thirds vote. The filibuster pivots were therefore located at the thirty-third and sixty-seventh positions.

Presidential veto power also contributes to gridlock. Either the president must support new legislation or a coalition of two-thirds of each chamber must vote to override it. Suppose that the president's position is on the left of the policy spectrum. Then he or the legislator at the thirty-third percentile must support any policy change. This legislator becomes the veto pivot. If the president is a rightist, the sixty-seventh-percentile legislator becomes the veto pivot.

Putting these institutional requirements together, a rough measure of the propensity for legislative gridlock is the ideological distance between the thirty-third senator and the sixtieth senator when the president is on the left and the distance between the fortieth senator and the sixty-seventh senator when the president is on the right. When these distances are great, passing new legislation will be difficult. The level of polarization and the width of this "gridlock interval" are closely related because the filibuster and veto pivots are almost always members of different parties. Thus, as the preferences of the parties diverge, so do those of the pivots. In fact, more than 75 percent of the variation in the width of the gridlock interval in the postwar period is accounted for by party polarization and the 1975 cloture reforms (McCarty 2007). Therefore, this "pivotal-politics" model of supermajoritarianism suggests that polarization reduces opportunities for new legislation and increases the status-quo bias of American politics (Krehbiel 1998).

It is important to note that these supermajority requirements may also lead to polarization-induced gridlock even during periods of unified government. As long as the majority party is not large enough to satisfy all the supermajority requirements, cross-party bargaining, negotiation, and coalition building are necessary for policy change.

This pivot perspective also underscores why the Senate's cloture rules have come under scrutiny and have produced calls for reform. Once an infrequently used tool reserved for the most important legislation, the filibuster has become—during the period of increasing polarization—one of the central features of American politics. Filibusters, both threatened and realized, have been used to kill many important pieces of legislation. Perhaps even more consequentially, the ease of the current filibuster has led the Senate to rely greatly on legislative tricks to avoid its effects. One such gimmick is using the budget-reconciliation process to pass new legislation; reconciliation bills cannot be filibustered. This was the approach taken to pass the major income- and estate-tax cuts in 2001, as well as major portions of the Affordable Care Act in 2009. To avoid points of order under the so-called Byrd Rule, however, such legislation can have deficit-increasing fiscal effects only for the term of the budget resolution (that is, five to ten years). Thus, many important pieces of fiscal policy require gimmicks such as "sunset" provisions (in which the law expires after a certain predetermined time) to avoid death by filibuster.

Legislative Productivity

Despite the strong theoretical case for a relationship between polarization and policy gridlock, few scholars have addressed the issue. In his seminal work on postwar lawmaking, Mayhew (2005) considered whether divided party control of the executive and legislative branches produces legislative gridlock, but he did not consider the effects of polarization and declining bipartisanship. Indeed, he attributed his finding that divided government produced little gridlock to the fact that bipartisanship was the norm during the postwar period. McCarty (2007) used data on landmark legislative enactments to assess polarization's effects on the legislative process. He found that the ten least polarized congressional terms produced almost sixteen significant enactments per term, whereas the ten most polarized terms produced only slightly more than ten. This gap would be even larger except for the enormous legislative output following the September 11 terrorist attacks during the most polarized congressional term of the era. Using a multivariate model that controls for other factors that contribute to legislative productivity, McCarty found substantively large and statistically significant effects of polarization on legislative productivity. At the upper end of the range of his estimates, Congress produced 166 percent more legislation in the least polarized congressional term than in the most polarized term. Even at the lower range of his estimates, there is still a large—60 percent—difference in legislative output. His estimates are robust to the use of other data sources, which extend the time-series back to the nineteenth century.

Binder (1999) also found that as the gridlock interval increases under divided legislatures (that is, when the distance between the House and Senate medians is largest), we observe less legislation passed. As these gridlock intervals grow owing to polarization, her prediction was that we will observe even less legislation created and eventually passed through Congress.

The current unprecedented distance between the parties, combined with divided government between the House and the Senate, has led many media outlets to note that the 112th Congress has passed fewer laws than any other since the late 1800s (Davis 2012; Kasperowicz 2012; Sides 2012; Steinhauer 2012), when polarization was at almost the same levels as today.

Case Study: Polarization, Gridlock, and the Politics of Immigration[18]

Historically, successful immigration legislation was characterized by bipartisan coalitions between Republicans and Democrats, in addition to coalitions across chambers within Congress (Gimpel and Edwards 1998). The last significant piece of comprehensive immigration legislation that successfully navigated the legislative process passed in 1986. The Immigration Reform and Control Act (IRCA), also known as the Simpson–Mazzoli Act, was brought forward by a Democratic representative from Kentucky and a Republican senator from Wyoming, both of whom were chairs of respective subcommittees on immigration in the two chambers. The legislation was partially informed by the bipartisan Commission on Immigration Reform, which is consistent with the use of commissions on immigration throughout the legislative history of this policy area (Tichenor 2002). The legislation

18. This section was written by task force member Sophia Wallace.

was considered comprehensive given the broad scope of the bill, which included criminalization of hiring undocumented immigrants, employer sanctions, and amnesty for a sizable portion of the undocumented immigrant population.

Attempts at reform since the passage of IRCA have been confronted with increased polarization on immigration both between and within the two political parties. Comprehensive immigration bills have had limited success in getting passed in one chamber, much less clearing the necessary hurdles in both chambers. Consequently, much of the legislation introduced during the 1990s and 2000s was piecemeal in nature, meaning that only one small component of immigration reform would be addressed. Three major legislative initiatives stand out in the post-IRCA era as attempts at broader immigration reform.

In 2006, Bill H.R. 4437, also known as the Sensenbrenner Bill, was introduced. Its language was wide in scope and reach because it criminalized being an undocumented immigrant as a felony (as well as the actions of anyone assisting an undocumented immigrant), required significant construction of border fences, and imposed employer penalties and sanctions. Party polarization on the issue was intense, as demonstrated by the bill being pushed only by the Republican Party and overwhelmingly opposed by Democrats. Mass mobilization of Latinos around the country occurred, leading to approximately 350 protests with millions of participants in an attempt to thwart support of the bill after it passed in the House (Wallace, Zepeda-Millán, and Jones-Correa 2014). Ultimately, the bill died, and scholars attribute the failure to the effects of the protests, as well as to a lack of consensus on this issue between the political parties and among the electorate (Zepeda-Millán 2011).

In 2010, the Development, Relief, and Education for Alien Minors Act (DREAM Act) was formally introduced by Dick Durbin (Democrat) and Orin Hatch (Republican) but was announced by a number of members across both chambers, demonstrating a bipartisan effort at reform—in contrast to the Sensenbrenner Bill. The purpose of the DREAM Act was to offer a pathway to citizenship for undocumented immigrants who had arrived in the country as minors, attended high school in the United States, and were now enrolling in college or the military. Although the bill was bipartisan in its creation, support in the

House split along party lines, with a vote of 216 to 198, with Democrats in favor. In the Senate, the bill failed to achieve the necessary sixty votes to end debate, thereby preventing its passage. The DREAM Act is an important indication of the state of party polarization on immigration when one considers the context of the actual bill. In many ways, it was viewed as the least potentially polarizing immigration bill because it involved people brought to the United States as minors. Thus, the assumption was that they bore little culpability for the choices of their parents, and it targeted only those willing to pursue college or the military, which are highly valued pathways for young people. If Republicans and Democrats were going to agree on the issue of immigration reform, then this bill should have been one of the most likely cases to pass muster. The defeat of this bill suggests that polarization within Congress had reached nearly insurmountable levels.

In January 2013, lawmakers announced bipartisan efforts to pursue comprehensive immigration reform, with acknowledgment from both political parties that the nation's immigration system was broken. In particular, attempts to smooth polarization were made through the use of a "gang"—in this case, a bipartisan group of senators—that could work with party leaders to try to appeal to and negotiate with their own party members (for more on gangs, see chapter 3). The Gang of Eight, in this case, devised a bill that contained individual provisions that appealed to both parties, such as a pathway to legalization for undocumented immigrants and increased border security. The bill was able to win two-thirds of the support of the Senate but was not advanced on the House legislative agenda by Speaker Boehner. Taken as a package, the bill was not popular among House Republicans. Moreover, the compromised version of the bill contained provisions that House Democrats believed were too restrictionist, such as substantially expanding border-security resources. This attempt at immigration reform demonstrated polarization on this issue not only across chambers and political parties but also within each party. Republicans diverged in opinion on the issue between the moderates and the Tea Party Caucus. Boehner lacked consensus within his party in the House, which limited his power as the speaker to move forward on this issue. For Democrats, there was enormous pressure to deliver immigration reform for the Latino electorate it so heavily relied on, to the point of excessive compromise in the view of some House Democrats. As a result, certain House Democrats were so angered by the bill that they withdrew support, including one Latino representative, Representative Filemon Vela, who resigned from the Congressional Hispanic Caucus in response to its support for the bill, despite the border-security provisions.

One explanation for the more general breakdown of bipartisan efforts on immigration legislation may be rooted in the fact that post-1992, Congress has experienced more changes of party control than in the prior forty years. Lee (2009) argues this leads each party to believe that in the next election, it may be able to win control of the chamber or increase its vote share; therefore, each party has little incentive to compromise. Rather, they have incentives to differentiate from the opposing party by taking distinctly different stands on many issues. Recent public-opinion data suggest that the public is also becoming increasingly polarized along partisan lines on many issues, including immigration (Pew Center 2012). Despite losing traction with Latino voters and struggling to win their support (Wallace 2012)—in large part because of its position on immigration—the Republican Party continues to take a restrictionist stance that is consistent with a very active component of its electoral base. This segment of its reelection constituency comprises Tea Party supporters who played a vital role in Republican Party dominance in the 2010 elections (Parker and Barreto 2013; Skocpol and Williamson 2012). When Republicans come to believe that their chances of winning elections will be greatly influenced by the Latino electorate, their legislative strategy on immigration may change. Until then, both parties will take positions most appealing to the coalitions of voters they have historically relied upon, and will likely continue to be highly polarized on the issue of immigration.

Policy Outcomes

Given the evidence that polarization has reduced Congress's capacity to legislate, we turn to the question of how this has affected public policy outcomes. The most direct effect of polarization-induced gridlock is that public policy does not adjust to changing economic and demographic circumstances.

There are a number of reasons to believe that these effects would be most pronounced in the arena of social policy. Given that one of the aims of social policy is to insure citizens against the economic risks inherent in a market system, it must be responsive to shifts in those economic forces. If polarization inhibits those responses, it may leave citizens open to the new risks created by economic shifts brought on by deindustrialization and globalization.

For example, consider the political response in the United States to increasing economic inequality since the 1970s. Most economists attribute increasing inequality to a number of economic factors, such as the rise in the returns to education, exposure to trade, immigration, and changes in family structure. Nevertheless, numerous Western European countries faced with the same economic forces developed policies to mitigate the consequences so that the level of inequality changed only marginally. Hacker (2004) has argued, for example, that in the United States polarization has been an important factor in impeding the modernization of several of the policies designed to ameliorate social risks. A second issue concerns the ways in which social policies in the United States are designed. Many policies, especially those aimed at the poor or near poor, are not indexed with respect to their benefits. Therefore, these programs require continuous legislative adjustment to achieve a constant level of social protection. McCarty, Poole, and Rosenthal (2006) provided evidence for the stagnating effects of polarization on, for example, the minimum-wage and welfare-policy outcomes.

Delays and Brinkmanship

The continuing battles over raising the federal government's debt limit and dealing with the so-called fiscal cliff of January 2013 have led many observers to blame partisan polarization for Congress's proclivity to miss deadlines, "kick the can down the road" to the next legislative session or another governmental body, and govern by (artificial) crises. These same concerns have been raised about Congress's ability to deal with longer-term problems such as reform to entitlements including Social Security and Medicare.

There is little doubt that partisan polarization played a major role in creating and shaping the fiscal governance "crises" of the past few

Figure 2-10. *The Percentage of Appropriation Bills Completed by Month.* Each observation shows the percentage of regular appropriation bills enacted prior to that month. The dark line is a lowess smoother, which illustrates the longer-term trends.

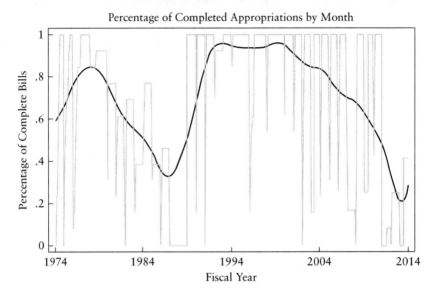

Percentage of Completed Appropriations by Month

years. Clearly, the parties remain far apart on the appropriate reforms for entitlement programs. However, many of these concerns predate the contemporary rise of polarization. For example, we consider the ability of Congress to pass the annual appropriation bills before the beginning of the fiscal year. Recently, Congress's track record on this score has been abysmal. From Fiscal Year 2011 to Fiscal Year 2013, Congress completed zero appropriations bills before the September 30 deadline. During the same period, Congress passed only nine of thirty-six regular appropriations bills. (The government was funded by continuing resolution in all of the unsuccessful cases.) It would be premature, however, to conclude that party polarization is the prime reason for this performance. Figure 2-10 plots for each month since 1974 the proportion of regular appropriation bills that have been passed prior to that month (a smoothing lowess curve is also provided to capture longer-term trends.) Congress's performance has declined significantly in the past decade, but it is important to note that it performed almost equally poorly in the late 1980s. With the exception of the 1995–1996 government shutdown, it performed quite well in the 1990s. Thus, the trends in congressional performance on appropriations do not closely match those of party polarization.

Legislative Deliberation and the Quality of Policy Outcomes

Although the quality of deliberation and policy outcomes is difficult to quantify, several studies have argued that polarization has altered Congress's deliberative and policymaking procedures and capacities (Hacker and Pierson 2006; Mann and Ornstein 2012; Sinclair 2006, 2008).

This literature identifies several changes in the norms and procedures in the U.S. House during the past two decades. First, a decentralized, committee-dominated system of policy development was replaced by a more centralized, party-dominated system. Decisions about policy development and strategy are increasingly likely to be made by party leaders. Moreover, the committee system itself has become more partisan, with much less input from the minority party. Second, the role of the minority party in legislative deliberations appears to be diminishing. The amount of legislation considered under rules that restrict the number of amendments by the minority party has increased since the 1990s. Third, the number of violations of seniority for committee leadership positions has risen. These violations generally reward partisan loyalists and punish defectors. Case studies often suggest that these changes have had deleterious effects on the quality of legislation, but the question awaits more systematic study.

On the Senate side, the focus has been on the increased use of dilatory and obstructionist tactics, such as the filibuster and the hold (Binder and Smith 1997; Koger 2010; Wawro and Schickler 2006). These procedures purport to improve legislative deliberation and minority participation. Although the effects of these procedures on delay and gridlock have been established, there is little evidence of their effects on the quality of legislative output.

Although it is often difficult to quantify claims about the effects of polarization on the quality of legislation, recent history is replete with examples that plausibly illustrate how polarized politics undermines the quality of legislation. We take as an example the lame-duck congressional session in 2010. The session directly followed a midterm election in which the Democrats lost sixty-three House seats, along with their majority, and narrowly maintained control of the Senate after losing six seats.[19]

Even with the healthy partisan majorities it held through 2009 and 2010, the Obama administration was unable to expand on its 2009 efforts at stimulus or to provide an extension of unemployment benefits. After the election, the administration was in an even more difficult bargaining situation. The pending loss of House control and trimming of its Senate majority meant that these agenda items would have to be taken up in a lame-duck session. Thus, Democratic legislators would be called on to move on many of the same policies that the voters had appeared to repudiate in the election. There was also pressure to avoid the across-the-board tax increases that would result from the expiration of the Bush-era tax cuts on December 31, 2010. The administration had pledged to keep the tax cuts for families making less than $250,000 and let the rest expire. This approach, the administration argued, balanced the need to avoid tax increases in a recession with the goal of adding progressivity to the tax structure to offset growing economic inequality.

The Republicans also faced a difficult situation. The party has a long-standing commitment to making the Bush cuts permanent at all income levels. If they let the tax cuts expire, they would have little hope of restoring cuts in the upcoming congressional term. So, the lame-duck session became a "game of chicken."

However, rather than push the dispute to the brink, the Obama administration reached out to Republican leaders to fashion a compromise. Yet, given the polarized environment, finding a middle ground on each of the issues—tax cuts, unemployment insurance, and other stimulus—would be impossible. Therefore, the underlying principle of the negotiation was to trade on differences in issue salience so that each side could get what it most valued and give on other issues (see chapter 5). The Republicans procured an extension of all of the tax cuts, albeit for only two years. The Republicans also received a favorable deal on the provisions for the estate tax, with a higher exemption and lower rate than would have prevailed without the legislation. The Democrats got fiscal stimulus and relief measures targeted at low-income and

19. This section draws heavily on McCarty (2012).

unemployed workers. The employee contribution to Social Security was reduced from 6.2 percent to 4.2 percent for one year, and $57 billion was appropriated for extended unemployment benefits.[20]

Reflecting the nature of a negotiated outcome of this sort, the opposition to the plan came from the ideological extremes of both parties. Progressives were particularly upset with the extension of tax cuts for high-income families and with the estate-tax provisions. Some even expressed concern that the payroll tax deductions would undermine the Social Security system. Conservatives were similarly dismayed not to receive a more permanent extension of the tax cuts, and worried that the extension of unemployment benefits would contribute to the deficit.[21]

Ultimately, polarization did not lead to gridlock, but it may have led to something far worse. Instead of a negotiated outcome that provided a targeted stimulus and a transition to a more efficient, fair, and certain tax code, the bill increased the deficit by almost $900 billion and postponed important decisions to the future.

Other Policy Consequences

Perhaps one of the most important long-term consequences of the decline in legislative capacity caused by polarization is that Congress's power is declining relative to the other branches of government.[22] Recent studies by political scientists demonstrate that presidents facing strong partisan and ideological opposition from Congress are more

---

20. Technically, the estate tax had been repealed in 2010; therefore, establishing any estate tax was a departure from the Republican goal of extending all of the tax cuts and not raising taxes in a recession. Nevertheless, liberal Democrats were especially incensed about the high exemption and low rates. Consequently, they forced a vote on an amendment to strike the estate-tax provisions, which—had it been successful—might have unraveled the negotiated agreement (Sullivan 2010).

21. The progressive opposition was somewhat more pronounced than that of the conservatives. Of the House members in the most liberal quartile, 71 percent opposed the agreement but only 25 percent of the most conservative quartile opposed. Support was highest among moderate Republicans in the third quartile, 88 percent of whom supported the bill.

22. For a set of recent examples, see Reich (2013).

likely to take unilateral action rather than pursue their goals through legislation.

Not only are presidents likely to become more powerful, polarization also increases the opportunities of judges and courts to pursue their policy goals because such judicial activism is unlikely to be checked by legislative statute. The courts have become the dominant arena for a wide swath of policy issues, from tobacco regulation to firearms to questions such as gay marriage.

Although most of this chapter concentrates on the effects of polarization within the legislative process, contemporary work in bureaucratic and judicial politics suggests that polarization also has detrimental effects at the policy implementation stage. First, polarization decreases Congress's willingness to delegate authority to administrative agencies. In a systematic study, Epstein and O'Halloran (1999) showed that Congress is far less willing to delegate policymaking authority to agencies when there are significant ideological disagreements between the president and congressional majorities. Because party polarization has exacerbated these disagreements (especially during divided government), Congress relies far less on the expertise of the bureaucracy in the implementation and enforcement of statutes. The result is often excessive statutory constraints or the delegation of statutory enforcement to private actors and courts rather than agencies (Farhang 2010). These outcomes further weaken the executive and legislative branches vis-à-vis the judiciary. In addition, polarization has now distorted the confirmation process for executive-branch officials and judges. In studies of all major executive branch appointments in the past century, McCarty and Razaghian (1999) found that heightened partisan polarization is the major culprit in the increasing delays in the Senate confirmation process. Consequently, long-term vacancies in the political leadership of many departments and agencies have become the norm. Because these problems are exacerbated at the beginning of new administrations, presidential transitions have become considerably less smooth. Polarization also has clearly contributed to the well-documented conflicts over judicial appointments, leading to an understaffing of the federal bench and more contentious and ideological battles over Supreme Court nominees (Binder and Maltzman 2009).

Conclusions

The negotiation failures resulting from polarization have done much to undermine governance in the United States through gridlock and lower-quality legislation and by harming the functioning of the executive and judicial branches. The goal of this volume is not only to rekindle scholarly interest in political negotiation and bargaining but also to make concrete suggestions on how to improve the negotiation infrastructure in ways that enhance good governance.

The central idea of this chapter is not only how badly U.S. Congress needs such medicine but also how unwilling a patient it is likely to be. Partisan and ideological divisions in Congress have grown significantly during the past three decades. Although the evidence suggests that the average voter may not have polarized significantly, engaged and attentive voters now hold issue positions that are more consistent with those of their party. Campaign funding from ideological individuals has increased and the media has also contributed to the increased ideological divisions.

These long-term trends have profound implications for successful negotiation. First, polarization has fundamentally altered legislators' incentives to negotiate. Expanding ideological differences and declining dimensionality have increasingly replaced win-wins with zero-sum outcomes. Increased teamsmanship has reduced the number of honest brokers who can effectively work "across the aisles" to create agreements. Moreover, polarization has exacerbated the incentives for strategic disagreement. It is difficult to negotiate when one or both sides think they are better off when bargaining fails.

Polarization has also transformed congressional institutions. The "textbook" Congress of decentralized committees has been replaced by a more partisan Congress, where much of the negotiation occurs among party leaders. As Binder and Lee (see chapter 3) point out, this change may have an ambiguous effect. On the one hand, with their near-universal jurisdiction, congressional leaders have more opportunities than committee chairs to form multi-issue integrative solutions. On the other hand, leaders will continue to be constrained to the extent that their members do not find such negotiated settlements politically advantageous.

Unfortunately, the existing political science literature suggests few opportunities for reducing polarization by electoral reforms. The evidence undermines the common arguments that reforming legislative districting or primary elections will materially reduce polarization. Because reforming campaign finance has been fraught with constitutional difficulties and unintended consequences, it does not seem to be a promising avenue for reducing polarization in the short run.

Given this dreary outlook, it is entirely appropriate that we turn our intellectual energies to exploring ways to negotiate and govern despite growing partisan differences. A new political science of negotiation that can suggest new mechanisms and protocols that help to "get the deal done," even in polarized times, would accomplish a great deal of good.

Note: This chapter was shaped profoundly by discussions of the American working group of the APSA Task Force on Negotiating Agreement in Politics. This group included Andrea Campbell, Thomas Edsall, Morris Fiorina, Geoffrey Layman, James Leach, Frances Lee, Thomas Mann, Michael Minta, Eric Schickler, and Sophia Wallace. We also thank Chase Foster for his assistance with the working group.

References

Abramowitz, Alan I. 2010. *The Disappearing Center: Engaged Citizens, Polarization, and American Democracy.* Yale University Press.

Aldrich, John. 1995. *Why Parties? The Origin and Transformation of Political Parties in America.* University of Chicago Press.

Aldrich, John, and David W. Rohde. 2010. "Consequences of Electoral and Institutional Change: The Evolution of Conditional Party Government in the U.S. House of Representatives." In *New Directions in American Political Parties,* ed. Jeffrey M. Stonecash. New York: Routledge.

Ansolabehere, Stephen, John M. de Figueiredo, and James M. Snyder. 2003. "Why Is There So Little Money in U.S. Politics?" *Journal of Economic Perspectives* 17 (1): 105–30.

Ansolabehere, Stephen, Jonathan Rodden, and James M. Snyder. 2006. "Purple America." *Journal of Economic Perspectives* 20 (2): 97–118.

Bafumi, Joseph, and Michael C. Herron. 2010. "Leapfrog Representation and Extremism: A Study of American Voters and Their Members in Congress." *American Political Science Review* 104 (3): 519–42.

Barber, Michael. 2013. "Ideological Donors, Contribution Limits, and the Polarization of State Legislatures?" Typescript. Princeton University.

Baron, David P. 1994. "Electoral Competition with Informed and Uninformed Voters." *American Political Science Review* 88 (1): 33–47.

Bartels, Larry. 2000. "Partisanship and Voting Behavior 1952–1996." *American Journal of Political Science* 44 (1): 35–50.

———. 2008. *Unequal Democracy: The Political Economy of the New Gilded Age.* Princeton University Press.

Binder, Sarah A. 1999. "The Dynamics of Legislative Gridlock, 1947–96." *American Political Science Review* 93 (3): 519–33.

Binder, Sarah A., and Forrest Maltzman. 2009. *Advice and Dissent: The Struggle to Shape the Federal Judiciary.* Brookings Institution Press.

Binder, Sarah A., and Steven S. Smith. 1997. *Politics or Principle? Filibustering in the United States Senate.* Brookings Institution Press.

Bishop, Bill. 2009. *The Big Sort: Why the Clustering of Like-Minded Americans Is Tearing Us Apart.* New York: Mariner Books.

Bonica, Adam. 2013. "Ideology and Interests in the Political Marketplace." *American Journal of Political Science* 57 (2): 294–311.

Brady, David W., Hahrie Han, and Jeremy C. Pope. 2007. "Primary Elections and Candidate Ideology: Out of Step with the Primary Electorate?" *Legislative Studies Quarterly* 32 (1): 79–105.

Brewer, Mark, Mack Mariani, and Jeffrey M. Stonecash. 2002. *Diverging Parties: Social Change, Realignment, and Party Polarization.* Boulder, CO: Westview Press.

Bullock, Will, and Joshua D. Clinton. 2011. "More a Molehill than a Mountain: The Effects of the Blanket Primary on Elected Officials' Behavior from California." *Journal of Politics* 73 (3): 915–30.

Burnham, Walter Dean. 1970. *Critical Elections and the Mainsprings of American Politics.* New York: W. W. Norton.

Canon, David T. 1999. *Race, Redistricting, and Representation: The Unintended Consequences of Black Majority Districts.* University of Chicago Press.

Carsey, T. M., and G. C. Layman. 2006. "Changing Sides or Changing Minds? Party Identification and Policy Preferences in the American Electorate." *American Journal of Political Science* 50 (2): 464–77.

Carson, Jamie L., Michael H. Crespin, Charles J. Finocchiaro, and David W. Rohde. 2007. "Redistricting and Party Polarization in the U.S. House of Representatives." *American Politics Research* 35 (6): 878–904.

Clinton, Joshua D. 2006. "Representation in Congress: Constituents and Roll Calls in the 106th House." *Journal of Politics* 68 (2): 397–409.

Clinton, Joshua D., Simon Jackman, and Douglas Rivers. 2004. "The Statistical Analysis of Roll Call Data." *American Political Science Review* 98 (2): 355–70.

Converse, Philip. 1964. "The Nature of Belief Systems in the Mass Public." In *Ideology and Discontent*, ed. David Apter. New York: Free Press.

Cox, Gary, and Mathew McCubbins. 2005. *Setting the Agenda: Responsible Party Government in the U.S. House of Representatives.* Cambridge University Press.

Cox, Gary W., and Keith T. Poole. 2002. "On Measuring Partisanship in Roll-Call Voting in the U.S. House of Representatives, 1877–1999." *American Journal of Political Science* 46 (3): 477–89.

Davis, Susan. 2012. "This Congress Could Be Least Productive since 1947." *USA Today*, August 15. http://usatoday30.usatoday.com/news/washington/story/2012–08–14/unproductive-congress-not-passing-bills/57060096/1.

DellaVigna, Stefano, and Ethan Kaplan. 2007. "The Fox News Effect: Media Bias and Voting." *Quarterly Journal of Economics* 122 (3): 1187–1234.

Edwards, Mickey. 2012. *The Parties versus the People: How to Turn Republicans and Democrats into Americans.* Yale University Press.

Eilperin, Juliet. 2007. *Fight Club Politics: How Partisanship Is Poisoning the House of Representatives.* Lanham, MD: Rowman & Littlefield.

Ensley, Michael J. 2009. "Individual Campaign Contributions and Candidate Ideology." *Public Choice* 138 (1): 221–38.

Epstein, David, and Sharyn O'Halloran. 1999. *Delegating Powers: A Transaction Cost Politics Approach to Policy Making under Separate Powers.* Cambridge University Press.

Farhang, Sean. 2010. *The Litigation State: Public Regulation and Private Lawsuits in the United States.* Princeton University Press.

Fiorina, Morris P. 2013. "Party Homogeneity and Contentious Politics." In *Can We Talk? The Rise of Rude, Nasty, Stubborn Politics*, ed. Daniel M. Shea and Morris P. Fiorina. New York: Pearson.

Fiorina, Morris P., and Samuel J. Abrams. 2008. "Political Polarization in the American Public." *Annual Review of Political Science* 11:563–88.

Fiorina, Morris P., Samuel J. Abrams, and Jeremy Pope. 2005. *Culture War? Myth of a Polarized America.* Upper Saddle River, NJ: Pearson Education.

Garand, James C. 2010. "Income Inequality, Party Polarization, and Roll-Call Voting in the U.S. Senate." *Journal of Politics* 72 (4): 1109–28.

Gelman, Andrew. 2009. *Red State, Blue State, Rich State, Poor State: Why Americans Vote the Way They Do.* Princeton University Press.

Gentzkow, Matthew, and Jesse M. Shapiro. 2006. "Media Bias and Reputation." *Journal of Political Economy* 114 (2): 280–316.

Gerber, Alan, Dean Karlan, and Daniel Bergan. 2009. "Does the Media Matter? A Field Experiment Measuring the Effect of Newspapers on Voting Behavior and Political Opinions." *American Economic Journal: Applied Economics* 1 (2): 35–52.

Gerber, Elisabeth R., and Rebecca B. Morton. 1998. "Primary Election Systems and Representation." *Journal of Law Economics and Organization* 14 (2): 304–24.

Gilens, Martin. 2012. *Affluence and Influence: Economic Inequality and Political Power in America.* Princeton University Press.

Gilmour, John. 1995. *Strategic Disagreement: Stalemate in American Politics.* University of Pittsburgh Press.

Gimpel, James, and James R. Edwards. 1998. *The Congressional Politics of Immigration Reform.* London: Longman Publishing Group.

Gimpel, James, Frances Lee, and Joshua Kaminski. 2006. "The Political Geography of Campaign Contributions in American Politics." *Journal of Politics* 68 (3): 626–39.

Gimpel, James, Frances Lee, and Shanna Pearson-Merkowitz. 2008. "The Check Is in the Mail: Interdistrict Funding Flows in Congressional Elections." *American Journal of Political Science* 52 (2): 373–94.

Groseclose, Timothy, Steven D. Levitt, and James M. Snyder Jr. 1999. "Comparing Interest Group Scores across Time and Chambers: Adjusted ADA Scores for the U.S. Congress." *American Political Science Review* 93 (1): 33–50.

Groseclose, Timothy, and Nolan McCarty. 2001. "The Politics of Blame: Bargaining before an Audience." *American Journal of Political Science* 45 (1): 100–19.

Groseclose, Timothy, and Jeff Milyo. 2005. "A Measure of Media Bias." *Quarterly Journal of Economics* 120 (4): 1191–1237.

Hacker, Jacob S. 2004. "Privatizing Risk without Privatizing the Welfare State: The Hidden Politics of Social Policy Retrenchment in the United States." *American Political Science Review* 98 (2): 243–60.

Hacker, Jacob S., and Paul Pierson. 2006. *Off Center: The Republican Revolution and the Erosion of American Democracy.* Yale University Press.

Hall, Robert L., and Frank W. Wayman. 1990. "Buying Time: Moneyed Interests and the Mobilization of Bias in Congressional Committees." *American Political Science Review* 84 (3): 797–820.

Hare, Christopher, Nolan McCarty, Keith T. Poole, and Howard Rosenthal. 2012. "Polarization Is Real (and Asymmetric)." Voteview Blog, May 16. http://voteview.com/blog/?p=494.

Hirano, Shigeo, James M. Snyder Jr., Stephen Ansolabehere, and John Mark Hansen. 2010. "Primary Elections and Partisan Polarization in U.S. Congressional Elections." *Quarterly Journal of Political Science* 5 (2): 169–91.

Hopkins, Daniel J., and Jonathan Ladd. 2014. "The Consequences of Broader Media Choice: Evidence from the Expansion of Fox News." *Quarterly Journal of Political Science* 9 (1): 115–35

Iyengar, Shanto, Gaurav Sood, and Yphtach Lelkes. 2012. "Affect, Not Ideology: A Social Identity Perspective on Polarization." *Public Opinion Quarterly* 763 (3): 405–31.

Jacobson, Gary C. 1990. "The Effects of Campaign Spending in House Elections: New Evidence for Old Arguments." *American Journal of Political Science* 34 (2): 334–62.

Kasperowicz, Pete. 2012. "Parties Trade Blame for 'Least Productive Congress' in Decades." *The Hill*, September 14. http://thehill.com /video/house/249597–cantor-hoyer-trade-barbs-on-the-way-out -the-door-to-2012–elections.

Kaufmann, Karen M., James G. Gimpel, and Adam H. Hoffman. 2003. "A Promise Fulfilled? Open Primaries and Representation." *Journal of Politics* 65 (2): 457–76.

Klinkner, Philip A. 2004. "Red and Blue Scare: The Continuing Diversity of the American Electoral Landscape." *The Forum* (2) 2. http://www.degruyter.com/view/j/for.2004.2.2_20120105083449 /for.2004.2.2/for.2004.2.2.1035/for.2004.2.2.1035.xml?format =INT.

Koger, Gregory. 2010. *Filibustering: A Political History of Obstruction in the House and Senate.* University of Chicago Press.

Krehbiel, Keith. 1998. *Pivotal Politics: A Theory of U.S. Lawmaking.* University of Chicago Press.

Layman, Geoffrey, and Thomas Carsey. 2002. "Party Polarization and 'Conflict Extension' in the American Electorate." *American Journal of Political Science* 46 (4): 786–802.

Layman, Geoffrey C., Thomas M. Carsey, John C. Green, Richard Herrera, and Rosalyn Cooperman. 2010. "Activists and Conflict Extension in American Party Politics." *American Political Science Review* 104 (2): 324–46.

Lee, Frances. 2009. *Beyond Ideology: Politics, Principles, and Partisanship in the U.S. Senate.* University of Chicago Press.

Lenz, Gabriel S. 2012. *Follow the Leader: How Voters Respond to Politicians' Policies and Performance.* University of Chicago Press.

Lessig, Lawrence. 2011. *Republic, Lost: How Money Corrupts Congress—and a Plan to Stop It.* New York: Twelve/Hachette Book Group.

Levendusky, Matthew. 2009. *The Partisan Sort: How Liberals Became Democrats and Conservatives Became Republicans.* University of Chicago Press.

Levendusky, Matthew S., Jeremy C. Pope, and Simon D. Jackman. 2008. "Measuring District-Level Partisanship with Implications for the Analysis of U.S. Elections." *Journal of Politics* 70 (3): 736–53.

Mann, Thomas E., and Norman J. Ornstein. 2012. *It's Even Worse Than It Looks: How the American Constitutional System Collided with the New Politics of Extremism.* New York: Basic Books.

Masket, Seth. 2008. "Where You Sit Is Where You Stand: The Impact of Seating Proximity on Legislative Cue-Taking." *Quarterly Journal of Political Science* 3:301–11.

Masket, Seth, Boris Shor, Steven Rogers, and Nolan McCarty. 2013. "A Primary Cause of Partisanship? Nomination Systems and Legislator Ideology." Typescript. Princeton University.

Mayhew, David R. 2005. *Divided We Govern: Party Control, Lawmaking, and Investigations, 1946–2002.* Yale University Press.

McCarty, Nolan. 2007. "The Policy Effects of Political Polarization." In *The Transformation of American Politics: Activist Government and the Rise of Conservatism,* ed. Paul Pierson and Theda Skocpol. Princeton University Press.

———. 2012. "The Politics of the Pop: The U.S. Response to the Financial Crisis and the Great Recession." In *Coping with Crisis: Governmental Responses to the Great Recession,* ed. Nancy Bermeo and Jonas Pontusson. Cambridge University Press.

McCarty, Nolan, Keith T. Poole, and Howard Rosenthal. 1997. *Income Redistribution and the Realignment of American Politics.* Washington, DC: American Enterprise Institute.

———. 2001. "The Hunt for Party Discipline in Congress." *American Political Science Review* 95 (3): 673–88.

———. 2006. *Polarized America: The Dance of Ideology and Unequal Riches.* MIT Press.

———. 2009. "Does Gerrymandering Cause Polarization?" *American Journal of Political Science* 53 (3): 666–80.

McCarty, Nolan, and Rose Razaghian. 1999. "Advice and Consent: Senate Responses to Executive Branch Nominations 1885–1996." *American Journal of Political Science* 43 (4): 1122–43.

McClosky, Herbert, Paul J. Hoffmann, and Rosemary O'Hara. 1960. "Issue Conflict and Consensus among Party Leaders and Followers." *American Political Science Review* 54 (2): 406–27.

Minta, Michael D. 2009. "Legislative Oversight and the Substantive Representation of Black and Latino Interests in Congress." *Legislative Studies Quarterly* 34 (2): 193–218.

Minta, Michael D., and Valeria Sinclair-Chapman. 2013. "Diversity in Political Institutions and Congressional Responsiveness to Minority Interests." *Political Research Quarterly* 66 (1): 27–140.

Moon, Woojin. 2004. "Party Activists, Campaign Resources and Candidate Position Taking: Theory, Tests and Applications." *British Journal of Political Science* 34 (4): 611–33.

Parker, Christopher S., and Matt A. Barreto. 2013. *Change They Can Believe In: The Tea Party and Reactionary Politics in America.* Princeton University Press.

Pew Center. 2012. "Partisan Polarization Surges in Bush and Obama Years." *Pew Research Center for the People and the Press.* www.people-press.org/2012/06/04/partisan-polarization-surges-in-bush-obama-years/.

Piketty, Thomas, and Emmanuel Saez. 2003. "Income Inequality in the United States 1913–1998." *Quarterly Journal of Economics* 118 (1): 1–39.

Poole, Keith. T. 2007. "Changing Minds? Not in Congress!" *Public Choice* 131:435–51.

Poole, Keith T., and Howard Rosenthal. 1997. *Congress: A Political-Economic History of Roll Call Voting.* Oxford University Press.

Prior, Markus. 2007. *Post-Broadcast Democracy: How Media Choice Increases Inequality in Political Involvement and Polarizes Elections.* Cambridge University Press.

Reich, Robert. 2013. "The Real Price of Congress's Gridlock." *New York Times*, August 13.

Roberts, Jason M. 2007. "The Statistical Analysis of Roll-Call Data: A Cautionary Tale." *Legislative Studies Quarterly* 32 (3): 341–60.

Roberts, Jason M., and Steven S. Smith. 2003. "Procedural Contexts, Party Strategy, and Conditional Party Voting in the U.S. House of Representatives." *American Journal of Political Science* 47 (2): 305–17.

Rohde, David W. 1991. *Parties and Leaders in the Postreform House.* University of Chicago Press.

Schattschneider, E. E. 1960. *The Semisovereign People.* New York: Holt, Reinhart, and Winston.

Shaw, Daron. 2012. "If Everyone Votes Their Party, Why Do Presidential Election Outcomes Vary So Much?" *The Forum* 3 (1): 1.

Shor, Boris, and Nolan McCarty. 2011. "The Ideological Mapping of American Legislatures." *American Political Science Review* 105 (3): 530–51.

Sides, John. 2012. "Your Do-Nothing Congress (in One Graph)." *Washington Monthly*, September 21. www.washingtonmonthly .com/ten-miles-square/2012/09/your_donothing_congress_in_one 040039.php.

Sinclair, Barbara. 2006. *Party Wars: Polarization and the Politics of National Policy Making*. University of Oklahoma Press.

———. 2008. "Spoiling the Sausages? How a Polarized Congress Deliberates and Legislates." In *Red and Blue Nation? Consequences and Corrections of America's Polarized Politics*. Washington DC: Brookings Press.

Skocpol, Theda, and Vanessa Williamson. 2012. *The Tea Party and the Remaking of Republican Conservatism*. Oxford University Press.

Smith, Richard A. 1995. "Interest Group Influence in the U.S. Congress." *Legislative Studies Quarterly* 20 (1): 89–139.

Snyder, Jr., James M., and Tim Groseclose. 2000. "Estimating Party Influence in Congressional Roll-Call Voting." *American Journal of Political Science* 44 (2): 193–211.

Snyder, Jr., James M., and David Stromberg. 2010. "Press Coverage and Political Accountability." *Journal of Political Economy* 118 (2): 355–408.

Steinhauer, Jennifer. 2012. "Congress Nearing End of Session Where Partisan Input Impeded Output." *New York Times*, September 18. www.nytimes.com/2012/09/19/us/politics/ congress-nears-end-of -least-productive-session.html.

Stone, Walt J., and Elizabeth N. Simas. 2010. "Candidate Valence and Ideological Positions in U.S. House Elections." *American Journal of Political Science* 54 (2): 371–88.

Sullivan, Paul. 2010. "Estate Tax Will Return Next Year, but Few Will Pay It." *New York Times*, December 17.

Sundquist, James L. 1983. *Dynamics of the Party System: Alignment and Realignment of Political Parties in the United States*. Brookings Institution Press.

Sunstein, Cass R. 2002. "The Law of Group Polarization." *Journal of Political Philosophy* 10:175–95.

Tate, Katherine. 2003. *Black Faces in the Mirror: African Americans and Their Representatives in the U.S. Congress*. Princeton University Press.

Theriault, Sean M. 2008a. *Party Polarization in Congress*. Cambridge University Press.

———. 2008b. "The Procedurally Polarized Congress." Presented at the Annual Meeting of the American Political Science Association, Boston, MA.

Tichenor, Daniel. 2002. *Dividing Lines*. Princeton University Press.

Tufte, Edward R. 1973. "The Relationship between Seats and Votes in Two-Party Systems." *American Political Science Review* 67 (2): 540–54.

Wallace, Sophia J. 2012. "It's Complicated: Latinos, President Obama, and the 2012 Election." *Social Science Quarterly* 93 (5): 1360–83.

Wallace, Sophia J., Chris Zepeda-Millán, and Michael Jones-Correa. 2014. "Spatial and Temporal Proximity: Examining the Effects of Protests on Political Attitudes." *American Journal of Political Science*. http://onlinelibrary.wiley.com/doi/10.1111/ajps.12060/abstract.

Wawro, Gregory, and Eric Schickler. 2006. *Filibuster: Obstruction and Lawmaking in the U.S. Senate*. Princeton University Press.

Zelizer, Julian E. 2006. *On Capitol Hill: The Struggle to Reform Congress and Its Consequences, 1948–2000*. Cambridge University Press.

Zepeda-Millán, J. Chris. 2011. "Dignity's Revolt: Threat, Identity, and Immigrant Mass Mobilization." Ph.D. dissertation, Cornell University.

CHAPTER THREE

Making Deals
in Congress

SARAH A. BINDER AND
FRANCES E. LEE

*There is one unavoidable fact about legislating in a
democratic system. No single person, faction, or interest can get everything it wants. Legislating inevitably means compromising, except in the rare circumstances when consensus is so strong that one dominant
view can prevail with ease.*

—ROBERT KAISER 2013, P. 174

Compromise may be the "unavoidable fact" about legislating in a democratic system. Yet scholars have few systematic answers to the question: How do legislators "get to yes"? To put the
question in language more familiar to students of politics: How do
politicians with diverse, often-conflicting interests and policy preferences reach agreements on public policy in a legislative body of co-
equals? In this chapter, we offer a perspective on deal making in
contemporary Congress, highlighting the impact of political and
partisan considerations on lawmakers' abilities to secure policy
agreements.

Negotiation in Congress is never solely about policy; politics and
policy are always intertwined. Congressional negotiations thus differ
from those in the private sector, in which actors seek to maximize

benefits and minimize costs, and the substantive terms of an offer are paramount. Congressional deal making occurs in a political context that shapes the willingness of party leaders and their "rank and file" to negotiate at all or to accept even favorable offers. Lawmakers must justify votes and policy compromises to their constituencies, whereas party leaders must attend to key groups in the party coalition and to the party's public image. Given the political context of congressional negotiations, we evaluate the tools and institutional arrangements that make deals in Congress more likely—emphasizing that conflicting incentives and interests place a premium on negotiating out of the public eye. We conclude with a broader assessment of the prospects for negotiation in a party-polarized Congress.

Distributive versus Integrative Models of Negotiation in Congress

Negotiation theorists typically distinguish between distributive and integrative solutions to public problems (see chapters 4 and 5). Distributive solutions involve zero-sum bargaining over extant benefits. As Riker (1962) emphasized in his work on political coalitions, what one party gains, the other must lose. Distributive models depict congressional bargaining as a matter of splitting differences over divisible policies. In contrast, integrative solutions emphasize expanding "the pie" rather than just doling out its pieces. Follett ([1925] 1942) first developed the logic of integrative solutions—that is, agreements that create value by taking advantage of differences in players' valuations of problems and solutions. Exploiting differences across players' priorities—achieved by "logrolling," vote trading, or crafting multidimensional agreements—allows negotiators to enlarge the pie, moving negotiators past narrow, distributive solutions.

Legislative scholars have developed a robust literature on bargaining and coalition building in Congress, almost all of which is predicated on a distributive model of politics. We suspect that congressional studies favor a distributive framework for both empirical and theoretical reasons. Readily available data and contemporary modes of modeling discourage a focus on integrative solutions. For decades, Sorauf's (1992, p. 164) "law of available data" has steered students to design their analyses of Congress at the individual level of the legislator. The entire floor roll-call record across congressional history is readily available, encouraging scholars to make congressional voting the focus of their studies. With the addition of Poole and Rosenthal's (1997, 2013) NOMINATE data, which provides robust estimates of legislators' revealed preferences, proxies for legislators' policy positions over the full course of congressional history are also at scholars' fingertips.

Analyses of such data yielded a wealth of knowledge about the forces that shape lawmakers' votes. Costs are also apparent: we know an enormous amount about the choices legislators face when they take positions on policy and procedural questions, but relatively little about the politics and processes that facilitate the underlying deals and terms of policy proposals. Arnold's (1990) analysis of leaders' strategies for forming successful coalitions provided an important exception. Focusing on the substance and politics of winning coalitions, of course, is challenging: no comparable databases track the formation of legislative deals. To make matters more difficult, virtually all such deals are negotiated out of the public eye. Subsequent reporting about what terms were offered or refused often is contested; therefore, it may be impossible to construct a consensus account of what transpired. Even if we knew which alternatives were on the table during negotiations, we would still need to know how lawmakers crafted and chose among them.

The influence of formal modeling also has encouraged a focus on distributive policymaking. For example, Baron and Ferejohn's (1989) foundational work in this area—"Bargaining in Legislatures"— focuses on divide-the-dollar games. Elaborations of such formal models include important work on vote buying, coalition formation, coalition sizes, and policy outcomes. These are significant contributions to our understanding of Congress. Still, these models emphasize a view of congressional bargaining as a matter of splitting differences rather than creating value. If successful negotiation often requires enlarging the pie, then existing formal models offer only a limited basis for understanding congressional deal making.

Congressional scholars' focus on the spatial model of politics also reinforces the primacy of distributive politics: players come to the table with exogenously fixed policy preferences, hold perfect information about fellow players' preferences, and either accept or reject proposals following a set of rules for play. This basic framework works well for reaching agreement on policy when bargaining occurs over who gets what at whose expense in splitting divisible benefits (for example, see Krehbiel and Rivers's exemplary 1988 study of changes to the minimum wage).

The key assumptions of the spatial model—especially fixed, exogenous preferences and complete information—are difficult to fit into models of negotiation that involve integrative solutions. The assumption of fixed preferences is incompatible with a view of politics that suggests lawmakers' preferences are endogenous to the legislative process (C. L. Evans 2011). Decades of research suggest that although lawmakers hold a set of core beliefs, their policy preferences (and, hence, the deals to which they are likely to agree) develop as they weigh input from various constituencies and stakeholders. Assuming complete information about players' preferences also limits the reach of the spatial model in settings that entail expanding the number of available solutions. As Arnold (1990) argued, lawmakers with similar preferences might reach different conclusions about the policy and electoral consequences of competing alternatives, raising uncertainty for leaders in negotiating agreements with opponents and partisans alike.

Students of Congress recognize that spatial and formal models, by design, offer stylized accounts of legislative politics. The empirical literature on Congress is replete with accounts of the messy dynamics that underlie legislative politics. Here, we note only the tip of the iceberg: in addition to Arnold (1990), Sinclair's (2006) work emphasizes how party leaders exploit procedural tools to construct multidimensional packages, allowing them to assemble complex bargains that meet competing demands. Smith's (2007) treatise on legislative parties in Congress encouraged more careful thought about how legislators' and leaders' multiple goals influence their strategic choices and shape policy outcomes. Diana Evans's (2004) exploration of pork barreling explained how legislative "lard" can be used to buy votes for broad-based national legislation. Arguably, distributive bargaining is more often an instrument for crafting integrative solutions than an end in itself.

Starting Premises

Politics and policy are tightly intertwined on Capitol Hill. Former Representative Barney Frank (D-Mass.) (2013) stated it well: "Nobody pushes for unpopular policies." This simple premise has important implications for understanding how coalition leaders build winning coalitions in Congress. Deal making is not merely a matter of finding the ideological "sweet spot" between competing coalitions. Instead, common ground is typically a joint function of lawmakers' policy views and political calculations. As we elaborate herein, three key political premises continually shape congressional negotiations over policy.

First, lawmakers represent constituencies. Stated more accurately, they represent political coalitions within the constituencies that elected them. Officeholders must manage these coalitions. These "intense demanders," who are critical to politicians' fundraising and activist base, often sharply constrain lawmakers' flexibility on key issues (Karol 2009). When legislators or their leaders negotiate over policy, they know that they will have to justify any deals to their active supporters. The catch, as Gilmour (1995, pp. 25–37) explained, is that such constituencies often have little understanding of what is and is not possible in Congress. Constituents will not be happy to hear that they must settle for less than what they wanted or that they must make unpalatable concessions to achieve desired goals. Not being a party to the negotiations themselves, they must trust what their representative tells them about what was achievable. Rather than accept disappointment, they may prefer to listen to other voices—such as those of activist group leaders or congressional hardliners—who tell them that a better deal was possible. As a consequence, lawmakers must continually cope with constituencies, activists, and supporters who push them to take a tougher line and refuse compromise. "On both sides, the task is dealing with all the people who believe that insufficient purity is the reason why their party hasn't won more elections," observed Representative Frank (2013).

Even if a particular deal is the best that can win sufficient support in Congress to pass—and would be an improvement, in their view, over the policy status quo—lawmakers still may conclude that they would be unable to defend it successfully with their constituencies. Lawmakers may well reject "half a loaf" and settle for nothing, if taking the half would be understood by constituents or denounced by important groups or activists as an unacceptable sellout. Pundits today call this a fear of being "primaried," although the electoral imperative to satisfy activist constituencies has deep roots in congressional politics.

Second, as Mayhew (1974) taught us, individual lawmakers are responsible for the positions they take (that is, their votes) but not for the resulting policy outcomes. In almost all cases, blame or credit for the outcome of negotiations in Congress does not attach to individual lawmakers, largely because a single lawmaker's vote rarely decides an outcome. Lawmakers therefore weigh vote decisions for their effects on their reputations as politicians, not only for their effects on public policy. Lawmakers will not necessarily vote for a deal that they support on policy grounds if the vote could harm their public image; conversely, they might vote in favor of a deal to which they object on policy terms if the vote would be helpful to their image.

Third, lawmakers affiliate with political parties in a highly competitive two-party system. Party leaders are responsible for stewardship of the party "brand"—that is, for protecting the party's public image on issues. Individual members, for their part, care about the party brand name to the extent that they perceive a favorable party image as important to their party's majority status in Congress or to their own electoral interests. In promoting a party's brand name, the question is often whether party leaders and members want a law or a political issue addressed. When a party perceives that it has an advantage with the public on an issue, it may prefer to keep its image unsullied by the compromises that are usually necessary to legislate. The party may see more political benefit in refusing to negotiate and in preserving the issue for future campaigns. Nearly two decades ago, Gilmour (1995, p. 9) termed this dynamic "strategic disagreement": parties to a potential deal "avoid the best agreement that can be gotten given the circumstances in order to seek political gain." In short, explicitly partisan political considerations condition the opportunities for deal making on policy issues.

The 2012 congressional negotiations over the so-called fiscal cliff offer an example of the complex interplay between politics and policy. With the tax cuts originally passed in 2001 under President George W. Bush set to expire at the end of 2012, Speaker of the House John Boehner (R-Ohio) sought support from his party's conference for legislation that would have made permanent all of the tax cuts for those with taxable incomes less than $1 million. Preserving the Bush tax cuts was unquestionably a consensus policy objective among congressional Republicans. Passage of Boehner's so-called Plan B proposal would have strengthened the House Republican leader's negotiating position vis-à-vis the Democratic-controlled Senate and President Barack Obama, who wanted to raise taxes on taxpayers at a much lower income level of $250,000. In addition, House passage of the bill would have enhanced the Republican public image by portraying the party as fighting for tax cuts that benefited those outside the richest 1 percent of Americans. Under circumstances in which the alternative was the imminent expiration of all of the Bush tax cuts, Boehner's proposal was a vast improvement over the status quo for all lawmakers who wanted low taxes; it also put the party more in tune with national public opinion. Nevertheless, Boehner could not win the support of a key contingent of Republicans who refused to cast a vote that allowed anyone's taxes to rise. As a result, Boehner was sidelined from further negotiation, with the eventual deal worked out between the White House and Senate leadership.

The Plan B episode illustrates that a proposal's policy effect is not the only matter at stake in congressional deal making. Members and party leaders continually take stock of political stakes as well. Moreover, congressional parties are not unitary actors, and party leaders have limited power to command followership from their rank and file. With respect to Boehner's Plan B, considerations of policy and the party brand pulled in the opposite direction from many lawmakers' political calculations. Regardless of the strength of party leaders' case in favor of Plan B, a group of Republicans would simply not allow themselves to be personally associated with a compromise on the issue: their individual reputations as authentic, principled conservatives took priority.

The premise that policy and political choices are tightly interwoven has implications for how we explain the dynamics of negotiating in Congress. If politics always took a backseat to policy considerations, then deal making in Congress would consist of distributive and integrative bargaining to locate a common zone of policy agreement. However, if both policy and politics matter, then the players' willingness to negotiate or sign on to compromises becomes a threshold matter. In the following section, we explore the politics of crossing that threshold and the implications for negotiations that often ensue.

Getting to Agreement: Key Elements

In this section, we outline key elements of congressional negotiations on major public problems. We explore the central players, the terrain of potential policy solutions, and the dynamics of interparty and intraparty bargaining. Collectively, these elements of congressional deal making lead to the expectation that successful negotiations in Congress usually revolve around the task of building integrative (or at least partially integrative) solutions to policy dilemmas.

Players. Generally, party and committee leaders of the majority party take the lead in negotiating policy deals. The rise of party leaders as pivotal negotiators reflects the emergence of "unorthodox lawmaking," a term coined by Sinclair (2012) to capture the nature of lawmaking in a polarized and increasingly centralized legislative institution. There is certainly room for issue entrepreneurship in some cases (see Volden and Wiseman 2009; Wawro 2000). Most recently, we see entrepreneurs emerging on the complex matter of immigration reform in 2013, although there seems to be more room for such activity in the Senate than in the House. Even when authority to negotiate deals devolves to committee or other coalition leaders and the involvement of party leaders is difficult to detect, in the contemporary Congress those leaders are rarely left uninformed.

Negotiation terrain. One of the most important differences between private negotiations and deal making in Congress is the broad—perhaps limitless—reach of congressional jurisdiction. As Representative Frank (2013) framed it, "The key to understanding deal making in Congress is to remember that the ankle bone is connected to the shoulder bone. Anything can be the basis of a deal. . . . In Congress, the jurisdiction is universal." The omnicompetence of congressional authority makes possible frequent integrative solutions to policy problems. Congress's broad reach allows leaders to enlarge the policy pie and to secure positive-sum solutions to otherwise intractable problems. Unrelated or loosely related issues can be addressed simultaneously, giving different lawmakers alternative reasons to sign on to a package. "Different priorities across issues," Representative Frank (2013) noted, "are often the basis of an agreement."

In a book subtitled "How Congress Really Works," Representative Henry Waxman (D-Calif.) views integrative, win-win negotiation as

the basis of most successful congressional deals. "The greatest mis-
conception about making laws is the assumption that most problems
have clear solutions, and reaching compromise mainly entails splitting the difference between partisan extremes," he wrote (Waxman
and Green 2009, p. 77). Waxman offered the Food Quality Protection Act of 1996 as one example. This law, a comprehensive new set
of regulations governing pesticides in food, was passed during conditions of divided government, despite long standing partisan stalemate
over regulatory policy in this area. According to Waxman, he and
Representative Tom Bliley (R-Va.), chair of the House Commerce
Committee, were able to negotiate a deal that took advantage of their
different priorities. Conservative Republican Bliley prioritized repeal-
ing a strict regulation of carcinogens in processed food—a regulation
that experts expected would be more rigorously enforced in the wake
of a court ruling. Liberal Democrat Waxman was most concerned
with the lack of regulations on carcinogens in raw foods—to his mind,
a greater problem given the impact of such pesticides on children.
Waxman, Bliley, and representatives of the affected industries struck
an accord that established a single standard governing pesticides in
food—raw or processed—that required a reasonable certainty of "no
harm" to consumers (including special considerations for infants and
children). Their solution won unanimous approval in the House, ver-
batim acceptance in the Senate, and President Bill Clinton's signature.

The search for win-win solutions is labor intensive, as this and
other case studies recount. Information must be gathered from many
sources—for example, interest groups, affected industries, policy experts, activists, and government agencies—before members and their
staffs can understand the causes and dimensions of a policy problem
and see a pathway to possible solutions. Lengthy discussions and negotiations are often needed for the different actors and stakeholders to
understand one another's interests. Many, probably most, such negotiations fail. However, these processes of information gathering, con-
sultation, and discussion lay the groundwork for creative problem solving
that can address the concerns of all key interests at once. The result
can be legislation that commands widespread support, even from
players who initially saw their interests and preferences as opposed.

Interparty negotiations. In interparty negotiations, there is no default presumption of cooperation. Given the two parties' diametrically

opposed electoral interests in winning and retaining control of Congress, members generally regard initiatives sponsored by the opposing party with suspicion and skepticism. In the contemporary Congress, there may even be a default presumption of opposition, such that the minority party will resist the majority's proposals unless it is actively courted and successfully co-opted. As one experienced congressional negotiator noted, "It is not uncommon for members of one party to oppose legislation merely because the other political party champions it" (Barry 2003, p. 434).

Before commencing negotiations across party lines, members and leaders of both parties ask the following questions: What are the political consequences of refusing negotiation? Who will suffer more politically from a deal not being done? The answers to those questions determine each side's bargaining power. The greater (lower) is the cost to the minority of saying no, the greater (lower) is the majority's bargaining leverage. Because both parties gauge the political fallout from a failure to produce a deal, Representative Frank (2013) explained, "It boils down to which side can message it better." Those who perceive themselves on the right side of public opinion will see themselves as having political leverage. A minority party that expects to win the message battle may disengage altogether. A majority party that expects to win the message battle will see less need for policy concessions to the opposition. In contrast, anticipation of losing the "blame game" can drive partisans to the negotiating table.

From the majority's perspective, coalition leaders must decide whether to try to include the minority. Given the differences in House and Senate rules, bipartisanship is typically more necessary in the upper chamber than it is in the House. A Senate majority party rarely can hope to legislate without at least some support from the minority. Reflecting on his long Senate career (1981–2011), former Senator Chris Dodd (D-Conn.) observed that on every major legislative success, "I've always had a Republican partner, every time" (quoted in Kaiser 2013, p. 204). Strictly speaking, a House majority party that can hold its ranks together does not need support from the minority to get legislation through the chamber. Even so, House majority leaders may nevertheless prefer to seek support from the minority party. Having bipartisan support in the House sends signals that can be beneficial for winning the necessary support elsewhere in the legislative process.

As Waxman (Waxman and Green 2009, p. 136) recounted about the Food Quality Protection Act of 1996, when his staffer called President Clinton's chief of staff, Leon Panetta, to inform him of the deal, Panetta stopped him. "If Waxman and Bliley are together on this, I don't need to know any more. We're for it."

Bipartisanship can also confer political legitimacy on a majority party's legislative efforts. A majority party may well be prepared to pay for such legitimacy by making substantive policy concessions to the minority. Barry (2003, p. 442) described the many efforts that House Judiciary Chairman F. James Sensenbrenner Jr. (R-Wisc.) made to obtain bipartisan support for the USA-PATRIOT Act in 2001. "The [George W. Bush] Administration wanted and needed overwhelming bipartisan support for its anti-terrorism proposal," she described. "Thus, the proposal's opponents were aware that in making public their disagreement with many of the provisions—and threatening the legitimacy of the Administration's proposal—they would receive some degree of leverage in the negotiations." Sensenbrenner and the Bush administration made policy concessions that were not strictly essential for House passage in order to secure broad bipartisan backing. Recognizing a similar political logic, Senate Minority Leader Mitch McConnell (R-Ky.) explained the strategy behind systematically withholding Republican support across the board for healthcare-reform legislation in 2009–2010: "It was absolutely critical that everybody be together because if the proponents of the bill were able to say it was bipartisan, it tended to convey to the public that this is OK, they must have figured it out," said McConnell. "It's either bipartisan or it isn't" (quoted in Hulse and Nagourney 2010). The minority party's ability to confer or withhold this kind of political legitimacy gives it leverage in interparty negotiations.

The majority must ask how much it has to give away to achieve its goals. As Representative Frank (2013) described the logic, "You start with the rational people. You order your preferences. You hope that you care more about more different things than they do, which gives you more flexibility in bargaining." A majority party may well decide that the price being demanded by the minority is too high. It may try to go it alone, even though it is rare that major legislation in the United States passes with support from only one party (Mayhew 2005). A majority party may eschew compromise altogether to keep an issue alive for the next election campaign, especially if it expects to gain additional seats in Congress.

At the same time, the opposition has its own calculations. As with the majority, the minority party also faces explicit trade-offs between politics and policy. As Representative Frank (2013) stated, "You think to yourself: 'They have the votes anyway. Am I better off making a deal and improving the policy? Or am I better off just opposing?'" In other words, do we want to use the issue to draw clear political distinctions between the parties, even at the cost of diminishing our influence over the substantive policy outcomes? Or do we prefer to influence the policy by trading our support in exchange for concessions, recognizing that doing so comes at the price of not being able to campaign as forcefully against the majority party on that issue? The minority may well prefer to use an issue for campaign purposes, even when the majority is willing to offer favorable substantive concessions on policy. Kaiser (2013, pp. 206–7), for example, reported that Senator McConnell was uninterested in a bipartisan deal on new Wall Street regulations in 2009–2010. Instead, McConnell considered Democrats' reform efforts a major opportunity for the Republican Party to raise campaign funds from financial interests.

In short, both parties must be willing to cross a threshold before any real bargaining is possible. When there are few or no political costs to saying no (or even benefits to saying no), then interparty negotiation will probably not even take place. How do the parties make their calculations about the costs of saying no to a pending matter? The desire to avoid blame for killing a deal strongly shapes lawmakers' and their leaders' incentives to cooperate. Past experience and polling results often lead both parties to come to the same conclusions about which side will shoulder the blame for failing to legislate. The government shutdown in 1995 under Speaker Newt Gingrich (R-Ga.) illustrates the consequence of underestimating the political costs of saying no. Gingrich grossly miscalculated who would be blamed for a government shutdown. Polling turned sharply against congressional Republicans, who eventually came to the table to negotiate an agreement with President Clinton and the Democrats. Since then, almost all lawmakers in Congress understand that the public may well assign blame to one party or the other if the government is shut down. Republicans apparently briefly forgot this lesson in October 2013 when they forced the closure of the federal government in a gambit to convince Democrats to defund their signature legislative achievement, the Affordable Care Act. Only when public views of Republicans tanked in mid-October did the GOP reconsider its stances and take a seat at the bargaining table to reopen the government.

Party members will sometimes reach different conclusions about the costs of saying no than party leaders. We consider, for example, the uncertain prospects for immigration reform in the summer of 2013. Many Republican elites and party strategists concluded that the electoral costs of blocking a deal on immigration reform were too great for the Republican Party over the long term. In this context, a bipartisan Senate "gang" was able to drive a comprehensive immigration reform to passage in the Senate Judiciary Committee and on the Senate floor. To be sure, less than a third of Senate Republicans signed on to the deal. However, the package safely cleared the Senate's supermajority requirements that in the past had blocked immigration reform. Given both parties' willingness to negotiate, the final Senate package was an integrative, win-win solution. Democrats cared the most about securing a path to citizenship for the nation's undocumented millions; the GOP cared most about securing the borders. A deal was reached when Democrats offered to *double* spending on border security. Even the prime GOP sponsor of the deal-making amendment called the border spending "almost overkill" (quoted in Blake 2013). Yet too many rank-and-file Republicans in the House were interested only in the parts of immigration reform that were popular with conservative constituencies back home. Can party elites convince their members that blame for blocking reform would be too costly for the party as a whole to shoulder? How Republicans answer that question will help determine when or if Congress will "get to yes" on immigration reform.

Intraparty negotiations. Rank-and-file members have many reasons to sign on to deals advocated by party and committee leaders. We might say that it is a default position for members to support their party leaders; they "go along to get along" and vote no only when they have a specific reason to do so. Members have a political interest in seeing the leaders of their party succeed. Party unity is usually seen as helpful to a party's brand-name reputation for competence and policy coherence. Substantive policy negotiation is also easier among party members because the barriers of mistrust and suspicion are lower than between the parties. Beyond the generalized trust and goodwill that are stronger within the political parties than between them, there are many extra-legislative favors that coalition leaders can provide to facilitate intraparty deal making.

First, leaders have procedural powers that can offer political benefits to members. As Representative Frank (2013) stated, "Members need protection." Sometimes such protection comes in the form of assurances that members will not have to face votes on controversial issues. Again, from Representative Frank: "I'd often have members come to me to say, 'Can you guarantee that a particular issue will not come up for a vote?' I'll say, 'Well, it's kind of a crazy idea, and it won't come up.' They'll respond, 'If you can guarantee that it won't come up, I can announce I'm for it.' "

Smoothing the way for a member on a difficult issue helps leaders to curry support on other issues. Similarly, party leaders can sometimes win support from recalcitrant members without making policy concessions to them. For example, they may grant a member a recorded vote on a favorite issue. The member may well be satisfied with winning political visibility as a "player" and a champion on that issue, even if his or her amendment fails in adoption. As Representative Frank (2013) explained with respect to House floor votes on Dodd–Frank financial regulatory reform: "I would go to leaders to ask for an amendment from Walt Minnick or Melissa Bean. The leadership will permit it if it can be defeated. . . . If so, then it can be offered. It's like the situation in Catch-22: 'Only schedule appointments when I'm not in the office.' "

Second, leaders' control of resources allows them to do favors for their rank and file that increase the likelihood of support from fellow partisans. Such favors include guaranteeing consideration of members' minor bills on the House floor, contributions from leadership political action committees (PACs) to members' campaign coffers, and even seemingly minor gestures such as showing up for members' fundraisers. "Always give people a vested interest in maintaining a good relationship with you," advised Representative Frank (2013).

In summary, the prospects and likely outcomes of congressional negotiation are very different within and between the congressional parties. With rare exceptions, rank-and-file partisans willingly engage in negotiations with their own party leaders. After all, members usually have a political interest in seeing their party leaders succeed. Furthermore, party leaders possess many resources to please their rank-and-file members even without making substantive policy concessions on a pending issue. Interparty dealing is far more limited: the opposition must first weigh the political incentives to negotiate at all. If they are unwilling to cross that threshold, strategic disagreement kicks in. Under such conditions, legislative deals are out of reach except for unusual political circumstances (for example, the short "window" running from 2009 into early 2010 when Democrats controlled both ends of Pennsylvania Avenue, bolstered by a filibuster-proof majority in the Senate). Under normal circumstances, interparty negotiations can begin and have a chance at success only when sufficient numbers of the opposition decide that they want to "get to yes."

Successful Negotiating: Instruments

This book identifies a set of institutional arrangements and policy tools that have facilitated successful negotiations in other contexts, including private meetings, penalty defaults, expertise, and repeated interactions (Martin 2013). In this section, we explore the relevance and effectiveness of these factors in the congressional context, as well as other factors informed by the congressional literature.

Secrecy. The move toward greater transparency in congressional operations—starting in the 1970s with a burst of "sunshine" laws for committees and the House floor in particular—has proven to be a double-edged sword. Greater openness of a legislative body might be considered a normative good: it increases the ability of the public and organized interests to hold accountable individual lawmakers and the institution as a whole for its decisions. However, the more transparent the legislative process is, the more the public dislikes Congress (Hibbing and Theiss-Morse 1995). Most people prefer to be "out of the kitchen" when legislators "grind sausage." Transparency does not necessarily lead to greater institutional legitimacy; in some cases, it may undermine it.

More worrisome, transparency often imposes direct costs on successful deal making. First, public attention increases the incentive of lawmakers to adhere to party messages, a step rarely conducive to setting aside differences and negotiating a deal. We consider, for example, what senators said as they emerged from the Senate's bipartisan retreat behind the closed doors of the old Senate Chamber in the summer of 2013, when Democrats were considering "going nuclear" to change the Senate's filibuster rule. "There was no rancor at all," Senator John Boozman (R-Ark.) noted about the closed-door session with ninety-eight senators in attendance. "I think if the American people were watching, the whole tone would have been different. It's different when the TV cameras are on. That might be part of the problem" (quoted in O'Keefe and Johnson 2013). Along these lines, Bessette (1994, p. 221) contended, "The duty to deliberate well may often be inconsistent with attempts to conduct policy deliberations on the plane of public opinion." Public settings encourage members to posture before external audiences rather than engage directly with their congressional interlocutors.

Second, transparency interferes with the search for solutions. Conducting negotiations of multidimensional, integrative solutions behind closed doors gives lawmakers more freedom to explore policy options. The genius of integrative solutions is that negotiating parties care unequally about different parts of the deal, requiring enlargement of the pie to secure competing parties' consent. The common mantra surrounding such negotiations is "nothing is agreed to until everything is agreed to" (Yglesias 2011), which reflects the conditional nature of most integrative solutions. Support for a provision that might be unpopular with your side is contingent on including a provision about which your side cares more. Leaking a less popular part of a deal—without linking it to what your party really cares about—is likely to kill the viability of the leaked provision, weakening the prospects for a deal. Waxman (Waxman and Green 2009, p. 137) attributed his successful pesticide negotiations with Bliley to a good mutual relationship and a common commitment to secrecy: "We implicitly trusted one another not to go public, had things not worked out, with the details of what the other had been willing to concede." Keeping negotiations secret until the whole package is unveiled allows both sides to justify the broader deal to constituencies and, in theory, avoid blame for unpopular giveaways. "The only way this type of negotiation can succeed is to tackle the whole problem in one fell swoop so that news of the deal arrives concurrently with the endorsements of all the major interests" (ibid.). This is also why—Representative Frank reminds us—serious negotiations rarely take place until very late in the game: early negotiations risk leaks of the parts of an integrative solution.

Despite the costs of transparency, private negotiations in Congress are increasingly difficult to secure. Repeated efforts to negotiate grand bargains on deficit reduction in the 112th Congress (2011–2012) were undermined each time by successful leaks about potential elements of a deal. Democratic-affiliated activists rejected reworking how the government calculates inflation for federal benefits (that is, the so-called chained Consumer Price Index proposal), whereas Republican-affiliated activists rejected any provisions that would raise revenue by increasing tax rates. Exceptions to the rule include the most recent bipartisan Senate gang on immigration reform, whose negotiations were shrouded in secrecy to the extent that participants could engineer it. The gang essentially made a pact to oppose deal-threatening amendments in committee and again during Senate floor consideration. Critical to the deal's success was its initial crafting in secret: that move gave senators the space to knit separate dimensions of immigration reform into a single package, exploiting the variation in senators' weighting of key issues and making support of one another's priorities conditional on support for the whole. The rarity with which House and Senate leaders can secure privacy complicates negotiations in Congress.

Penalty defaults.[1] Congress rarely acts in the absence of a deadline. Congress seems to recognize this and therefore regularly builds deadlines into the design of policies. Such deadlines often take the form of "sunset dates," which are limited authorizations for public programs that force the parties to reconsider policies when an appointed time arrives (Adler and Wilkerson 2013). At times, Congress crafts temporary fixes, requiring reconsideration at a later date. Congress tries to "rig" many such penalty defaults to guarantee action from itself at a future date, such as when it agrees to only a small increase in the government's legal borrowing limit. Other times, penalty defaults are beyond Congress's control: courts or states can

---

1. The origins of the concept of penalty defaults stem from contract law (Ayres and Gertner 1989).

impose policy changes that create an unacceptable status quo. Perhaps the most familiar penalty default is embedded in the U.S. Constitution: "No money shall be drawn from the Treasury but in consequence of appropriations made by law."[2] Failure to enact annual spending bills to fund the government's discretionary programs forces a government shutdown.

Regardless of the origin or structure of a penalty default, the underlying concept is the same. In the congressional context, such default provisions are expected to be action forcing. In theory, Congress will move to avert an unacceptable penalty imposed by the default. The default fallback provisions create "must-pass" bills because failure to legislate would produce what is deemed to be an extreme (and, thus, politically unacceptable) reversion policy. However, as we argue herein, policy and politics are always intertwined. When we think about the potential for penalty defaults to force lawmakers to make a deal, we must consider the political consequences of blocking an agreement.

At times, the penalty defaults engineered by Congress work. Hacker and Pierson (2005, pp. 61–62) called them policy "time bombs." The fiscal cliff "worked" to get Congress to act on tax policy because the restoration of Clinton-era middle-class income-tax rates was deemed a political nonstarter by both parties; neither party wanted to shoulder the blame for raising middle-class taxes. Other times, penalty defaults are a bust. The Joint Committee on Deficit Reduction (aka the "Supercommittee") of 2011 failed to produce a budget grand bargain even when the penalty default was *sequestration*—that is, blanket cuts across discretionary federal spending. Sequestration—at the time considered a sword of Damocles that would give both parties an incentive to cooperate—failed in practice as a penalty default. Lawmakers individually escaped blame for the draconian cuts, even as Congress came under fire for its failure to act. In short, there was little incentive for Republicans (and perhaps for Democrats) to avoid the penalty outcome. Congress did act to avert cuts at the Federal Aviation Administration but only after a well-organized air travel industry (including pilots, flight attendants, passengers, and shippers) raised the political costs of saying no for both parties. The conditional success

2. Article I, Section 9, Clause 7.

of penalty defaults keeps them from being an easy solution for securing major deals in Congress.

Expertise. Congress relies on information and expertise but not of a technocratic sort. Neutral expertise bodies established within the legislative branch, including the Government Accountability Office and the Congressional Budget Office, have limited impact on negotiating deals in Congress. Lawmakers cite these agencies when the experts produce favorable results for their own agenda; however, such expertise is heavily discounted when unfavorable.

That said, Congress is anxious for expertise of a more politicized sort. It seeks out input from affected interests on the possible effects of legislative proposals. It wants to know whether interest groups are "on board." Kaiser (2013, p. 166) wrote that the first responsibility of congressional staff in crafting major legislation is "to hear out and sometimes to seek out the opinions of every party that would be significantly affected by it." Information gathering (for example, from groups, industry, and agencies) allows members to discern different valuations across issues that allow potential win-win deals to be made. If all affected groups can coalesce around a policy—and settle the controversies among themselves—Congress often will ratify the result.

Repeated interactions. Current and former members and staff testify to the importance of relationships and getting to know one another on a personal basis. Political scientists are often skeptical of such claims. However, a sizable literature shows that senior legislators are more legislatively successful (Cox and Terry 2008) and that their effectiveness in office increases across their careers in the House (Volden and Wiseman 2009). Lawmakers who have been in office longer have more specific human capital that enhances their legislative success. Female legislators in the minority party seem to outshine their male colleagues in legislative effectiveness (Volden, Wiseman, and Wittmer 2013), a function perhaps of their superior collaborative skills (see, for example, Rosenthal 1998).

Institutional arrangements that encourage repeated interactions may thus promote successful deal making in Congress. The standing committees of Congress comprise the primary congressional institution fostering repeated interactions and expertise among members, although committee chair term limits imposed by Senate Republicans and by House chamber and Republican Party rules have disrupted repeated relationships in both chambers. Most major legislative deals emerge from committee work. In the case of the Dodd–Frank financial-regulatory reforms, the key committee chairs—Representative Frank and Senator Dodd, both longtime institutional loyalists—had built relationships of trust during their many years of service that assisted them in constructing durable coalitions (Kaiser 2013). All else equal, repeated interactions—across lawmakers, their staffs, and lobbyists for key organized interests—undoubtedly facilitate deal making.

The rise of partisanship, however, has weakened congressional committees and contributed to the breakdown of "regular order." For example, the Senate Finance panel's slow start in 2013 in getting tax reform off the ground testifies to the difficulties that committee leaders now face in tackling policy challenges without the support of party leaders (Lesniewski 2013). Lawmakers often resort to ad hoc or "unorthodox" procedures to achieve major deals in the contemporary context. Sometimes small bipartisan groups of legislators (or "gangs") assume responsibility outside of the formal committee system for generating bipartisan measures. Some of these are successful (for example, the Finance Committee gang that worked to generate the Senate healthcare proposal in 2009); others are not (for example, the Gang of Six that met in 2011 and 2012 to negotiate a grand bargain on debt and deficit reduction). Ad hoc arrangements sacrifice many of the negotiating advantages afforded by long-standing repeated interactions, but they are sometimes the only pathways to success under contemporary conditions.

Messaging and communications. The "messaging game" shapes the public's views of legislative battles in Washington (Malecha and Reagan 2012; Sellers 2010). Episodes of messaging and communication strategies more generally can put pressure on the opposition party to come to the table to negotiate a deal. However, messaging typically must be blunt and often becomes little more than an effort to demonize the opposition; it then can impede negotiations. This is yet another reason why secrecy often improves the prospects for a deal, although party messaging tends to continue right up to the eleventh hour, even when lawmakers find themselves cloistered behind closed doors in the final moments before an impending deadline.

Leadership from the president. The president unquestionably has a central role in setting the stage for congressional negotiations. When presidents focus on an issue, they can set the legislative agenda "single-handedly" (Kingdon 1995, p. 23). Presidents surpass any individual lawmaker in their ability to garner media attention. Strategic appeals from the president—which, in turn, are shaped partially by the disposition of public opinion on an issue (Canes-Wrone 2001)—can help a president win more in bargaining with Congress (at least with respect to budget battles over spending). At the same time, presidential appeals can be a double-edged sword: they potentially commit lawmakers to particular positions, a move that limits legislators' bargaining flexibility (Kernell 2006). More generally, Edwards (2003), in his book *On Deaf Ears*, warned that presidential appeals almost always fail to move public opinion.

Presidential leadership is more helpful with members of the president's party than with the opposition. Members of the president's party have a political stake in the president's success, separate from their views on the underlying policy issues involved. As a consequence, a president who is publicly championing an issue undoubtedly puts pressure on members of his party in Congress. By the same logic, however, presidential leadership alienates the opposition party (Lee 2009). After all, a president's policy successes are not politically beneficial to his party's opposition. As one White House aide in the George W. Bush administration observed, "It seems like if the President is publicly 'for' something, the Democratic leaders [in Congress] are automatically against it" (quoted in Andres 2005, p. 764). Senator Pat Toomey (R-Pa.) observed this dynamic among his fellow Republicans during the Obama presidency: "There were some on my side who did not want to be seen helping the president do something he wanted to get done, just because the president wanted to do it" (quoted in Brandt 2013). Do quieter appeals make a difference for congressional negotiations? Perhaps, although it is a more difficult conjecture to evaluate, given the low visibility and traceability of an administration's behind-the-scenes role in deliberations over policy.

Conclusions

In tribute to one of his principal staff negotiators, Senator Mitch McConnell (R-Ky.) said, "I assure you it is rare in this business to come across somebody who combines a brilliant mind for policy and a brilliant mind for politics in one package."[3] McConnell's comment captures a truth about negotiation in Congress. The outcome of congressional negotiations depends on more than policy considerations. Negotiation in Congress is also driven by politics. Members and leaders negotiate with an eye to deals that they can defend successfully to constituencies outside of Congress. In this light, a good deal on policy merits still may be judged too politically risky. Members and leaders also consider whether it is in their party's interests to strike a deal or whether it seems more politically advantageous to preserve the disagreement for electoral purposes. Politics will often lead members to reject compromises that would be acceptable if public policy were the only consideration. By the same token, members sometimes accede to undesirable policies when the politics of holding out becomes too difficult to sustain.

One obvious implication is that negotiation in Congress is far more complex than negotiation in the private sector. As chapter 4 points out, many cognitive obstacles stand in the way of successful negotiation, including fixed-pie bias, self-serving bias, and general difficulties of perspective taking. All of these difficulties inevitably affect negotiation in Congress as well. Making success even more problematic, congressional negotiation also occurs in a political context, in which members must evaluate deals for their effects on their individual reelection efforts and political reputations, as well as for their party's broader interests in winning and maintaining institutional control. Members of Congress frequently confront trade-offs between their political interests and their policy goals.

On the other side of the ledger, there is more room in Congress for integrative solutions than in most other negotiation settings. Congress's broad jurisdiction allows for a wide array of unrelated issues to be considered simultaneously, affording players with different priorities a reason to come together and shake hands on a deal. This suggests that scholars need to do more to investigate how integrative negotiation works in Congress rather than relying so heavily on a congressional literature that emphasizes models of "splitting the difference." Undoubtedly, splitting the difference can be the basis of agreement in Congress when the conflict is over divisible goods, such

3. Congressional Record, July 31, 2013, S6085.

as budgets, appropriations, and taxes. However, many issues are not amenable to this kind of resolution. At the same time, the broad range of issues available to congressional negotiators gives wide scope for creative legislators to strike deals.

The contemporary Congress labors under remarkably high barriers to success in negotiations. As described by Barber and McCarty (see chapter 2), Congress today is strongly polarized by party in terms of members' policy preferences. During the 1950s, 1960s, and 1970s, the broader range of policy positions held by members of both parties in Congress facilitated interparty negotiation. In the contemporary Congress, there is far less overlap between the policy preferences of Republicans and Democrats. As the parties have moved further apart in policy terms, they also have tended to become internally more homogeneous. Increased party cohesion in the House can make intraparty negotiation in the House more efficient and successful. (However, since 2011, a House GOP majority increasingly *divided* between mainstream and hardline elements has struggled to reach deals within their conference.) At the same time, increased party cohesion can undermine deal making in the Senate. Given the Senate's supermajority procedures, increased intraparty homogeneity coupled with partisan conflict has rendered Senate obstruction rampant, with the minority party deploying the filibuster as a veto against the majority party's legislative agenda. Even parties under unified government rarely have a clear shot to legislative success. In short, party polarization has greatly complicated the task of legislating (Binder 2003; Sinclair 2006, 2012).

Today's political context is unfavorable for congressional negotiations. Political competition between the parties for control of national institutions creates electoral incentives for the parties to engage in "strategic disagreement." The United States is also in the midst of a ferociously party-competitive era, in which the two major parties stand at near parity in terms of their prospects for winning or holding control of national institutions. Since 1980, control of the Senate shifted seven times, with Democrats and Republicans each in the majority for nine Congresses. Control of the House of Representatives reversed three times, also with Democrats and Republicans each in the majority for nine Congresses. Between 1981 and 2017, Republicans will have held the presidency for twenty years and Democrats for sixteen years. When control of Congress or the White House hangs in the balance, lawmakers weigh more heavily the partisan political consequences of negotiations. Such zero-sum competition fuels antagonism between the parties beyond the policy-based obstacles to agreement fostered by ideological polarization.

In the United States, both political and policy considerations complicate successful negotiation, especially in periods of polarized parties. Our political system's many veto points and extensive array of checks and balances demand considerable negotiating skill among officeholders to make government function. Yet, "Congress is becoming more like a parliamentary system," observed former Senator Olympia Snowe (R-Maine), "where everyone simply votes with their party and those in charge employ every possible tactic to block the other side" (quoted in Kaiser 2013, p. 398). The outcome is a Congress and a national government in which deals are more elusive than ever.

Note: We thank former chair of the House Financial Services Committee, Representative Barney Frank, for his valuable insights on congressional negotiation. Frank's examples and analyses were most helpful in orienting our thinking from the outset. We also benefited from a discussion with Gary Andres, staff director of the House Energy and Commerce Committee.

References

Adler, E. Scott, and John D. Wilkerson. 2013. *Congress and the Politics of Problem Solving.* Cambridge University Press.

Andres, Gary. 2005. "The Contemporary Presidency: Polarization and White House/Legislative Relations: Causes and Consequences of Elite-Level Conflict." *Presidential Studies Quarterly* 35 (4): 761–70.

Arnold, Douglas. 1990. *Logic of Congressional Action.* Yale University Press.

Ayres, Ian, and Robert Gertner. 1989. "Filling Gaps in Incomplete Contracts: An Economic Theory of Default Rules." *Yale Law Journal* 99:87–130.

Barber, Michael, and Nolan McCarty. 2013. "Causes and Consequences of Polarization." In *Negotiating Agreement in Politics*, ed. Cathie Jo Martin and Jane Mansbridge. Washington, DC: American Political Science Association.

Baron, David, and John Ferejohn. 1989. "Bargaining in Legislatures." *American Political Science Review* 83 (4): 1181–1206.

Barry, Mindy. 2003. "Principled Negotiating: Breeding Success and Protecting Public Interests behind Closed Doors." *Georgetown Journal of Law and Policy* 1:431–44.

Bessette, Joseph M. 1994. *The Mild Voice of Reason: Deliberative Democracy and American National Government.* University of Chicago Press.

Binder, Sarah A. 2003. *Stalemate: Causes and Consequences of Legislative Gridlock.* Brookings Institution Press.

Blake, Aaron. 2013. "Corker: My Border Security Deal Is 'Almost Overkill,'" *Washington Post*, June 20. www.washingtonpost.com /blogs/post-politics/wp/2013/06/20/corker-my-border-security -deal-is-overkill?wprss=rss_politics&wpisrc=pl_wonk.b.

Brandt, Evan. 2013. "Toomey Doubts Second Senate Gun-Control Vote Any Time Soon." *Times Herald*, May 1.

Canes-Wrone, Brandice. 2001. "The President's Legislative Influence from Public Appeals." *American Journal of Political Science* 45 (2): 313–29.

Cox, Gary W., and William C. Terry. 2008. "Legislative Productivity in the 93rd–105th Congresses." *Legislative Studies Quarterly* 33 (4): 603–18.

Edwards, George. 2003. *On Deaf Ears.* Yale University Press.

Evans, C. Lawrence. 2011. "Congressional Committees." In *The Oxford Handbook of the American Congress*, ed. Eric Schickler and Frances E. Lee. Oxford University Press.

Evans, Diana. 2004. *Greasing the Wheels: Using Pork Barrel Projects to Build Majority Coalitions in Congress.* Cambridge University Press.

Follett, Mary Parker. [1925] 1942. "Constructive Conflict." In *Dynamic Administration: The Collected Papers of Mary Parker Follett*, ed. H. C. Metcalf and L. Urwick. New York: Harper.

Frank, Barney. 2013. Interview with authors, June 24. Washington, D.C.

Gilmour, John B. 1995. *Strategic Disagreement: Stalemate in American Politics.* University of Pittsburgh Press.

Hacker, Jacob S., and Paul E. Pierson. 2005. *Off Center: The Republican Revolution and the Erosion of American Democracy.* Yale University Press.

Hibbing, John, and Elizabeth Theiss-Morse. 1995. *Congress as Public Enemy*. Cambridge University Press.

Hulse, Carl, and Adam Nagourney. 2010. "Senate GOP Leader Finds Weapon in Unity." *New York Times*, March 16, A13.

Kaiser, Robert. 2013. *Act of Congress: How America's Essential Institution Works, and How It Doesn't*. New York: Knopf.

Karol, David. 2009. *Party Position Change in American Politics: Coalition Management*. Cambridge University Press.

Kernell, Samuel. 2006. *Going Public*. 4th ed. Washington, DC: CQ Press.

Kingdon, John W. 1995. *Agendas, Alternatives, and Public Policies*. 2nd ed. New York: HarperCollins.

Krehbiel, Keith, and Douglas Rivers. 1988. "The Analysis of Committee Power: An Application to Senate Voting on the Minimum Wage." *American Journal of Political Science* 32 (4): 1151–74.

Lee, Frances E. 2009. *Beyond Ideology: Politics, Principles, and Partisanship in the U.S. Senate*. University of Chicago Press.

Lesniewski, Niels. 2013. "Reid Dismisses Baucus' Tax Overhaul Efforts." *CQ/Roll Call*, July 25. http://blogs. rollcall.com/wgdb/reid -dismisses-baucus-tax-reform-efforts/.

Malecha, Gary Lee, and Daniel J. Reagan. 2012. *The Public Congress: Congressional Deliberation in a New Media Age*. New York: Routledge.

Martin, Cathie Jo. 2013. "Conditions for Successful Negotiation: Lessons from the EU and the European States." In *Negotiating Agreement in Politics*, ed. Cathie Jo Martin and Jane Mansbridge. Washington, DC: American Political Science Association.

Mayhew, David. 1974. *Congress: The Electoral Connection*. Yale University Press.

———. 2005. *Divided We Govern: Party Control, Lawmaking, and Investigations, 1946–2002*. 2nd ed. Yale University Press.

O'Keefe, Ed, and Jenna Johnson. 2013. "No Filibuster Deal, but Senators Agree They Should Meet More Often." *Washington Post*, July 15. www.washingtonpost.com/blogs/post-politics/wp/2013/07 /15/no-filibuster-deal-but-senators-agree-they-should-meet-more -often/.

Poole, Keith T., and Howard Rosenthal. 1997. *Congress: A Political-Economic History of Roll Call Voting*. Oxford University Press.

———. 2013. *NOMINATE and Related Data*. Voteview.com, Department of Political Science, University of Georgia. http://voteview.com/downloads.asp.

Riker, William. 1962. *The Theory of Political Coalitions*. Yale University Press.

Rosenthal, Cindy Simon. 1998. *When Women Lead: Integrative Leadership in State Legislatures*. Oxford University Press.

Sellers, Patrick. 2010. *Cycles of Spin: Strategic Communication in the U.S. Congress*. Cambridge University Press.

Sinclair, Barbara. 2006. *Party Wars*. University of Oklahoma Press.

———. 2012. *Unorthodox Lawmaking: New Legislative Processes in the U.S. Congress*. 4th ed. Washington, DC: CQ Press.

Smith, Steven S. 2007. *Party Influence in Congress*. Cambridge University Press.

Sorauf, Frank J. 1992. *Inside Campaign Finance: Myths and Realities*. Yale University Press.

Volden, Craig, and Alan E. Wiseman. 2009. "Legislative Effectiveness in Congress." Typescript. Ohio State University.

Volden, Craig, Alan E. Wiseman, and Dana E. Wittmer. 2013. "When Are Women More Effective Lawmakers Than Men?" *American Journal of Political Science* 57 (2): 326–41.

Wawro, Gregory. 2000. *Legislative Entrepreneurship in the House*. University of Michigan Press.

Waxman, Henry, and Joshua Green. 2009. *The Waxman Report: How Congress Really Works*. New York: Twelve.

Yglesias, Matthew. 2011. "Eric Cantor Takes Bargaining Positions out of Context, Poisoning the Atmosphere of Future Negotiations." Think Progress. http://thinkprogress.org/yglesias/2011/07/12/267092/eric-cantor-takes-bargaining-positions-out-of-context-poisoning-the-atmosphere-of-future-negotiations/.

Part II

THE PROBLEM
AND THE
SOLUTION

Chapter Four

Negotiation Myopia

Chase Foster, Jane Mansbridge,
and Cathie Jo Martin

In this chapter, we use the term *negotiation myopia* to cover the many ways in which negotiators fail to see their own advantage, sometimes right in front of them, thereby missing an opportunity for coming to agreement. The forms of myopia range from innate cognitive biases that are highly resistant to change to volatile emotional states. All of these forms can sink a negotiation when the issues are in fact tractable and outcomes exist that would benefit all participants. This analysis does not discuss the moments in which parties think that such positive-sum outcomes might exist but in fact the interests of the parties are incompatible.

We begin with "fixed-pie bias," which many experts consider one of the two most harmful forms of negotiation myopia. Fixed-pie bias keeps negotiators from seeing the ways that they can share information and think together to "create value" for both sides. Several other forms of bias contribute to fixed-pie bias. Yet even a simple set of instructions to "take the perspective of the other side" can reduce this bias dramatically.

We next consider "self-serving bias," which ranks with fixed-pie bias as one of the two most harmful forms of negotiation myopia. Elements of this bias may be innate. The bias comes in many forms, running from natural overoptimism to deep-seated convictions about justice. Self-serving bias can be greatly reduced through ongoing trustful relationships with others who hold opposite perceptions.

Finally, we consider the anger that often can impede negotiations and we briefly mention other biases that also can interfere with negotiation.

To help legislators combat these biases, we distill many of the lessons from forty years of study of negotiation in business and law schools. A simple way to do this is to summarize a key chapter from a best-selling book on negotiation by David Lax and James Sebenius, *3–D Negotiation: Powerful Tools to Change the Game in Your Most Important Deals*. In that book, the authors first provide useful advice on how to set up a negotiation and design the deal. They conclude with advice for the negotiation process itself, which is the focus of this chapter. Following are their mostly self-explanatory titles from that section, which take the form of condensed, one-sentence pieces of advice (we provide brief explanations and translations to political negotiation where necessary).

Move from positional to interest-based conversations. This is their first and perhaps most important piece of advice. A "position" is the negotiation specialists' word for the demand one brings to a negotiation. The "interests" are the wants and needs that underlie a position. The goal is to try to determine what the other side really wants and needs and to be open to exploring what you and your constituents really want and need. Work with the other side to get below the surface, with the expectation that the process can help craft solutions to problems that are good for both, find trades that are least costly for each side, and settle on compromises that both sides think are fair.

Move from blaming and past actions to problem-solving and the future. This statement requires no explanation.

Move from high-level assertions to fact-based statements. In the context of political negotiation, this means moving from generalizations—particularly negative ones about the other side and positive ones about your side—to the facts in the case and the specific needs of constituents or groups that conflict or coincide with the needs of others.

Adopt a persuasive style. This recommendation has several important components. A "persuasive negotiator," according to Lax and Sebenius, "understands the other side's story," "is open to persuasion," "uses reciprocity to build trust," "matches appeals to the other side's circumstances," seeks "agreements that feel fair to both sides," "recognizes how people process information" through stories as well as analysis, builds "substantive and relationship credibility," understands and responds to the best arguments against his or her own side, responds to the other side's emotions, deals with his or her own feelings, and responds empathetically to the other side's culture. Crucially, a good negotiator can "write *their* victory speech," actively helping design some "wins" that the other side can deliver.[1]

Taken together, these recommendations come close to what in this book we call "deliberative negotiation." In fact, we argue, if *negotiation myopia* is the problem, then *deliberative negotiation* is the solution.

Successful Negotiation

Oversimplifying here, we have two criteria for a successful negotiation, as follows:[2]

1. If there is a deal to be done, the negotiators do it. That is, if there is a "zone of possible agreement" (ZOPA) between the parties, they in fact agree on an outcome within that zone.[3]

2. If redefining or expanding the issues to be negotiated could improve the outcome for both sides, the negotiators find and exploit those possibilities. In the relatively rare event that the parties can find solutions to conflict that bring benefits to both parties with no loss, the parties find or create those solutions. In the more

---

1. Distilled and quoted from Lax and Sebenius (2006, pp. 205–24; emphasis added).

2. See chapter 7 for another statement of these two criteria. Each of these criteria requires benefit to both (or all) parties in a negotiation. From the perspective of every party in any negotiation, therefore, these are clear and obvious criteria for success, and all analyses of negotiation success include these two. As chapter 7 points out, we do not discuss herein two other potential criteria—namely, successfully claiming more from the other than the other claims from you, or successfully including all those affected by the decision on fair terms of participation (on this issue see also chapter 5).

3. The ZOPA is sometimes called simply the "zone of agreement," the "contract zone" or "bargaining range." It refers to the zone between the two parties' reservation values (that is, the points at which it would be better for the party to walk away from the deal). Agreements that have only win-lose zero-sum possibilities within a ZOPA are called *distributive* agreements or solutions, with distributive negotiation "*claiming*" value within that range.

common case in which the problem contains several issues or other issues that can be brought into the negotiation to create overall benefit, the negotiators find those issues and trade the high priorities of one side against the low priorities of the other side.[4]

Over time, negotiation scholars have discovered that ordinary people and even trained professionals sometimes have trouble coming to agreement, even when there is a clear zone of agreement on the table. They most frequently have trouble discovering or even looking for the other possible issues on which mutually beneficial trades can be conducted. These problems result from the forms of negotiation myopia that we discuss in this chapter.

Fixed-Pie Bias

At least in the United States, many people enter into even commercial negotiations with the expectation that "their gain is our loss."[5] They see the "pie" to be negotiated as of a fixed size and all outcomes as zero-sum. In almost every negotiating course in the United States, whether in business or law or policy schools, this is the first bias that an instructor tries to address. The environment of competitive politics accentuates this bias.

However, in many negotiations—particularly legislative ones—the pie is not fixed. The parties can improve the benefits for *both* sides by delving more deeply into the wants and needs of each of the sides and by looking for issues on which the parties have different valuations. If they can find any such issues, they are in a good position to craft a

---

4. Agreements that expand beyond the original ZOPA are called *integrative* agreements or solutions, with integrative negotiation "*creating* value" outside that original zone. In chapter 5, we distinguish between "*fully* integrative" solutions, in which a solution is good for all with no loss, and "*partially* integrative" solutions, in which mutually beneficial trades can be made but each side also loses something. In chapter 5, we also show that deliberative negotiations may have what we call "purely deliberative" moments, in which the parties, for example, simply are trying to ascertain the facts or to coordinate on conceptions of justice. At the same time, those negotiations may have distributive zero-sum moments in which the parties try to find or craft a fair compromise.

5. Bazerman, Baron, and Shonk (2001, chap. 2).

solution that allows the parties to trade on issues of high value to them but of low value to the other—or even occasionally devise a solution that is good for all with no loss to any. This process generates integrative solutions that, in the standard negotiation language, "create value," "expand the pie," or produce "joint gains."

A commercial example from an examination in a course on negotiation clarifies the point. In this example, the owner of a service station is willing to sell it for anything more than $500,000, but the buyer is unwilling to buy it for more than $400,000. Thus, there is no ZOPA. However, the description of the case mentions in passing that the seller also wants a job when he returns from an extended trip that he is planning. The buyer could offer $395,000 plus a job as manager of the service station when the seller returns, thereby obtaining an agreement. In an experiment using this question, only 39 percent of the pairs of MBA students playing the roles of buyer and seller in this situation discovered the integrative possibility and concluded the deal. However, simply giving the students playing the buyer instructions to "take the perspective" of the seller in the negotiation and to "try to understand what he is thinking, what his interests and purposes are in selling the station; try to imagine what you would be thinking in that role" increased the likelihood of their making a deal from 39 percent to 76 percent.[6]

To obtain these joint gains, negotiation texts instruct students to ask many questions and look for differences in valuation between the parties. In the service station case, the future job was valuable to the seller but relatively costless to the buyer, who would have had to hire someone to manage the station anyway. The most important differences to look for are those in the valuation of the issues; the expectations of uncertain events; and the attitudes toward risk, time preferences, and capabilities.[7]

---

6. Example and data are from Galinsky et al. (2008). Instructions to "take the perspective of the service-station owner; try to understand what he is feeling, what emotions he may be experiencing in selling the station; try to imagine what you would be feeling in that role" proved less effective, generating a nonstatistically significant improvement (that is, an increase to 54 percent of those seeing the possible joint gains).

7. Thompson (2005, p. 84).

The point of fixed-pie bias is that many people entering into a negotiation are not looking for ways to "create value" or "expand the pie." Thus, on average, people fail to see the issues in the negotiating situation on which they have compatible interests about half the time.[8] The fixed-pie assumption is in place before the parties even meet or begin to talk with one another.[9] It also can be difficult to challenge.[10] Describing the task as "problem solving" rather than "bargaining" has no effect.[11] Without the appropriate background in mutual trust and commitment to a solution, few parties to a negotiation will offer information about their own interests, and fewer still will ask about the other's interests, even though such an information exchange has been shown repeatedly to improve negotiation performance.[12]

In politics, fixed-pie bias is likely to be even stronger than it is in commercial negotiations. First, "the fixed-pie perspective is more likely to be a problem in group negotiations than in dyadic [that is, two-person] negotiations."[13] Second, competitiveness increases the bias. Simply being told to take a side in a negotiation increases fixed-pie bias, compared with being told simply to observe,[14] and the competitive dynamic in politics is far stronger than simply being assigned a

---

8. In a meta-analysis of thirty-two experiments, Thompson and Hrebec (1996) found that on average the parties in a negotiation failed to identify 45.5 percent of the compatible issues. In an average of 20 percent of the cases, the parties did not conclude deals that would have left both better off (see also chapter 7).

9. Thompson and Hastie (1990).

10. Thompson and DeHarpport (1994).

11. Ibid.

12. Thompson, Peterson, and Brodt's (1996) experiment revealed that only about 20 percent of the parties to the negotiation offered any information about their own situation and only 7 percent asked the other side for information. For experiments demonstrating how greatly information exchange contributes to improved performance, see Pruitt and Lewis (1975); Thompson, Peterson, and Brodt (1996); and Weingart et al. (1990), cited in Thompson and Hrebec (1996, p. 405).

13. Neale and Bazerman (1991, p. 107).

14. Among the subjects who were induced to become relatively involved in the negotiation, those told to assume a side were "most likely to maintain the fixed-pie belief; in contrast, highly involved nonpartisan observers were the most accurate" (Thompson and Hrebec 1996, p. 405).

role in an experiment. Bazerman and his colleagues concluded that "the 'myth of the fixed pie' is pervasive in many political situations."[15]

It turns out, however, that the fixed-pie bias has a relatively easy fix. If the negotiating parties trust one another, they will not necessarily see the pie as fixed. If they have a solid problem-solving orientation, they will look for creative ways of obtaining joint gains. As chapter 5 reports, in helping to craft the Clean Air Act of 1990, Senator Timothy E. Wirth, a Democrat, and Senator John Heinz, a Republican, both found it perfectly natural as longtime friends to engage in what we call "deliberative negotiation."[16] As a matter of course, they did everything that Lax and Sebenius suggest a "persuasive negotiator" should do. They asked questions, they interacted openly with each other, and they shared information; the result was a greatly expanded pie.

Self-Serving Bias

Self-serving bias is the tendency of the human psyche to interpret the world through a lens that favors our own position or self-image. Everyone has this bias. More accurately, almost all of us have this bias: research shows that depressed people have more accurate self-assessments than the average overly optimistic person does.[17] This

---

15. Bazerman, Baron, and Shonk (2001, p. 46).

16. Individuals who are *too* close (for example, married and romantically involved couples) may achieve fewer joint gains because they compromise too soon instead of pushing for creative solutions in which they could both get more of what they wanted (Fry, Firestone, and Williams 1983; Schoeninger and Wood 1969). Negotiating partners who are simply friends, however, tend to produce more joint gains than others (Thompson and DeHarpport 1990; Valley, Neale, and Mannix 1995). In one set of experiments, the greatest joint gain came from subjects playing the role of representatives who were both accountable to others (for example, constituents) *and* had good relations with one another based on the expectation of future cooperation (Pruitt 1983). For an overview, see Bazerman and Neale (1995).

17. See Taylor and Brown (1988); Seligman (1991); Greenberg et al. (1992). Kahneman and Tversky (1995), however, point out that in the executing of a plan, optimism tends to increase effort, commitment, and persistence in the face of difficulty; in the setting of goals and plans, it tends to favor excessive risk taking.

bias is strongest when there is ambiguity—as there so frequently is in politics—about the very nature of the problem, the relevant facts, and which conceptions of justice or fairness apply.[18]

Self-serving bias applies to many features of a negotiation: from the selection and perception of facts, theories of reality, and concepts of justice and the common good to recollections of past events, to estimates of our own and others' motivations, to the reasons we give for our own and others' successes and failures, and even to estimates of our own and others' biases.

Most people, for example, are unrealistically optimistic about their chances for success. On election night in 2012, when Karl Rove refused to recognize the Fox News analysts' expertise and disputed their decision that Ohio had gone for Obama, he was responding the way most of us respond under uncertainty: he overestimated the strength of his position. Not surprisingly, when both parties in a negotiation overestimate how much they can get in a negotiation, they are less likely to reach agreement. This overoptimism applies across the board. Babcock and Loewenstein have pointed out that people generally overestimate their personal contribution to joint tasks, and "well over half of survey respondents typically rate themselves in the top 50 percent of drivers, ethics, managerial prowess, productivity, health, and a variety of desirable skills."[19] In their experiments, simply being given a role on one side or the other before—rather than after—making one's initial assessment in a negotiation created a self-serving bias and reduced the eventual agreement rate from 28 percent to 6 percent. Neither reading a paragraph "on the extent and consequences of the self-serving bias" nor writing an essay "arguing the opponent's case as convincingly as possible" resulted in a significant improvement.[20]

---

18. Bazerman, Curhan, and Moore (2002).

19. Babcock and Loewenstein (1997, p. 111). See also their real-world examples from negotiation. In one example, the degree of difference between the self-serving factual estimates by school board presidents and union leaders of the annual salaries in school districts they considered "comparable" to their own predicted the number of past strikes in the district.

20. Ibid. (pp. 114–15). In another experiment, however, listing the weaknesses in one's own case substantially reduced the rate of impasse from 35 percent to 4 percent. We would expect rules, institutions, and friendly interactions that

Self-serving bias applies as strongly, or more so, to perceptions of justice and fairness. Self-serving judgments of fairness can keep negotiators from reaching agreement in several ways.[21] First and most obviously, self-serving judgments of what is fair to expect from the other side may simply eliminate any ZOPA, even when a third party might identify such a zone from the underlying interests. Worse yet, people's perceptions of fairness make them dig in because most people "are strongly averse to settling even slightly below the point they view as fair."[22] Finally, if the parties believe that their own understanding of fairness is impartial and the other side *must* see that, then each will interpret the other side's bargaining moves not as an attempt to get what they see as fair but rather only as an attempt to gain strategic advantage. This perception dangerously undercuts a negotiation because, as Babcock and Loewenstein have explained, negotiators usually care not only about what the other side offers but also about its motives.[23]

Judgments of motivation are highly susceptible to self-serving bias. People tend to attribute injurious intentions to their adversaries even when the adversary's behavior could have been plausibly attributed to other motivations. They also tend to interpret their own motivations as pure. This mismatch does not help the parties constructively explore their options.

Everyone falls prey to these biases, including individuals of good will and public spirit. We all find self-serving bias particularly difficult to detect in ourselves because we tend to see our own views as close to objective reality, whereas our adversaries' views are influenced by biases.[24] Our biases about our biases then escalate the spiral of conflict,

---

make one aware of the weaknesses in one's case to have the same effect in the political world.

21. We take the following paragraph directly from the analysis of ibid. (p. 110).

22. Ibid., citing Loewenstein, Thompson, and Bazerman (1989).

23. Ibid., citing Blount (1995), Rabin (1993), and Kagel, Kim, and Moser (1996).

24. Pronin, Lin, and Ross (2002). This bias is reinforced by *confirmation bias*, which leads people to interpret events in ways that confirm their earlier theories. It is also reinforced by *attribution bias*, which leads people to interpret the negative qualities of adversaries as fundamental to their person or ideology rather than produced by the situation, but their own negative qualities as situational rather than personal.

which works as follows. First, our faith in our own lack of bias leads us to view our adversaries as even less rational and more immune to reasoned argument than they actually are. Therefore, judging them as biased, we tend to use threats and bribes in our interactions rather than cognitive appeals to what we see as the benefits the deal can give them. They then perceive us as nonresponsive to good arguments and respond with threats and bribes. This behavior confirms our perception of them as not working on the plane of rational argument.[25]

A physical experiment with two people putting pressure on each other's fingers shows how unconscious assessments of one's own purity and the others' relative malevolence can create a spiral of conflict. In this experiment, each participant was instructed to apply pressure to the other's finger with "the same force on the other participant that had just been exerted on them." As each pressed the other's finger, each consistently overestimated the amount of outgoing force required to match the incoming force. The result: a 38 percent mean escalation at each turn.[26] We overestimate others' negative actions toward us and underestimate our own negative actions toward them, while also overestimating our own positive actions toward others and underestimating their positive actions toward us.

What can be done to correct self-serving bias? Quite a lot. Any form of "anchor" located outside ourselves can help overcome self-serving bias. In politics, governmental fact-finding bodies, independent think tanks, bipartisan commissions, relatively neutral media commentators, and even elections can serve the function of giving both sides in the negotiation a mutually acceptable set of facts.

In chapter 3, Binder and Lee report that the nonpartisan fact-finding bodies established within the legislative branch, including the Government Accountability Office and the Congressional Budget Office, have only a limited impact on current negotiating processes in Congress. Yet many negotiation specialists report that impartial fact-finding institutions can play a key role in negotiation by allowing participants to work from mutually accepted facts (Bazerman et al. 2000, p. 284). If such institutions are not available, the parties must spend much of their negotiation time simply agreeing on the facts and not working

25. Kennedy and Pronin (2008).

26. Shergill et al. (2003).

out possible deals. In such instances, negotiation specialists often advise spending the first part of a negotiation—perhaps even the first year—in a joint fact-finding exercise.[27] This exercise not only provides the set of facts from which the parties can then negotiate; it also involves the parties in a task that, to a certain degree, provides a common good (even when that good is contested), thereby building mutual trust in the process. When society as a whole is so polarized that no fact-finding group, third party, or institution can be considered nonpartisan, this crucial resource becomes unavailable.

The most important anchors outside the self, however, are not usually institutions but rather other people. When people engage in trusting interactions with others who have different perspectives, interests, and opinions, they typically soon realize that people of intelligence and goodwill can hold different conceptions of both the facts and justice. Thus, one key anchor to perceptions outside one's own brain is simple contact with the opposing parties in any context that facilitates accurate communication. By contrast, discussion with only members of one's own party tends to (1) increase subjective certainty at the same time that it (2) decreases objective accuracy and (3) moves the group assessments toward opposite extremes.[28] For this reason, informal ongoing interactions across party lines in legislatures should play a major role in decreasing self-serving bias.

Other Forms of Cognitive and Emotional Myopia

We have focused here on only two of the most salient cognitive biases that reduce negotiators' capacities to reach agreement when it is possible. Researchers have demonstrated a host of other biases.

Loss aversion. This bias leads us to value outcomes that are framed in terms of loss more than we value exactly the same outcomes framed in terms of gain. Thus, we value what we have (even if we were randomly given it only a minute ago) more than we value what we can get; therefore, we find it difficult to envision future gains.[29]

---

27. See Karl, Susskind, and Wallace (2007) and citations therein.

28. Mnookin and Ross (1995, p. 18); Sunstein (2006).

29. Kahneman, Knetsch, and Thaler (1991).

Availability bias. This bias leads us to extrapolate forecasts and judgments from easily accessible cases—our own histories or sensational stories in the media—rather than from a systematic study of similar events. It also makes it easy to ignore second- and third-order effects; therefore, we find it difficult to move beyond the evidence of our own stories.[30]

Reactive devaluation. This bias leads us to devalue an offer only because it was made by an opponent; therefore, we reject such offers without exploring their potential.[31]

Regret aversion. This bias leads us to distort our decisions to avoid facing evidence later that might cause regret.[32] This aversion is multiplied many times both as a bias and as recognition of reality when a challenging candidate might capitalize on a mistake at the next election.

Emotions, although less well studied, also interfere with our capacity to reach agreement. When negotiators are in a positive mood, they are more likely to discover the possibilities that lead to joint gains in a negotiation. Anger, in tandem with lack of compassion, demonstrably reduces the capacity to achieve joint gains.[33] Malhotra and Bazerman (2007) concluded, as most of us can attest from personal experience: "Anger prevents people from staying focused on the substantive issues about which they care deeply."[34]

Like fixed-pie and self-serving bias, most of these cognitive and emotional barriers to agreement can be reduced, sometimes dramatically, by repeated positive interactions with parties on the opposing side whose perspectives and personal and constituent stories differ from one's own.

30. Tversky and Kahneman (1973).

31. Ross (1995).

32. Malhotra and Bazerman (2007, pp. 136–38).

33. For the classic experiment, see Allred et al. (1997); they cite Carnevale and Isen (1986) and Kramer, Newton, and Pommerenke (1993) on mood.

34. Malhotra and Bazerman (2007, p. 272).

Strategic Overreaching

Strategic overreaching, common when parties are in difficult competition, compounds the constraints on negotiation that derive from the
fixed-pie and other cognitive biases. Individuals in negotiation rightly
recognize that the tactics of intransigence and deception can sometimes improve their bargaining positions. Yet these tactics often keep
participants from making deals that are to the benefit of all.

Intransigence. This is an obvious winning "hardball" strategy when
one party rightly sees deadlock as a good alternative to a negotiated
agreement. However, even when deadlock is costly in the present, skilled
strategists may choose intransigence as a strategy, accepting immediate losses for future gains. Those who strategically use intransigence
by refusing to compromise are usually trying to weaken their counterpart's position and set themselves up for larger gains in the future.[35]

Deception. This tactic, including the misrepresentation of one's
goals or reservation price through silence and innuendo, is a relatively
common and often successful hardball move in commercial negotiation. In legislatures, where ongoing interactions and reputations are
at stake, outright deception is relatively rare. However, negotiators
may guard closely the information they have regarding intensity of
preferences—suggesting, for example, that party members or constituents for whom they are negotiating have stronger preferences than
in fact they have. Parties and factions within parties in Congress may
also have an incentive to appoint a negotiator with intense and possibly extreme views, falsely signaling greater intransigence than the
party median, to improve their bargaining positions.[36]

In the long run, these tactics can harm both parties. First, aggressive negotiators have been shown to see fewer value-creating opportunities that come from creative ways of bringing new issues into the
negotiation.[37] Second, hardball tactics inspire reciprocal hardball

35. Ross and Stillinger (1991, pp. 390–91).

36. King and Zeckhauser (2002). For hardball tactics more generally, see
Mnookin and Ross (1995) and Mnookin, Peppet, and Tulumello (2000,
pp. 24–25).

37. Lax and Sebenius (1986) give the name "negotiator's dilemma" to the tension between the open, inquiring, creative, and disclosing stance required to

responses that increase transaction costs. In politics, the pattern is familiar and in the United States has become more intense since the 1990s. When one party breaks established norms of reciprocity, the other party retaliates, and the norms disintegrate.[38] Third, in politics as in commerce, irreversible investments in hardball reputations may escalate conflict even after all of the parties consciously realize that a resolution based on compromise would leave them better off.[39]

If Negotiation Myopia Is the Problem, Deliberative Negotiation Is the Solution

Chapter 5, which discusses deliberative negotiation, argues for the democratic value of deliberation based on mutual respect and mutual justification and the search for fair processes and outcomes. Here we suggest that such deliberation also has clear practical advantages for uncovering and creating joint gains.

In U.S. national politics in an earlier era—that is, Congress from at least 1940 to 1970—long stays in Washington, cross-cutting cleavages within the parties, a multiplicity of venues for informal interaction, closed committee hearings, and many informal norms of civil interaction made what we call deliberative negotiation a daily possibility. As chapter 2 demonstrates, however, the polarization of the parties and the closeness of their electoral competition for control of the House and Senate have destroyed many of these cross-cutting cleavages while increasing the strategic incentives for obstruction. Today, the party system is less likely to produce legislators like Jack Heinz and Tim Wirth, discussed in chapter 5, who engaged in highly constructive negotiation to help craft the Clean Air Act. Instead, congressional leaders at the head of polarized and highly competitive parties currently play the main roles in negotiation, with the assistance at cru-

---

"create value" by bringing in new issues in the "integrative" moments of a negotiation and the closed, competitive stance required to "claim value" in the "distributive" moments.

38. Moe (1987).

39. Bazerman et al. (2000); Fukuno and Ohbuchi (1997); Thompson and De-Harpport (1994); Thompson and Hastie (1990); Bizman and Hoffman (1993); Diekmann, Tenbrunsel, and Bazerman (1999); Keltner and Robinson (1993).

cial moments, particularly in the Senate, of ad hoc "gangs"—that is, small bipartisan groups of legislators outside of the formal committee system (see chapters 2 and 3).

The journalist Ronald Brownstein (2013) recently commented that these gangs "represent an evolutionary adaptation to Congress's increasing rigidity." The congressional committees, he wrote, "were never entirely immune from the partisan gales that buffeted Congress, but historically many were somewhat sheltered from the storms. Through long hours mastering complex issues, panel members built personal relationships across party lines that didn't always produce agreement but did allow for candid and substantive negotiation." Now that the committees have been open to the public for decades and are "as balkanized and as ideologically divided as the parties in general,"[40] some of the responsibility for what we call deliberative negotiation has passed to the small ad hoc gangs whose members often have ongoing personal relationships and therefore can discuss issues in a way that is respectful, based on mutual justification, and open to both new ideas and fair compromise. This is what we call deliberative negotiation.

Deliberative negotiation is our solution to negotiation myopia. Respect, mutuality, openness, and a commitment to fairness on both sides open up participants to exploring new ideas that can create joint gains and "expand the pie." These conditions also undermine self-serving bias because parties with repeated, strong, and informal as well as formal relationships soon discover that their selection and interpretations of the facts or the justice of a situation are not always the same as those of their counterparts. Although we have no laboratory research on this subject, it is highly likely that discussions with respected others also help overcome the framing effects of loss aversion and availability bias. When participants think of the members of other parties less as opponents and more as partners in a problem-solving venture, they also will be less subject to reactive devaluation. When they are aware of the political needs of members of the other parties, they can help craft wins for the others to use when they and

40. Brownstein (2013), quoting Michael Franc, vice president for government studies at the conservative Heritage Foundation, on the balkanization in congressional committees.

their parties face reelection. Embedded in ongoing relationships and at respectful ease with one another, they will be less likely to feel anger at the others' suggestions or positions and more likely to ask questions and explain their own positions. In settings of deliberative negotiation, in short, they can more easily put campaigning behind them and get on with the business of governing.[41]

As chapter 2 demonstrates, the United States is in a structural position today that, more than any time in the past century, promotes stalemate. Thus, Congress accomplishes less; as crises build, the legislative branch is not able to solve them. By default, the power to do so will migrate to the presidency and the courts. We know this to be true. This analysis of negotiation myopia shows, in addition, that the conditions for stalemate in Congress not only produce inaction; they also stifle the creativity, innovation, and capacity to forge solutions that take into account more features of reality. The loss is in our capacity to act and, even more problematically, in our capacity for collective intelligence. Human beings already suffer from a natural myopia as they enter negotiations. Our democratic institutions should help us collectively to see better, not further fog our vision.

Note: We thank George Loewenstein of the cognitive working group of the APSA Task Force on Negotiating Agreements in Politics for the central concept in this report. We also thank Linda Babcock, Max Bazerman, Emile Bruneau, Robert Frank, Robert Mnookin, David Rand, Laurie Santos, Rebecca Saxe, and Cass Sunstein for their insightful comments at the working group meeting.

References

Allred, Keith G., John S. Mallozzi, Fusako Matsui, and Christopher P. Raia. 1997. "The Influence of Anger and Compassion on Negotiation Performance." *Organizational Behavior and Human Decision Processes* 70 (3): 175–87.

Babcock, Linda, and George Loewenstein. 1997. "Explaining Bargaining Impasse: The Role of Self-Serving Biases." *Journal of Economic Perspectives* 11 (1): 109–26.

41. Gutmann and Thompson (2012).

Bazerman, Max H., Jonathan Baron, and Katherine Shonk. 2001. *You Can't Enlarge the Pie: Six Barriers to Effective Government.* New York: Basic Books.

Bazerman, Max H., Jared R. Curhan, and Don A. Moore. 2002. "The Death and Rebirth of the Social Psychology of Negotiations." In *Blackwell Handbook of Social Psychology: Interpersonal Processes,* ed. G. Fletcher and M. Clark. Malden, MA: Blackwell Publishers.

Bazerman, Max H., Jared R. Curhan, Don A. Moore, and Kathleen L. Valley. 2000. "Negotiation." *Annual Review of Psychology* 51 (1): 279–314.

Bazerman, Max H., and Margaret A. Neale. 1995. *Cognition and Rationality in Negotiation.* New York: Free Press.

Bizman, Aharon, and Michael Hoffman. 1993. "Expectations, Emotions, and Preferred Responses Regarding the Arab-Israeli Conflict: An Attributional Analysis." *Journal of Conflict Resolution* 37 (1): 139–59.

Blount, Sally. 1995. "When Social Outcomes Aren't Fair: The Effect of Causal Attributions on Preferences." *Organizational Behavior and Human Decision Processes* 63:131–44.

Brownstein, Ronald. 2013. "Can Bipartisan Cooperation Save Us from Stalemate?" *National Journal,* May 9.

Carnevale, Peter J. D., and Alice M. Isen. 1986. "The Influence of Positive Affect and Visual Access on the Discovery of Integrative Solutions in Bilateral Negotiation." *Organizational Behavior and Human Decision Processes* 37 (1): 1–13.

Diekmann, Kristin, Ann E. Tenbrunsel, and Max H. Bazerman. 1999. "Escalation and Negotiation: Two Central Themes in the Work of Jeffrey Z. Rubin." In *Negotiation Ethics: Essays in Memory of Jeffrey Z. Rubin,* ed. David A. Kolb. Cambridge, MA: PON Books.

Fry, William R., Ira J. Firestone, and David L. Williams. 1983. "Negotiation Process and Outcome of Stranger Dyads and Dating Couples: Do Lovers Lose?" *Basic and Applied Social Psychology* 4:1–16.

Fukuno, Mitsuteru, and Ken-Ichi Ohbuchi. 1997. "Cognitive Biases in Negotiation: The Determinants of Fixed-Pie Assumption and Fairness Bias." *Japanese Journal of Social Psychology* 13 (1): 43–52.

Galinsky, Adam D., William W. Maddux, Debra Gilin, and Judith B. White. 2008. "Why It Pays to Get inside the Head of Your

Opponent: The Differential Effects of Perspective Taking and Empathy in Negotiations." *Psychological Science* 19 (4): 378–84.

Greenberg, Jeff, Tom Pyszczynski, John Burling, and Karyn Tibbs. 1992. "Depression, Self-Focused Attention, and the Self-Serving Attributional Bias." *Personality and Individual Differences* 13 (9): 959–65.

Gutmann, Amy, and Dennis Thompson. 2012. *The Spirit of Compromise: Why Governing Demands It and Campaigning Undermines It.* Princeton University Press.

Kagel, John, Chung Kim, and Donald Moser. 1996. "Fairness in Ultimatum Games with Asymmetric Information and Asymmetric Payoffs." *Games and Economic Behavior* 13 (1): 100–10.

Kahneman, Daniel, Jack L. Knetsch, and Richard H. Thaler. 1991. "Anomalies: The Endowment Effect, Loss Aversion, and Status Quo Bias." *Journal of Economic Perspectives* 5 (1): 193–206.

Kahneman, Daniel, and Amos Tversky. 1995. "Conflict Resolution: A Cognitive Perspective." In *Barriers to Conflict Resolution*, ed. Kenneth Arrow, Robert H. Mnookin, Lee Ross, Amos Tversky, and Robert Wilson. New York: W. W. Norton.

Karl, Herman A., Lawrence E. Susskind, and Katherine H. Wallace. 2007. "A Dialogue, Not a Diatribe." *Environment* 49 (1): 2–34.

Keltner, Dacher, and Robert J. Robinson. 1993. "Imagined Ideological Differences in Conflict Escalation and Resolution." *International Journal of Conflict Management* 4 (3): 249–62.

Kennedy, Kathleen A., and Emily Pronin. 2008. "When Disagreement Gets Ugly: Perceptions of Bias and the Escalation of Conflict." *Personality and Social Psychology Bulletin* 34 (6): 833–48.

King, David C., and Richard J. Zeckhauser. 2002. "Punching and Counter-Punching in the U.S. Congress." Paper delivered at "Leadership 2002: Bridging the Gap between Theory and Practice," Cambridge, MA, March 14–15.

Kramer, Roderick M., Elizabeth Newton, and Pamela L. Pommerenke. 1993. "Self-Enhancement Biases and Negotiator Judgment: Effects of Self-Esteem and Mood." *Organizational Behavior and Human Decision Processes* 56 (1): 110–33.

Lax, David A., and James K. Sebenius. 1986. *The Manager as Negotiator: Bargaining for Cooperative and Competitive Gain.* New York: Free Press.

———. 2006. *3–D Negotiation: Powerful Tools to Change the Game in Your Most Important Deals.* Harvard Business School Press.

Loewenstein, George, Leigh Thompson, and Max Bazerman. 1989. "Social Utility and Decision Making in Interpersonal Context," *Journal of Personality and Social Psychology* 57:426–41.

Malhotra, Deepak, and Max H. Bazerman. 2007. *Negotiation Genius.* New York: Random House/Bantam Dell.

Mnookin, Robert H., Scott R. Peppet, and Andrew S. Tulumello. 2000. *Beyond Winning: Negotiating to Create Value in Deals and Disputes.* Harvard University Press.

Mnookin, Robert H., and Lee Ross. 1995. "Introduction." In *Barriers to Conflict Resolution,* ed. Kenneth Arrow, Robert H. Mnookin, Lee Ross, Amos Tversky, and Robert Wilson. New York: W. W. Norton.

Moe, Terry M. 1987. "Interests, Institutions, and Positive Theory: The Politics of the NLRB." *Studies in American Political Development* 2:236–99.

Neale, Margaret A., and Max H. Bazerman. 1991. *Cognition and Rationality.* New York: Free Press.

Pronin, Emily, Daniel Y. Lin, and Lee Ross. 2002. "The Bias Blind Spot: Perceptions of Bias in Self versus Others." *Personality and Social Psychology Bulletin* 28:369–81.

Pruitt, Dean G. 1983. "Achieving Integrative Agreements." In *Negotiating in Organizations,* ed. Max H. Bazerman and Roy J. LeWicki. Beverly Hills, CA: Sage.

Pruitt, Dean G., and Steven A. Lewis. 1975. "Development of Integrative Solutions in Bilateral Negotiations." *Journal of Personality and Social Psychology* 31:621–33.

Rabin, Matthew. 1993. "Incorporating Fairness into Game Theory and Economics." *American Economic Review* 83:1281–1302.

Ross, Lee. 1995. "Reactive Devaluation in Negotiation and Conflict Resolution." In *Barriers to Conflict Resolution,* ed. Kenneth J. Arrow, Robert H. Mnookin, Lee Ross, Amos Tversky, and Robert Wilson. New York: W. W. Norton.

Ross, Lee, and Constance Stillinger. 1991. "Barriers to Conflict Resolution." *Negotiation Journal* 7 (4): 389–404.

Schoeninger, Douglas W., and William D. Wood. 1969. "Comparison of Married and Ad Hoc Mixed-Sex Dyads Negotiating the

Division of a Reward." *Journal of Experimental Social Psychology* 5 (4): 483–99.

Seligman, Martin E. P. 1991. *Learned Optimism*. New York: A. A. Knopf.

Shergill, Sukhwinder S., Paul M. Bays, Chris D. Frith, and Daniel M. Wolpert. 2003. "Two Eyes for an Eye: The Neuroscience of Force Escalation." *Science* 301 (11): 187.

Sunstein, Cass R. 2006. *Infotopia*. Oxford University Press.

Taylor, Shelley E., and Jonathon D. Brown. 1988. "Illusion and Well-Being: A Social Psychological Perspective on Mental Health." *Psychological Bulletin* 103 (2): 193–210.

Thompson, Leigh L. 2005. *The Mind and Heart of the Negotiator*. 3rd ed. Upper Saddle River, NJ: Pearson/Prentice Hall.

Thompson, Leigh, and Terri DeHarpport. 1990. "Relationships, Goal Incompatibility, and Communal Orientation in Negotiations." *Basic and Applied Social Psychology* 20 (1): 33–44.

———. 1994. "Social Judgment, Feedback, and Interpersonal Learning in Negotiation." *Organizational Behavior and Human Decision Processes* 58 (3): 327–45.

Thompson, Leigh, and Reid Hastie. 1990. "Social Perception in Negotiation." *Organizational Behavior and Human Decision Processes* 47 (1): 98–123.

Thompson, Leigh, and Dennis Hrebec. 1996. "Lose-Lose Agreements in Interdependent Decision Making." *Psychological Bulletin* 120 (3): 396–409.

Thompson, Leigh, Erika Peterson, and Susan E. Brodt. 1996. "Team Negotiation: An Examination of Integrative and Distributive Bargaining." *Journal of Personality and Social Psychology* 70:66–78.

Tversky, Amos, and Daniel Kahneman. 1973. "Availability: A Heuristic for Judging Frequency and Probability." *Cognitive Psychology* 5 (1): 207–33.

Valley, Kathleen L., Margaret A. Neale, and Elizabeth A. Mannix. 1995. "Friends, Lovers, Colleagues, Strangers: The Effects of Relationships on the Process and Outcome of Dyadic Negotiations." *Research on Negotiation in Organizations* 5:65–94.

Weingart, Laurie R., Leigh L. Thompson, Max H. Bazerman, and John S. Carroll. 1990. "Tactical Behavior and Negotiation Outcomes." *International Journal of Conflict Management* 1:7–31.

Deliberative
Negotiation

MARK E. WARREN AND
JANE MANSBRIDGE

*with André Bächtiger, Maxwell A. Cameron,
Simone Chambers, John Ferejohn,
Alan Jacobs, Jack Knight, Daniel Naurin,
Melissa Schwartzberg, Yael Tamir,
Dennis Thompson, and Melissa Williams*

In this normative analysis of negotiation, we have several objectives. First, we establish that the capacity to act is an integral part of the meaning of democracy. When legislatures deadlock because of their inability to negotiate, their inaction undermines key democratic values. Second, we make the simple point that a negotiation process is unlikely to be fully just unless it incorporates two elements often viewed as normatively essential to democracy: (1) inclusion on fair terms of the affected parties, and (2) the equal power of the negotiators. Negotiations rarely meet these criteria, of course, but the criteria provide standards at which to aim. We note further that although these two criteria are both intuitive and widely held, they also remain contested. Third, we distinguish the possible components that may appear in the legislative negotiating process. Between the two extremes of pure deliberation and pure bargaining, we specify three forms of what we call *deliberative negotiation* and detail the characteristics of each. We then explain why we believe the phenomenon of deliberative negotiation has been neglected, both empirically and normatively, and why it should receive more attention in politics. Finally, we undertake a normative investigation of three practices—long incumbencies, closed-door meetings, and side payments—that make political negotiation more effective, thereby enabling democracies to act. We specify the criteria we can use to judge when these practices are justifiable from a democratic perspective.

The normative theory of democratic negotiation and compromise is in its infancy. The theory of deliberative democracy has been evolving over the past thirty years, but it is not necessary to accept deliberative democratic theory to appreciate the value of deliberative negotiation. The case we advance here for the capacity for collective action as essential to democracy, for the deliberative negotiations that enable legitimate collective action, and for the institutional conditions that support deliberative negotiation is part of a first stage in a process of theory building.

Action

The collective capacity to act is a crucial component of democracy. That capacity is surprisingly undervalued in both popular and academic democratic theory. When problems in the polity demand action and the legislature fails to act, the demand for action is displaced onto the executive, the administrative agencies, and the courts. In the United States, the president, the agencies, and the courts are not, of course, undemocratic. They all have democratic justification in the sense that the citizens directly elect the executive, the agencies are duly appointed, and the citizens have constitutionally authorized their elected officials to appoint the members of the judiciary. Yet the legislature—the official law-giving body—has a unique and central role in a democracy. In the United States, Congress alone has the authority to make and fund laws and the programs and policies that follow from them. Because Congress is composed of many representatives, elected from every part of the country, it also can come far closer than the executive to representing and communicating with the people in all of their plurality. When Congress is unable to act in the face of urgent collective problems, power flows to other parts of the political system, often diminishing the system's democratic capacity and legitimacy.

Some failures of a legislature to act are democratically justified by a majority decision, whether explicit or implicit, not to act. Other failures to act are democratically justified by deep divisions among the citizenry on what course of action to take, even when most agree that some action should be taken. The failures to act that most concern us arise when the members of the legislature could craft policies that would improve on the status quo, not infringe minority or individual rights, and be backed by a majority of the public—but the legislators still fail to agree and thus fail to act. These kinds of failures are not normatively neutral: they favor the status quo and disempower collective responses to both long-standing and emerging problems. Privileging the status quo is not the sole province of one side or another on the political spectrum; even partisans who want small government have to pass legislation to accomplish that goal (Gutmann and Thompson (2012, p. 32). When a majority of the citizenry favors an action that would not curtail individual rights, legislative paralysis begins to rob the legislature—and even the polity as a whole—of its legitimacy.

The capacity to act is built into the very meaning of democracy, or rule (*kratos*) by the people (*demos*). Whereas much normative political theory to date has explored what it might mean to say that the *people* rule, we focus on what it might mean to say that they *rule*— that is, have the capacity to act and implement decisions (see Ober 2008, p. 7).

Sometimes both ordinary citizens and democratic theorists take for granted the action component of democracy and therefore neglect it because action per se is not distinctively democratic. Both ordinary citizens and democratic theorists also may forget to value action because we are habituated to focusing on the resistance to tyranny. Key features of our political system (for example, the separation of powers) were designed to avoid the dangers of tyranny.

Many democratic practices, based on sound democratic ideals, can impede democratic action. The establishment of minority rights, with strong and independent court systems to protect those rights, can impede democratic action. The checks and balances among separate branches of government, instituted to protect against the abuse of power, can impede democratic action. Rules intended to promote deliberation, such as unlimited debate, can impede democratic action. The practice of resistance in civil society, which both blocks tyranny and is one of the few sources of pressure for the inclusion of excluded or marginalized groups in the polity, also can impede democratic action. We value these practices and ideals for their inclusionary functions. Our goal, however, is to point out that inclusions are not sufficient to democracy: if collectivities lack the capacity to act, inclusions remain powerless. We stress that the capacity for action is *part* of democracy, insofar as a political system should empower collectivities to respond to their collective problems and aspirations. We therefore underscore the damage that political gridlock can do to a democracy's capacities to get things done—that is, the damage to democracy as collective self-rule. We want to redress the balance between resistance and collective action by drawing attention to the ways that institutions intended to empower resistance can undermine democratic capacities to solve collective problems.

In contemplating the trade-offs between resistance to tyranny and the capacity to act, we emphasize that the failure to come to agreement often harms inclusion, collective-will formation, efficiency, collective trust, and legitimacy.

First, a gridlocked system tends to defeat emerging claims. Failed negotiations freeze existing patterns of inclusion and exclusion into place, while failing to respond to problems and opportunities driven by social and economic change. Social change may occur, but the forces of change must do their work outside the political system.[1]

Second, although the media, interest groups, and social movements help shape the perspectives and interests of the members of the polity through advocacy and discussion, and political parties, political campaigns, and candidates help shape these perspectives, interests, needs, and desires into agendas that are actionable, legislatures then do the detailed work of crafting policies that can attract a majority of the representatives' votes. If a democracy is working well, its institutions transform conflicts into potential agreements that at least a majority of participants could find substantively acceptable and most others could find procedurally acceptable and thus legitimate. Legislative gridlock amounts to a failure to convert the wills of those who should be included in any decision into something that constitutionally could be considered a collective will and decision.

1. Gutmann and Thompson (2012, pp. 30–32).

Failed agreements also entail efficiency costs, borne by members of the collectivity. Some forms of what we call deliberative negotiation can help participants discover efficient outcomes that capture more common interests, overlapping interests, and positive-sum solutions to problems than had previously appeared possible. Such agreements then can save the polity significant costs. Classic compromises, another feature of deliberative negotiation, also save on the ongoing costs of conflict, with overt war the limiting case.

Failed agreements often have costs in the reduction of mutual trust, which affects the possibilities for future agreements. Every failure to agree when agreement is possible tends to induce participants to withhold respect from their opponents and to demonize them. The failure to agree can breed a culture and mind-set of animosity, which in turn makes future agreements less likely (Gutmann and Thompson 2012, chap. 2). In contrast, successful agreements often produce positive ethical externalities: they generate the trust among opponents necessary for the next agreement.

These failures together take their toll on legitimacy. We distinguish between *normative legitimacy* and *perceived legitimacy*. Normative legitimacy exists when a process can be justified with well-founded reasons. Perceived legitimacy exists when a process is actually accepted by most of the people in the relevant collectivity.

Deadlock undermines normative legitimacy when the practice emanating from institutions established to promote democratic ideals is no longer justifiable in terms of either those ideals themselves or a reasonable balance with other ideals, such as democratic action. We previously noted that legislative deadlock encourages migration of power away from the legislature. If the legislature is the most "democratic" of the branches—in view of its capacities to represent the pluralism of a collectivity and to enable two-way communication between constituents and representatives—then deadlock produces a less democratic process. Deadlock also produces undemocratic results. As political scientists have pointed out since the 1960s, a "nondecision" is as much a decision as any overt decisive act.[2] If a significant majority favors action and the opposition to that action is not based on individual or minority rights, then inaction is undemocratic. Inaction

2. Bachrach and Baratz (1962, 1963).

is particularly worrying when for external reasons a situation is already developing in one direction and inaction allows that "drift" to continue, or when strong majority preferences change in response to new circumstances but the existing political bodies do not change the relevant policies.[3] In the United States today, long-standing structural budget deficits, increasing inequality, and uneven investment in physical and human capital exemplify several kinds of drift. Internationally, the increasing extremes in climate exemplify drift. If the decisions to act in each case were deliberatively thought through and potential negotiated outcomes were contemplated and rejected, the resulting inaction would be democratically legitimate. However, when a polity's institutions consistently block decisions that otherwise would have been made democratically and action taken, the result is democratically illegitimate.

Deadlock also undermines perceived legitimacy. A political system that cannot perform in the judgment of its people risks losing its legitimacy, which in turn can risk its stability. In the United States, trust in Congress is at an all-time low, in part because of the recent stalemate.[4] Although the system as a whole does not seem to be losing its legitimacy in the eyes of its people, its democratic core—Congress—is in such danger. In newer democracies, the incapacity to act democratically often provides a major reason for the return to authoritarian rule.[5] In the United States, the danger to democracy is more subtle but also quite real: in addition to the great losses from simple inaction and its consequences, as the core of the political system loses its legitimacy, those powers of collective action that remain migrate into

3. Gutmann and Thompson (2012, pp. 30–34). On "drift," see Burns (1963); Hacker and Pierson (2010); Mansbridge (2011). On "utility drift," see Rae (1975, p. 1289); Shapiro (2003); Schwartzberg (2013).

4. For Gallup data on 9 percent approval of Congress in November 2013, see Newport (2013). By contrast, governors are much more popular, perhaps because they are more able to act (M. Cohen 2013).

5. Before World War II, critics attacked not only the Weimar Republic in particular but also democracy in general for the inability to act. Mussolini ([1932] 1935, p. 7) began his encyclopedia article on fascism by writing, "Like all sound political conceptions, Fascism is action" as well as thought. In contrast to democracy, "Fascism was . . . born of the need of action, and was action" (p. 12).

less fully democratic parts of the system: executive agencies, the Federal Reserve, and the judicial system.

Democracy, in short, includes both "the people" and their "rule." In a healthy democracy, people are able to provide collective goods for themselves and to respond collectively to emerging challenges, problems, and opportunities. A gridlocked legislative system damages democracy by undermining these capacities.

The Ideals of a Just Negotiation[6]

In this chapter, we argue for negotiation as an important democratic tool through which citizens and their representatives make collective decisions that affect their lives. Before we discuss the normative qualities of what we call "deliberative negotiation," we address the question of how negotiation processes might be assessed from the standpoint of justice—a question that is related but not identical to the question of democratic criteria. Although we do not offer an extended discussion of justice, we suggest that negotiation processes can be judged as more or less just in relation to two simple ideals: the ideal of including all affected parties and the ideal of equal power in the negotiation. Both ideals are related to the justice of the *process*, not the *outcomes*. And both ideals are closely related to and support democratic ideals of inclusion.[7] They are also "regulative ideals," meaning ideals that provide standards at which to aim, not ideals that if not met disallow the process.[8] We recognize that these ideas about justice are contested. We discuss them here not to settle any of the contested questions but rather to put the issues on the table for further deliberation.[9] Our overall criterion for justice in negotiation is that

6. This section must be taken as a placeholder for a more thorough discussion that we hope to have in the future and that if we as a collective do not have, we hope that the larger community of normative theorists will.

7. Young (2000).

8. Kant ([1781] 1998, p. 552); see also Rawls (1971) on most societies in practice being at best "nearly just."

9. The question of the ideals of a just negotiation has not yet been much discussed. In the one treatment that we know, Albin reported being "struck by the dearth of any comparable research" (Albin 2001, p. 12). Yet even Albin's

in a meta-deliberation over the conditions of just negotiation, free and equal participants would be likely to adopt these understandings of the application of justice to the conditions of negotiation.

Including Affected Parties

The simplest statement of the inclusion norm of a just negotiation is that all affected parties should be included in a negotiation. Democratic theorists have begun to discuss some of these issues under the rubric of "all affected interests."[10] The question is highly contested and not sufficiently resolved for us to take a stand on it. We believe, however, that whatever complexities it entails, it remains highly intuitive that all parties affected by a negotiation should have a rightful claim to have their interests represented in the negotiation and that to the extent that those interests are not represented, the negotiation is to that degree less just. In practice, it is particularly important to attend to the interests of less powerful and marginalized groups whose interests might easily be ignored.

There are, of course, many practical difficulties in actually bringing to the literal table all those who might in any way be affected. Moreover, this formulation would seem to ignore the special claims to be party to the negotiation of those who are members of the polities who will be legally bound rather than merely affected by the ensuing laws. It also ignores the special claims to be party to the negotiation of those who, as citizens, have contributed individually and whose family members and neighbors have contributed to bringing about the larger polity that undergirds the specific negotiation. For

---

treatment confines the normative philosophical discussion to the introductory chapter and defines the purpose of the book as investigating empirically how parties to negotiations perceive fairness in negotiation, how negotiators take into account such considerations, what effect the values have on the negotiation process, and how those values eventually influence the terms of international agreements. For Albin's purposes, "the formulation of principles for the conduct of negotiations" falls "outside the scope" of that work (ibid., p. 13). Other works that might take up the subject (for example, Menkel-Meadow and Wheeler 2004) address only the question of ethics within the negotiation.

10. See Goodin (2007), Shapiro (2003), and Fung (2013). As Goodin (2007) and others have noted, the principle of affected interests does not provide determinate boundaries.

these reasons, among others, citizens of the United States may have a greater claim to be parties to a negotiation over the U.S. laws on carbon emission than citizens in China, even beyond their claims on the grounds of being more directly affected. However, although these kinds of questions of degrees of concern and contribution remain to be worked out, it is likely that negotiations that exclude the interests of those affected will fall short of justice.

Equal Power

The simplest statement of the equality norm of a just negotiation is that all parties to a negotiation should have equal power. One way of understanding power in the context of negotiation is to consider power of one party to the negotiation, in general, as the preferences of that party causing or changing the probability of the outcomes. Coercive power, which we consider in regard to negotiation, is then the capacity of one party to cause or change the probability of outcomes for another party through the threat of sanction or the use of force. Threats of sanction would include the threat to leave the negotiation.[11] The bargaining component of negotiation includes not only threats of sanction but also promises of reward, which have a more positive normative status than threats of sanction but are also components of equal or unequal power. What might it mean to have equal power in a negotiation? When Habermas first approached the subject, he concluded that for a negotiation to be just in the absolute sense, "bargaining power should at least be disciplined by its equal distribution among the parties."[12] He then modified this point to read that the procedures should "provide all interested parties with an equal opportunity for pressure, that is, an equal opportunity to influence one another during the actual bargaining, so that all the affected interests can come into play and have equal chances of prevailing."[13] The problem is that equal bargaining resources, the equal exercise of power,

---

11. For more on a version of this definition, see Mansbridge et al. (2010, pp. 80ff.), drawing on Nagel (1975).

12. Habermas ([1992] 1996, pp. 165–66, see also pp. 108–9).

13. Ibid. (pp. 166–67).

the equal opportunity to exercise power, and the equal chance of prevailing are all different concepts and produce different outcomes.

Power also can be defined individually or as a matter of numbers of allies. An actor may individually have equal power with all other individuals (for example, an equal vote), but if the rule is majority rule (unlikely in a negotiation) and the actor is in a minority—particularly a permanent minority—the "equal opportunity for pressure" will not translate into an equal or even a proportionate chance of "prevailing." Neither will it even translate into outcomes in which all interests have equal consideration. An actor may have an equal veto with others in the group, as is characteristic of a negotiation that requires the agreement of all parties, but pay heavier costs if the agreement is not concluded. As Beitz (1989) pointed out, the procedures for producing political equality are multiple and indeterminate. Thus, what constitutes equal power, equal opportunity to exercise power, or the equal chance of prevailing will often be intrinsically contestable.

In addition to these problems with what "equal power" might mean in a negotiation, equal power is also not the only ideal-regarding criterion appropriate to negotiation. For the pure deliberative moments, the ideal of "no power" may be more appropriate.[14] For some purposes, Aristotelian proportionality is most appropriate, that is, that parties should be treated in the same way only if they are, in fact, equal in the respects relevant to the negotiation. There may be arguments for giving greater weight to those more greatly affected or to those who have contributed more to the goods in question. Issues such as compensatory justice and need may well be relevant.[15]

Nonetheless, like the affected-interests principle, the equal-power principle captures the robust intuition that those who have rightful *claims* to inclusion should also have the *means* for inclusion. Despite the many difficulties of interpretation, we retain this simple criterion when assessing the justice of negotiation processes.

From the perspective of democratic theory, the question of justice in the process of negotiation is ultimately part of the question of the justice in democratic representation—or, more generally, what should

14. See Mansbridge et al. (2010).

15. Albin (2001).

count as a just democratic process.[16] The question of justice in the results or outcomes of negotiation (either in legislation or a treaty) is ultimately a matter for the general theory of justice. Here, we intend to call attention only to the various and contestable ways that such questions can be addressed; we do not attempt to resolve the controversies about the meaning of inclusiveness and equality. Fortunately, it is not necessary to do so to make progress on the project of evaluating various types of negotiation. Our aim here is to find normatively acceptable forms of negotiation within a larger democratic process that is assumed to be reasonably just. To the extent that the larger process is unjust, the results of negotiations that it produces will usually be less just as well. And the results can be unjust even if the process is just. Within a relatively just democracy, individual negotiations may be considered less just to the extent that they are less inclusive and less equal if the departures from those ideals have not been deliberated and otherwise legitimized in that democracy. With this as background, we believe that to find effective forms of negotiation that are normatively acceptable in an ongoing democracy, it is more productive to operate at a less general level, employing criteria that refer specifically to the process of negotiation itself, such as those that balance confidentiality and transparency.

Deliberative Negotiation

Congress seems to be losing its capacity for what we call "deliberative negotiation." By *negotiation* in the political realm, we mean a practice in which individuals, usually acting in institutions on behalf of others, make and respond to claims, arguments, and proposals with the aim of reaching mutually acceptable binding agreements.[17] By *deliberative negotiation*, we mean negotiation based on processes of mutual justification, respect, and reciprocal fairness. Such negotiation includes elements of arguments on the merits made by advancing considerations that the other parties might accept; searching for zones of agreement and disagreement; and arguing about the terms of fair processes as well as outcomes, with a background of sufficient mutual

16. Young (2000, chap. 1).

17. Cf. Odell (2012, p. 27); and Odell and Tingley, chapter 7 in this book.

respect for those arguments to have motivating force. Deliberative negotiation takes place in a context of relative openness and disclosure about interests, needs, and constraints.[18]

Much of what became known as "deliberative political theory" in the second half of the twentieth century began by distinguishing between "deliberation," meaning a process of mutual justification, and "bargaining," meaning a process in which individuals or groups say they will do or give something in exchange for something else, with each trying to give the least and get the most in the bargain.[19] Elster (1986) summed up this distinction when he distinguished between political "bargaining" and political "arguing" (or deliberation). He placed bargaining and the vote in the same nondeliberative (or antideliberative) category, identifying bargaining as "instrumental," "private," based in "the individual and secret vote," and resulting in a "compromise between given, and irreducibly opposed, private interests." On the other side of his dichotomy, he identified "arguing" with "rational agreement rather than compromise" and with "public debate with a view to the emergence of a consensus."[20]

Since that time, many deliberative democratic theorists have argued that deliberation and voting are complementary rather than contradictory activities. They also have argued that the goal of deliberation is not only to reach unanimity but also to clarify and structure conflict.[21] We expand these points to cover negotiation, pointing out that in negotiation, arguing and bargaining not only frequently go together empirically but also are normatively compatible. In deliberative negotiation, the parties recognize conflicting interests but pursue mutual

18. On deliberative negotiations, see also Mansbridge (2009) and Mansbridge et al. (2010).

19. The definition of *bargaining* is drawn in part from the Merriam-Webster definition (see www.merriam-webster.com/dictionary/bargain). Three separate strands of early deliberative theory stressed this distinction: the Habermasian (Habermas [1981] 1984, 1987), the civic republican (for example, Sunstein 1988), and the Rawlsian (Cohen 1989).

20. Elster (1986, p. 103).

21. On the congruence between voting and deliberation, see, for example, Thompson (2002), Mansbridge et al. (2010). On clarifying and structuring conflict, see, for example, Goodin (2008), Mansbridge (2009), Knight and Johnson (2011), and List et al. (2013).

justification and respect and the search for fair terms of interaction and outcomes. They are relatively open and disclosing with one another. Instead of rational agreement on the substance of an issue, they may produce either a negotiated "integrative" agreement, a compromise, or a mixture of the two, as described below. We suggest that in the political world the prevalence of the deliberative forms of negotiation has been insufficiently noticed.

Table 5-1 arrays five types of agreement seeking procedures on a spectrum from pure deliberation to pure bargaining, with three types of deliberative negotiation in between.

Most actual political negotiations include interactions of several of these five types; a few include all of the types. Both this table and the analysis in this chapter apply to only agreement-seeking procedures when a problem is "tractable." A problem may be tractable in two ways: either a "zone of possible agreement" among the parties already exists (that is, there are various positions along a spectrum of possibilities on which the parties could agree that are better for all of them than the status quo), or other issues can be brought into the negotiation to create a package so that all could benefit compared with the status quo.[22] This table, therefore, does not cover all instances of negotiation. An exhaustive table covering all negotiations would include those in which there is no zone of possible agreement but in which the parties enter into negotiations because they have not discovered this fact or because they want to use the vehicle of negotiation itself (for example, in buying time or demonstrating commitment to their constituents) to improve the facts on the ground from their perspective.

For purposes of this analysis, we use *negotiation* as an umbrella term to include all the processes in this table, ranging from pure deliberation through the three forms of deliberative negotiation to pure bargaining. Deliberative elements in negotiations in practice may intertwine with the threats and promises characteristic of pure bargaining. Simply for ease of presentation and not for important analytic

22. See chapter 3 for these two possibilities. We use the status quo as our normative baseline rather than a party's Best Alternative to a Negotiated Agreement (BATNA)—the traditional baseline in negotiation theory—because of the normative problems involved when one party changes the other's best alternative to a position less desirable for the other party than the status quo.

Table 5-1. *Types of Agreement-Seeking Procedures*

		Agreement-seeking procedures			
	Pure deliberation	Deliberative negotiation			Pure bargaining
		Integrative		Distributive	
Background	Common interests, in which all gain, with identical or overlapping benefits, for example, in greater understanding	**Full mutual advantage, in which each party gains but with distinct benefits; no losses**	**Partial mutual advantage, in which each gains but with trades to add value**	No mutual creation of value, with fair offers, based on reasonableness, in which each gains, each loses	No mutual creation of value, with strategic demands, in which each aims at maximum
Outcomes	Informed consensus or clarified and structured conflict	**Fully integrative agreement, in which no party loses**	**Partially integrative agreement, in which parties have traded lower for higher values; at least one bears some loss**	Fair compromise, in which each has sacrificed something of value	**Power-based compromise, in which each loses something of value** *or* **capitulation, in which one side appropriates all the surplus**

purposes, the first row in table 5-1 depicts the background expectations that parties have going into the process and the claims that they make, while the second row depicts the outcomes that derive from the agreement.

The first column in table 5-1 identifies *pure deliberation*—that is, deliberation aimed at both deep agreement and clarifying conflicts.[23] Deliberation can take place without any negotiation, particularly in circumstances of relatively common interests, when participants are trying to ascertain facts about the world or to forge or discover instances of a common good. More importantly for our discussion, however, moments of pure deliberation can occur within the larger interaction that legislators and analysts call a negotiation. In those moments, one or more of the parties—coming into the interaction with a willingness to be persuaded—may change their minds for reasons of principle or by simply seeing that new means better achieve their ultimate ends than the means they had originally promoted.

The next four columns of the table can be divided in two ways, and we use both. First, we adopt the standard distinction in the negotiation literature between *integrative* and *distributive* negotiations. In the integrative moments in negotiation, participants discover or create joint gains beyond those demarcated by the original zone of possible agreement. By contrast, in distributive moments, all joint gains have been captured and only zero-sum distributions remain. Thus, in table 5-1, the second and third columns refer to the integrative moments and their corresponding integrative agreements, whereas the fourth and fifth columns refer to the distributive moments and their corresponding distributive agreements. In addition and more importantly, however, we distinguish between the three forms of deliberative negotiation and both pure deliberation and pure bargaining. Deliberative negotiations, whether integrative or distributive, are characterized by mutual justification and respect and the search for fair terms of interaction and outcomes.

In column two of table 5-1, we introduce the concept of *fully integrative* agreements. Most negotiation theorists currently refer only to

23. For definitions of deliberation, see, inter alia, Gutmann and Thompson (2004); Chambers (2003); Goodin (2008); Fishkin (2005); Stokes (1998); Przeworski (1998); Knight and Johnson (1994); Dryzek (2000); and Manin (2005).

"integrative" negotiations and agreements. We deploy a distinction between "fully" and "partially" integrative because fully integrative agreements are rare, in both commercial and legislative negotiations.[24] Follett ([1925] 1942), who developed the concept of "integration" in negotiation and coined that term in 1925, used as an example a small everyday negotiation in which she wanted the window in a Harvard library closed to avoid a draft but another patron wanted it open to get more air in the room. Her solution, opening the window in the next room, gave both parties what they wanted.[25] Textbook examples of fully integrative agreements include a fight over an orange that is resolved by discovering that one party wants only the inside for its juice and the other only the rind for cooking, or a similar fight over a cake resolved by discovering that one wants only the cake part and the other only the frosting. With a fully integrative agreement, the parties have no need to compromise; no party loses. Such an agreement might be said to "dissolve" a conflict or show that a perceived conflict was only apparent. Any integrative agreement, whether full or partial, is possible only when the parties have differing valuations of the different aspects of the good or goods about which they are negotiating. Such differing valuations usually appear in the course of relatively open conversations about underlying needs, interests, and constraints.[26]

A high-stakes actual example of an agreement that comes close to being fully integrative occurred in the 1979 settlement after the Egypt–Israel war, when Israel as the victor demanded land on the border from Egypt to protect its territory. The problem as originally defined involved two points on the same scale, a clear zero-sum conflict in which the more land Israel got, the more Egypt lost. However, Egypt most wanted to maintain its national pride and sovereignty, whereas Israel most wanted security. A demilitarized zone under Egyptian sov-

24. See Walton and McKersie (1965, p. 129) for the distinction between fully integrative (which they called "absolutely integrative") and partially integrative agreements. For the rarity of fully integrative agreements, see Wetlaufer (1996).

25. Follett ([1925] 1942, p. 32).

26. As Follett put it, "The first rule, then, for obtaining integration is to put your cards on the table, face the real issue, uncover the conflict, bring the whole thing into the open . . ." (Ibid., p. 37).

ereignty gave each of the two parties most of what they wanted.[27] It was thus an almost fully integrative agreement.

Column three of table 5-1 identifies what we call *partially integrative* agreement. Such agreements in negotiation are far more common, achievable in many situations that present multiple issues. As in fully integrative agreements, these are possible only when the parties have differing valuations of the different aspects of the negotiation and can discover a way of exploiting those differing valuations for joint gain. Unlike fully integrative agreements, however, the conflict is not dissolved, and significant distributive (that is, zero-sum) issues remain. The parties are able to achieve joint gains not by dissolving the conflict but rather by prioritizing their desires and trading on items that are low priority for one party and high priority for the other. Accomplishing these joint gains often will involve bringing in issues that were not originally on the table.

Chapter 4, "Negotiation Myopia," suggests the example from the commercial world of a seller of a service station and a potential buyer, whose reservation values are too far apart to make a simple deal good for both of them but who can add to the deal a job for the seller because the buyer in any case would need someone to fill that job. These kinds of instances, which we call "partially integrative," are what the vast majority of writers on negotiation mean when they use the terms *integrative, joint gains, creating value,* and *expanding the pie.* They depend on seeing more than one facet to the negotiation or bringing in other issues on which to trade. Political negotiations are more complex than in this two-person commercial deal because the representatives in Congress who are chosen to negotiate with representatives of the other parties (or with representatives in the other house or with the president) over a policy must then come back and negotiate with members of their own party regarding the outcome, creating what we could consider a "two-level game."[28] If the negotiators are successful in getting a majority in Congress, then a third level emerges in what we call a *three-level game,* because at this point the members of Congress must, in a sense, negotiate with their constituents to get

27. Fisher, Ury, and Patton (1991, pp. 41–42).

28. We borrow the term *two-level game* from Putnam's 1988 analysis of negotiation in international relations.

agreement on the negotiated outcome. Their communications with their constituents are often constrained by the positions that they and their parties have taken for other purposes, such as campaigning. In this complex process, the simple points we take from the negotiation literature are that mutual gains may be discovered or created through negotiations; that these gains often build on taking the perspective of the others; and that those perspectives often can be obtained in the course of informal, friendly, repeated, and relatively open relationships.

Walton and McKersie (1965), who first introduced the formal distinction between integrative and distributive negotiation, made it clear that the problem-solving approach of integrative negotiation requires "trust and a supportive climate" so that participants will be more likely to do the following: not anticipate threat and therefore behave defensively, which will then create defensive postures in others; not try to "control information"; hear more accurately what others are saying; and experiment with attitudes and ideas, and test and retest perceptions and opinions.[29] They point out, therefore, that the parties to a negotiation usually find it hard to shift from an integrative stance to what we call "pure bargaining" and then back again. The difficulty arises

> from the contradictory nature of the tactical operations required for integrative bargaining and [pure bargaining]. The two processes differ in important respects: in terms of the amount of information the parties share with each other at every stage in arriving at decisions and in terms of the amount of consideration each gives to the information about the other's problems. In the integrative process Party makes maximum use of voluntary, open, accurate discussion of any area which affects both groups. . . . Just the opposite is involved in [pure bargaining]. Party attempts to gain maximum information from Opponent but makes minimum disclosures himself.[30]

29. Walton and McKersie (1965, pp. 141–143). Walton and McKersie adopted the concept of "integration" from Follett ([1925] 1942).

30. Ibid. (p. 166). In the quotation, where we have inserted "[pure bargaining]," Walton and McKersie wrote "distributive bargaining." Neither they nor subsequent negotiation theorists have distinguished as we do between our third form

Columns four and five in table 5-1 identify forms of "distributive" negotiation, which—in contrast to forms of integrative negotiation—do not provide the possibility of bringing in other issues and "expanding the pie." In these two columns, whatever one party gains, the other loses. It is important to remember, however, that in this table, the term *zero-sum* refers only to the division of the surplus in a situation that is already positive-sum, such that the problem is already "tractable." All of the situations described in table 5-1 are ones in which both parties (and those they represent) will be better off with a negotiated agreement than with the status quo. In the distributive cases, there is a zone of possible agreement, but within that zone, the parties' losses and gains are zero-sum. To take another example from a two-party interaction in the commercial world, if a seller is willing to sell a house for anything more than $500,000 and a buyer is willing to buy that house for anything less than $600,000, the $100,000 difference between the two is the zone of possible agreement. Any deal in this area will benefit both. Within that area, however, any amount that the seller gets, the buyer loses. If this is all that is or can be at stake, the negotiation is purely distributive because it is zero-sum regarding the "surplus" of $100,000. However, the context is positive-sum for both parties because both benefit if the house is sold within that zone.

In the fourth column of table 5-1, within the zone of possible agreement, the parties look for a "fair compromise." They make claims that require their adversaries to give up something of value but offer concessions that involve sacrificing something of value themselves. Their practices and claims are "deliberative" in the sense that parties are relatively open with each other in their interactions, they do not take unfair advantage of their opponents, they signal their understanding of fairness as part of their claims, and they come to a mutual

---

of deliberative negotiation, which we call *fair compromise*, and *pure bargaining* (see below on columns 4 and 5 of table 5-1). In fair compromise, the potential outcomes within the zone of agreement are zero-sum and distributive but the goal is mutual sacrifice and fairness in the compromise, not each trying to achieve the maximum possible gains (Gutmann and Thompson 2012, p. 10). The "mindset and practices" that encourage fair compromise "are often the same as those that offer the best chance of finding common ground and integrative agreements" (p. 16). The mindset and practices are deliberative.

understanding about the fairness of the terms in ways that motivate and legitimize agreement. Gutmann and Thompson recommended in such interactions that parties adopt "mindsets of compromise" that include principled prudence and mutual respect, while avoiding the "principled tenacity" and mutual mistrust that make fairness in negotiations all but impossible.[31] These kinds of negotiations are possible and especially necessary in political institutions, such as a legislature like the U.S. Congress or a negotiating committee in the European Union (EU), in which the parties will have repeated interactions that would be disrupted by a series of outcomes that some of the parties considered unfair.[32] The outcome in this type of negotiation is typically a fair compromise. We define a *compromise* as an agreement in which all sides sacrifice something of value (that is, make concessions) to improve on the status quo from the perspective of each.[33] We define a *fair compromise* as one that both (or all) sides in the negotiation perceive as fair.

The fifth column of table 5-1 represents what we call "pure bargaining." It too typically produces a compromise, although in some cases, when one of the parties or group of parties can take an intransigent stance through greater power or bluffing, one party gets the entire surplus within the zone of agreement and the other capitulates.

31. Gutmann and Thompson (2012, pp. 16–24).

32. Conceptions of fairness are notoriously open to self-serving bias (see chapter 4 in this book). Yet when third parties also agree that a compromise is relatively fair, representatives can use this fact to convince their constituents that the compromise as a whole should be accepted. We note also that a compromise may fail to capture all possible joint gains because individuals who are concerned primarily with their ongoing relationship may compromise before pressing forward to see what further gains could be made. Representatives concerned only with their relationships with their colleagues might compromise too soon. In experiments that tested an approximation to the representative-constituent relationship, the greatest joint gain came from "representatives" who were both accountable to their "constituents" and had good relations with one another based on the expectation of future cooperation. Accountability alone tended to produce impasse; good relations alone tended to produce compromise without exploiting all the possibilities for joint gain (Pruitt 1983; see chapter 4, note 16, in this book). In many real-world situations, it may be better (for example, more efficient given transaction costs) to settle for a relatively quick and fair compromise than to press forward for joint gains.

33. Gutmann and Thompson (2012, pp. 10–16); see also Van Parijs (2012).

In the case of pure bargaining, both the negotiation process and the negotiators' claims lack deliberative elements. Rather than disclosing information to find ways of achieving joint gains, the negotiators will take advantage of any information asymmetries in the situation to reveal no more than what is strategically useful. They make what they perceive to be fair offers only when their opponent will reject anything else.[34] In addition to the outcomes being zero-sum within the zone of possible agreement, in this mode, the parties are merely trying to exercise power, exploit institutional advantages, and gain as much as possible at the expense of the other.

Successful legislative negotiation often incorporates over time many of the elements we identify. The negotiations in Congress about the Clean Air Act of 1990—especially as related to acid rain, which produced a policy widely viewed as highly successful—contained most of these elements, as discussed in the following section.[35]

Clean Air Act of 1990

Pure deliberation leading to informed consensus. In the case of the Clean Air Act, much of the pure deliberation did not take place in Congress but rather in the scientific community. The work of scientists who had achieved a consensus on the causes of acid rain by the late 1980s provided the key backdrop to successful congressional negotiation. These scientific findings were disseminated both inside and outside Congress via hearings and reports, and the consensus among scientists made possible common understandings across a range of policymakers in Congress and the executive branch. The shifting understanding produced by the scientific deliberation and the deliberative reception of those findings in Congress altered the politics of the issue and paved the way for new regulations. In Congress itself, certain members seem to have engaged in relatively pure deliberation.

34. The distinction we draw between fair offers and strategic demands in some respects tracks Rawls's distinction between the reasonable and the rational (Rawls 2001, pp. 6–7, 81, 191).

35. We are grateful to Frances Lee, a member of the U.S. working group of the Task Force and coauthor of chapter 3, "Making Deals in Congress," in this book, not only for the suggestion of the Clean Air Act as an example but also for the thought and most of the wording in the following section.

Toward an almost fully integrative agreement. One agreement in the legislation was to mandate "technology forcing standards." The idea was that advances in technology can make regulatory issues far less burdensome on affected interests. The catalytic converter was an example of this approach. In the case of the Clean Air Act, Congress mandated that industry develop technology to meet specific standards for reducing air pollution—technology that could make the goals of the legislation feasible at reasonable cost to industry. If the technology were not developed, the Environmental Protection Agency would be empowered to modify the standards. In other words, improved technology could make for solutions capable of transcending existing conflicts and reducing the extent to which interests were opposed to one another. The agreement was not fully integrative because industry had to bear the burden of research on the appropriate technologies; however, the goal was to find a agreement that would allow the reduction of pollution with a cost that was acceptable to the polluting industries.

A partially integrative agreement. The legislation's use of tradable emissions credits rather than mandates to bring pollution under control allowed affected industries to "trade lower values for higher ones," provided that they came in below the targets. This flexibility allowed industry to be creative in finding lower cost solutions to emissions controls. Jeffry Burnam (2010), a political scientist present at these discussions, summed up that aspect of the negotiation as follows:

> As an observer and a participant in that process, I can testify that there was very little bargaining in the sense of "horse trading" in the Senate back room. The discussions there were based on efforts by key leaders to find mutually acceptable solutions that were right for them in accordance with [the] view that politicians have much to gain by seeking common ground and sharing credit for measures that are in their mutual interest to support.[36]

36. Burnam (2010, p. 318). Using the status quo as a benchmark, from the perspective of the industry this was probably not a partially integrative agreement because they might have gained more by staying at the status quo. Using the lesser normative standard of the best available alternative to a negotiated agreement as a benchmark, however, it probably was partially integrative. With President George H. W. Bush, a Republican, pushing for clean-air improvements,

Compromise. The Clean Air Act provides many examples of compromise that aim at a rough concept of fairness. Burnam (2010) again reported:

> Senator John Breaux of Louisiana (who was involved in negotiations over the toxic air emissions title) entered the negotiating room on Wednesday morning and asked: "What's going on?" Senator Mitchell explained that there was a dispute between the two sides as to how many cities outside of California had to be out of compliance with the ozone attainment standard in the year 2000 in order to trigger the second stage of automobile tailpipe controls: "We say 10 and they say 12," Mitchell told Breaux. "Well," Senator Breaux replied, "there has to be a number between 10 and 12."[37]

Bargaining to win. According to the account of Henry Waxman, a key player in the process, successful negotiation with John Dingell, an opponent of tougher regulation, became possible only after Waxman's side had made a show of strength on a test vote in committee, forcing Dingell to realize that he could not prevail on the issue:

> For more than a decade, Dingell and I had battled ferociously over the Clean Air Act, and we had often tried to get him to sit down and work out a deal. Dingell never budged, and so neither did I, each of us believing that we would prevail when matters came to a vote. Seeing that this was now unlikely to happen on the issue so important to him, Dingell did what any good congressman would do, and sat down to negotiate the best possible deal for his constituents. Two hours later, we had settled on the outline of an agreement.[38]

Mixing the elements. In 1986, then-Senator Timothy E. Wirth, Democrat from Colorado, and Senator John Heinz, Republican from

---

the industry's alternative to a negotiated agreement might have been more draconian regulations.

37. Ibid. (pp. 315–16).

38. Waxman (2009, 98).

Pennsylvania—who had been friends since attending the same preparatory school and playing on its basketball team together—realized while attending a meeting sponsored by the Environmental Defense Fund (EDF) that although the two of them "were both very interested in the environment . . . we weren't paying enough attention to the economic side." They "got some money from the Carnegie Corporation," a private foundation, and hired a young Harvard economist, Robert Stavens, who had been the staff economist for the EDF, to work with other economists and business leaders to develop a plan for an economically sustainable approach to clean air ("Project 88") aimed at the 1988 elections. The interest of the two representatives in the facts was purely deliberative; they wanted to understand the situation better and worked together to do so. They believed that they already understood the conflicts between their constituencies' interests. As Wirth put it, "I was West; he was East. I was clean coal; he was dirty coal. I was new power plants; he was old plants."[39] They knew that fair compromise would be required, and they looked as well for integrative agreements. It would be difficult to disentangle the elements of deliberation, fully and partially integrative negotiation, and fair compromise in this mix. Power was in no way absent from the process, as suggested by the backgrounds of the protagonists, the importance of business interests, the role of private foundations and public-interest advocacy groups, and the dominating frame of the 1988 election. At the same time, in the parts of the negotiation that these two conducted together, they seem to have come close to being "completely open with one another; [with] total honesty, full disclosure, no strategic posturing."[40] Their official relationships as legislative representatives mandated concern for the interests of their districts and for the good the nation as a whole. In the negotiation taken overall, the representatives' roles were complex, changing subtly over time in response to the demand for different elements in the mix. Even "bargaining in the sense of 'horse trading' " entered the picture when, as

39. Jane Mansbridge interview with Timothy E. Wirth, April 22, 2013.

40. This is Raiffa's (1982, p. 18) description of a "fully cooperative" negotiation, characteristic, for example, of "a happily married couple or some fortunate business partners."

noted previously, Dingell agreed to negotiate the best deal he could for his constituents only when he realized that he would lose the vote.

As this example shows, interactions in negotiations may combine (1) purely deliberative elements (offering considerations that others might accept on their merits); (2) fully integrative elements (exploiting the different interests underneath the expressed demands or positions of each party to find a creative solution that gives each what that party really wants with no need for compromise on either side); (3) partially integrative elements (created by, for example, expanding the number of issues considered and trying to conduct trades on issues to which one party gives a high priority and another a low priority); (4) compromises in instances of zero-sum conflict in which the parties intend to act fairly; and (5) pure bargaining in instances of zero-sum conflict in which the aim of each party is only to win.

The Neglect of Deliberative Negotiation

Citizens, political scientists, and (increasingly) lawmakers in Congress are likely to mistake for pure bargaining the many dimensions of deliberative negotiation involved in successful agreements. These mistakes have been mirrored in political theory. In 1962, in his first major work, Habermas wrote scathingly of legislative action in the Weimar Republic that "compromise literally had to be haggled out, produced temporarily through pressure and counterpressure and supported only through the unstable equilibrium of power constellations between state apparatus and interest groups." Such "bargaining," he proclaimed, bore the mark of its "origins in the market."[41] In 1988, Sunstein wrote similarly from the civic-republican tradition that virtuous citizens "will attempt to design political institutions that promote discussion and debate among the citizenry; they will be hostile to systems that promote lawmaking as 'deals' or bargains among self-interested private groups."[42] In 1989, Cohen, writing from the Rawlsian tradition, argued that public "collective decision-making

41. Habermas ([1962] 1989, p. 198).

42. Sunstein (1988, p. 1549; see also "[civic] republicans will be hostile to bargaining mechanisms in the political process and will instead seek to ensure agreement among political participants," p. 1554).

ought to be different from bargaining, contracting, and other market-type interactions, both in its explicit attention to considerations of the common advantage and in the ways that that attention helps to form the aims of the participants."[43]

Each of these early deliberative theorists, from three different traditions, positioned the normative goals of deliberation as antithetical to "bargaining." As we have seen, in 1986 Elster, echoing much of the thought of his time, also positioned "arguing," or deliberation, in sharp contrast to "bargaining." Although Habermas ([1992] 1996) later changed his stance on bargaining, giving it more positive democratic status when the bargaining partners are equal, at the time those three theorists drew easily on a publicly accepted denigration of "bargaining." They overlooked the democratic value of negotiation generally and deliberative negotiation in particular.

Pure bargaining has generated most of the strongly negative connotations attached to negotiation. Bargaining often includes threats, including the threat of exit, as a matter of course. The standard use in one-shot bargaining of "strategic misrepresentation"—particularly not revealing one's reservation price—leads bargaining, or "haggling" as Habermas called it, to border on the unethical. Some market-oriented writers on negotiation underscore this interpretation. White (1980, p. 928), among others, argued that negotiation is like a poker game: "To conceal one's true position, to mislead an opponent about one's true settling point, is the essence of negotiation."[44] A handbook on business negotiation suggests that "an individual who confuses private ethics with business morality does not make an effective negotiator. A negotiator must learn to . . . subordinate his own personal sense of ethics to the prime purpose of securing the best deal possible for the client."[45] So too in legislatures: some legislators consider the use of parliamentary procedure to put one's opponents at a disadvantage, or to call a vote when one's opponents are absent, no more than savvy playing within the rules.

43. J. Cohen (1989, p. 17).

44. See also Carr (1968, p. 145), allowing "cunning deception" and "concealment."

45. Beckmann (1977), quoted in Lax and Sebenius (1986, p. 146).

None of these practices that are characteristic of pure bargaining—threat, strategic misrepresentation, and the strategic use of asymmetric information—meets the normative criteria for *deliberative* negotiation that the negotiation be based on mutual justification and respect and the search for fair terms of interaction and outcomes, all of which assume a reasonable degree of openness and disclosure among the parties.[46] A commitment to these practices also tends to overlook the practical value of deliberative negotiations. Repeated interactions, for example, undermine the usefulness of purely strategic bargaining by making it less likely that others will engage in future negotiations with those who have deceived them. Such practices, therefore, are often inefficient. Ulbert and Risse's cases of negotiation in the EU confirm "the crucial role" in repeated interactions of the "credibility and truthfulness of speakers."[47] Particularly to play the role of "knowledge broker," a position that grants significant influence in a negotiation, the speaker "must be perceived as honest and impartial." Personal reputation or representing an organization with a long history of dedication to a cause perceived to be in the common good can

46. Such practices in the "pure bargaining" phases of a negotiation might be considered democratically legitimate on the grounds that all players have agreed, explicitly or tacitly, to specific forms of "role-morality" that are restricted to the rules of a specific "game." Applbaum (1998, p. 123) has argued to the contrary that if the "rules of the game" are invoked to justify a role-morality that permits what would otherwise be morally prohibited, the game in question must meet certain stringent criteria, including that the rules must be "necessary for the continued success and stability of the game as a mutually advantageous cooperative venture . . . [that] provides all its players positive expected benefits" and "distributes benefits and burdens justly to its players" while imposing "no unjust externalities on those who are not players." In legislative negotiation, strategic misrepresentation in negotiation is unlikely to help create a mutually advantageous cooperative venture. The best argument for allowing "sharp dealing" in legislative negotiation is that because it is not possible to monitor intent or private knowledge, it may be better to accept openly, as part of the game, the behaviors that cannot be monitored, so that ethical individuals, adopting a role-morality suitable to this specific arena, may have an even playing field with the unethical. When repeated interactions, as is typical in legislatures, make such monitoring easier, there is no normative justification for strategic misrepresentation.

47. Ulbert and Risse (2005, p. 359).

also anchor a speaker's credibility.[48] The incentive structures created by repeated interaction reduce the likelihood of most instances of manipulation, deceit, and even the strategic use of asymmetric information.

It is worth underscoring that we are not equating "private" or "market" transactions with any of the categories in table 5-1. Market transactions can include all of these categories, as can political negotiations. Many early normative analyses drew a dichotomy between "deliberation" and "bargaining" that equated "bargaining" (or what we call "pure bargaining") with the "market." The negotiation literature in business and law may have reinforced this equation. The equation originally took root because the purest bargains typically are one-shot interactions among parties who need not be concerned with any of the deliberative virtues, and such interactions are likely to take place more in the market than in a legislature or committee with repeated interactions. Market transactions also typically do not involve attentiveness to broad, public, or common goods but instead only to the goods internal to the transaction. Nevertheless, even in the market realm, many transactions may have deliberative elements—if only because both parties may have an interest in obtaining better purchase on a particular factual situation. Repeated market transactions also usually rely on elements of reputation, trust, and fairness, often backed by the regulative norms and institutions that underwrite markets. For our purposes, the worst effect of the equation of negotiation=bargaining=market is to "tar" political negotiation, which often takes the form of deliberative negotiation, with the one-shot bargaining brush. The frequent implicit or explicit condemnation of negotiation and compromise in this equation deflects attention from the importance of deliberative negotiation for democratic action.

Negotiation also classically entails opprobrium because both in the market and in the political arena it is often based in self-interest or, more commonly, the self-interests of constituents. Equally important, negotiations are seen as deriving from conflicting interests that undermine or even corrupt the common good. Self-interest has recently been rehabilitated as an important input to democratic pro-

48. Ibid.

cesses.[49] Moreover, although sometimes negotiations that end in compromise do reflect failures to find common interests, thereby representing a second-best outcome, such failure can occur only when common interests exist actually or potentially and thus could be found or forged. In all other cases, including most of the difficult cases in politics, participants will not get everything they want from the political process. A negotiated compromise may be second best but good enough. Because conflicting interests are an ineradicable part of political life in a pluralist society, negotiation and compromise are essential features of political systems that maximize democratic goods.[50]

The concept of compromise attracts condemnation for another reason. In most of the world, the term *compromise* carries the connotation that one who compromises is "unprincipled" and thus morally suspect, as in the French phrase, "to put in compromise" (*mettre en compromis*).[51] This connotation of compromising one's principles in turn derives in part from the assumption that certain goods—moral principles in particular—should never be bargained or compromised. Although this judgment is sometimes right, the general and familiar point made by Schumpeter ([1942] 1962) and others that ideals and ideological interests cannot be compromised is wrong. Gutmann and Thompson (1996) have pointed out that compromises can be wrought in which each party respects the other's deepest moral values, and that successful compromises can include mutual principled gains even when parties hold opposing principles.[52]

Some of the most important legislative compromises are unattractive not only because they involve sacrificing principle but also because they combine conflicting principles. In the United States, the

49. Mansbridge et al. (2010).

50. See, for example, Gutmann and Thompson (2012, chap. 2).

51. Fumurescu (2013) compares the relatively neutral or even positive use of the word historically in Great Britain and the United States with the usually pejorative use of the term in French, which often occurs in the phrase *mettre en compromis*. The difference from France may arise from the normative and practical grounding in contracts of the British "nation of shopkeepers" and the American "commercial republic."

52. Gutmann and Thompson (1996; 2012, pp. 73–85). For a somewhat different position also arguing for the possibility of compromise on principle, see Richardson (2002).

Comprehensive Immigration Act of 2007, a compromise that had strong bipartisan support but ultimately failed, illustrates the disorderly nature of classic compromises. It combined a form of amnesty (which in the view of conservatives violated a principle of retributive justice) and a form of discrimination against illegal immigrants (which in the view of liberals violated distributive justice). Senator Arlen Specter, Republican of Pennsylvania, who spoke passionately in favor of the compromise, acknowledged the problem: "This amendment was characterized by the Senator from New Mexico as the politics of compromise. Well, that might sound bad, but that happens to be the reality of what goes on in the Senate all the time. It goes on in all political bodies . . . There is nothing inappropriate about the politics of compromise. That means we sacrifice the better for the good."[53]

On the issue of abortion, for example—an issue long thought to be resistant to compromise—proponents on each side can make concessions that respect both the claim that even an embryo has elements of human life and the claim that bringing an unwanted child into the world is a tragedy. Opponents have found that they can agree about the desirability of reducing unwanted pregnancies, particularly among teenagers. In cases such as these, talking together helps parties not only investigate their own commitments and convey them to others but also test whether they might discover possible agreements on some commitments and make concessions on others, such that they could craft agreements that might partially integrate what seemed to be absolutely irreconcilable differences. Ideological as well as material oppositions sometimes are fully incompatible. However, it takes argument (or deliberation) and often the attempt at negotiation to find this out.

---

53. Congressional Record 153 (June 6, 2007), S7099. For a discussion, see Gutmann and Thompson (2012, pp. 92–98). The Comprehensive Immigration Act of 2007 ultimately failed due to party polarization, as did the 2010 "DREAM Act" and the 2013 bipartisan effort to produce an immigration bill, both documented in the case study of "Polarization, Gridlock, and the Politics of Immigration" in chapter 2. The 2007 bill does not appear in that case study because the bill did not move beyond the introduction stage. Like the 2013 bipartisan effort, however, it was originally negotiated by a "gang" of individual representatives from each party who had built up sufficient mutual understanding over time to be able to talk through the issues constructively (see also chapters 3 and 4 for the current role of "gangs" in the U.S. Congress).

Negotiation-Facilitating Institutions and Practices

If deadlock undermines democracy and deliberative negotiation supports it, why do we not have more deliberative negotiation? Deliberative negotiation is resisted not only because its distinctive values are misunderstood but also because some of the practices that make it possible can conflict with democratic norms. Although many kinds of reforms would enhance conditions favorable to deliberative negotiations—nonpartisan primaries or independent electoral district commissions, for example—we focus on three practices that are both effective and can conflict with democratic norms: repeated interaction promoted by long incumbencies, closed-door negotiations, and provision of side payments for the constituency of a specific member of Congress. All three facilitate deliberative negotiation, but all have significant normative trade-offs. In the following discussion, we suggest circumstances in which the costs in these trade-offs are reduced or even become nonexistent.

One general circumstance likely to minimize the trade-offs between democratic norms and the three negotiation-supporting institutions discussed here is a relatively uncorrupt polity, in the sense of both illegal corruption and more pervasive institutional corruption such as that caused by massive inequalities in campaign funding.[54] The more corrupt the polity, the higher are the costs of the "cozy" relationships created by repeated interaction and the opportunities for self-dealing (or privileged-constituency dealing) afforded by closed-door sessions and the provision of side payments. Relatively uncorrupt polities allow political representatives to engage more freely in deliberative negotiations for the public good.

A major challenge confronting all efforts to facilitate legislative negotiation is the rise of the permanent campaign.[55] Campaigns are zero-sum contests, not occasions for negotiation, even less for deliberative negotiation. Elections are not intended to produce win-win solutions. The attitudes and practices of campaigns are not conducive

54. For institutional corruption, see Thompson (1995) and Lessig (2012).

55. Gutmann and Thompson (2012, pp. 3–5, 160–67) explicitly connect the permanent campaign to the difficulty of negotiating compromises. On the permanent campaign, see also Ornstein and Mann (2000) and King (1997).

to the negotiation necessary for governing. As campaigning increasingly intrudes into governing, negotiations become increasingly difficult. Representatives have their minds set on winning the next election more than on reaching constructive agreements. The practices we discuss here, if properly structured, can help representatives stay focused on governing. Long-term relationships, closed-door deliberations, and side payments that smooth collegial cooperation can be seen as ways of enabling legislators to concentrate their minds on governing. We focus on these three only as examples of facilitating mechanisms that raise normative questions, hoping that the examples will spur further research into the institutional and normative frameworks conducive to deliberative negotiation.

Repeated Interaction

Many negotiation theorists, as well as many active and former elected representatives, stress the importance of long-term repeated interactions, in which opposing parties can get to know one another personally, particularly in contexts separate from those involving the issues on which they are opposed. Such relationships are especially important in legislative bodies. As Gutmann and Thompson (2012) wrote:

> When adversaries know each other well, they are far more likely to recognize whether the other side's refusal to compromise on a principle is a negotiating tactic or a real political constraint. They are less likely to act as players in the classic bargaining game who hold out for their maximum individual payoff, producing an outcome that makes both sides worse off. In longer-term relationships, legislators have a better sense of their colleagues' intentions, their trustworthiness, and the political constraints they are facing—and their colleagues know that they do. They are repeat players. That enables all to make more confident judgments about when to compromise and when not to.[56]

---

56. Gutmann and Thompson (2012, p. 170; see also pp. 177–79, 200–9).

When repeated interactions involve working together on a common problem, they are particularly likely to increase the mutual respect and understanding that support deliberative negotiation.[57]

The solution of repeated interaction among representatives implicitly endorses long incumbencies. Yet long incumbencies often involve relatively uncontested elections, and the democratic accountability of representatives to their constituents is often thought to require genuinely contested elections. Empirical indexes of democracy often count relatively uncontested elections as a clear indicator of lack of democracy. The normative tension between the benefits of long incumbencies and the benefits of contest reflects to some degree the tension between action (deriving from negotiation) and resistance (deriving from suspicion of long incumbencies and the potentially corrupt or "shirking" motives of representatives). An increasingly disillusioned public in the United States increasingly demands term limits, short incumbencies, and a tight tether to public opinion. These demands are often (although not always) bad for negotiation.

What kinds of circumstances, then, support repeated interactions in ways consistent with democratic norms—especially the norm of responsiveness by representatives to those who elect them? Although a full theory of these circumstances is beyond the scope of this chapter, we believe that long incumbencies are more or less acceptable to the degree that the constituency is relatively informed and not manipulated, has potential alternatives to the incumbent, and has the capacity to act on alternatives. Thus, the more the following conditions are achieved or approached, the better a long incumbency conforms to democratic norms:

—The representative, by and large, promotes policies and a broad political direction of which the majority of constituents approves.

—Most constituents consider themselves relatively satisfied with their representative.

—The minority of constituents is not deeply unsatisfied with the representative.

57. See Sherif et al. (1961) on the null effects on opposing groups of contact alone in undermining prejudice and mutual animosity, in contrast to the dramatic effects of working together on a problem that will benefit both sides.

—The existing media system, interest-group system, and party system (through either an opposing party or internal-party dynamics) are healthy, able to present alternative policies, and able to publicize departures from citizen preferences or interests.

—The citizens are active in other forms of politics and therefore able to inform themselves easily and take action skillfully if their current representative no longer seems appropriate.

Although it may not be easy to ascertain whether these conditions hold in any given case, we must investigate them before we treat high rates of incumbency as prima facie evidence of democratic failure. The resulting judgment is a matter of degree. However, the underlying concept is not complicated: these kinds of indicators suggest that constituents can have enough warranted trust in their representatives to allow the representatives to form long-standing relationships with other representatives without thereby breaking or in some way betraying their representative relationships with constituents. Representatives should be able to use their long-term relationships to support deliberative negotiations on behalf of their constituents.

Closed-Door Interactions

Deliberative negotiation does not thrive, it seems, in highly public settings. Political representatives and negotiation scholars agree that relatively private interactions behind closed doors provide the moments, sheltered from publicity—particularly the constant monitoring and oversight of intensely interested and well-organized interest groups or a sensation-seeking press—in which opposing parties can share their perspectives freely and come to understand the perspectives of others.[58] As Ulbert and Risse (2005) noted in the EU, "Private in camera settings . . . such as the 'confession talks' during European Council summits allow actors to explore potential compromises, to seek out the justifiability of their interests, and the like. These

---

58. See Gutmann and Thompson (1996, pp. 115–16), arguing that deliberative secrecy is a "justifiable way of encouraging better discussion and fuller consideration of legislation. . . . Legislators remain freer to change their minds about a Bill in response to continuing discussions." See also Chambers (2009) for the most extensive treatment of the issue to date.

settings allow for arguing and persuasion, because negotiators do not have to stick to their fixed preferences behind closed doors and are allowed to 'think out loud' about possible negotiating solutions."[59]

Sheltering negotiations from publicity so they may be more productive has a long-standing history. At the Federal Convention to design the new U.S. Constitution, the sessions were closed and secret. As James Madison said later, he did not believe that the delegates could have come to agreement on the Constitution if the proceedings had not been behind closed doors. In his analysis, "Had the members committed themselves publicly at first, they would have afterwards supposed consistency required them to maintain their ground, whereas by secret discussion no man felt himself obliged to retain his opinions any longer than he was satisfied of their propriety and truth, and was open to the force of argument."[60]

Madison was right on being "open to the force of argument." After comparing the interactions in the U.S. Federal Convention, which met behind closed doors, and the French Assemblée Constituante, which met in public, Elster concluded: "Many of the debates at the Federal Convention were indeed of high quality: remarkably free from cant and remarkably grounded in rational argument. By contrast, the discussions in the public Assemblée Constituante were heavily tainted by rhetoric, demagoguery, and overbidding."[61]

Today, the positive effects of closed-door interactions are just as clear. In the United States, after the 1976 Government in the Sunshine Act opened committee meetings to the public, several senators interviewed on the larger subject of the growing "individualism" in the Senate blamed opening the committees to the public for part of the loss of their capacity to negotiate and their former spirit of "political self-sacrifice":

59. Ulbert and Risse (2005, pp. 357–58). See also Lewis (1998) and Wallace (2002).

60. Madison reported in an interview with Jared Sparks (1830), cited in United States Constitutional Convention (1937, p. 478), quoted in Elster (2000, p. 386). See also Stasavage (2004, p. 688).

61. Elster (1995, pp. 251, 244). Elster's comments raised in shorthand a number of issues that we do not discuss here. We quote his conclusion only to note his attribution of several positive attributes to the closed-door format and several negative attributes to the open-door format. See also Elster (1998).

Most senators seem to agree that [the recent changes in the rules] have made negotiation and political self-sacrifice infinitely more difficult. Open meetings are singled out most often. . . . "There was an enormous give and take," Pearson [former Senator James B. Pearson, Republican from Kansas] says of the old closed-door committee system. "People could change their minds—as a result of hard bargaining and deliberation. But nobody wants to admit in public that he was wrong."[62]

In their studies of the transcripts of parliamentary deliberation in Switzerland, Steiner and colleagues (2004) found that indications of one representative's listening to the others were far more frequent in in-camera proceedings in the Swiss parliament than in proceedings that were open to the public.[63] In a study that compared publicly available and private lobbying letters to governmental regulatory bodies, Naurin (2007b) found more "self-regarding" justifications in the publicly available letters, presumably because the groups the letter writers were representing could see those letters but not the private ones. The paid consultants (that is, lobbyists) that Naurin interviewed also pointed out that a public audience encourages posturing through adopting uncompromising positions and playing to one's own constituents. As one consultant stated, "The leaders of these types of organizations [business and public interest groups] have a fairly difficult task. On the one hand, they have to keep their own comrades happy and 50 percent of their own group, maybe more, demand blood. . . . If the [head] of the organization is up for re-election six weeks later, his tone . . . may be [even] sharper."[64]

62. Ehrenhalt (1982, pp. 2177–78).

63. Steiner et al. (2004).

64. Naurin (2007b, p. 222). In the same study, Naurin showed that when impartiality norms are relatively strong and the degree of corruption is relatively low, there need be no trade-off between secrecy and deals that are capable of withstanding public scrutiny. Through his interviews with consultants and his discovery of private letters that later became unexpectedly open to the public, he found that business lobbyists acting under closed-door conditions in their relationships with the European Commission had realized that "in order to promote their interests they have to argue carefully with reference to public interests and ideals rather than bargain from self-interest" and that "the industry

In studies of negotiations in the EU, Ulbert and Risse (2005) identified many instances in which negotiators had agreed on controversial passages in papers drafted behind closed doors because, in that
context, they were able to go beyond their instructions to explore possibilities for compromise.[65] As early as 1945, on the basis of many
years of labor negotiations, the pathbreaking negotiation specialists
Walton and McKersie concluded:

> [The parties] will not engage in problem-solving behavior unless
> the activity is relatively safe. Both Party and Opponent need to
> be assured that if they freely and openly acknowledge their prob-
> lems, if they willingly explore any solution proposed, and if
> they candidly discuss their own preferences, this information will
> not somehow be used against them. . . . The use of transcripts
> or a stenographer may inhibit exploratory and tentative discus-
> sions. Large galleries and disclosure to outside persons have the
> same effect.[66]

By now, the empirical evidence on the deliberative benefits of closed-
door interactions seems incontrovertible.[67]

---

lobbyists studied here sounded better, with respect to self-interest, behind
closed doors than in public" owing to constituency pressure toward a self-
interested stance in public settings (Naurin 2007a, pp. 9, 8).

65. Ulbert and Risse (2005, p. 358). The Council of Ministers of the EU explicitly made this point in its rejoinder to the Court of First Instance when *The
Guardian* newspaper demanded access to their minutes: "The Council normally
works through a process of negotiation and compromise, in the course of which
its members freely express their national preoccupations and positions. If agreement is to be reached, they will frequently be called upon to move from those
positions, perhaps to the extent of abandoning their national instructions on a
particular point or points. This process, *vital to the adoption of Community
legislation*, would be compromised if delegations were constantly mindful of
the fact that the positions they were taking, as recorded in Council minutes,
could at any time be made public through the granting of access to these documents, independently of a positive Council decision" (Council of the European
Union 1994, cited in Stasavage 2004, pp. 690–91; emphasis in original).

66. Walton and McKersie (1965, p. 159) quoted in Naurin (2007b, p. 211).

67. See, for example, Groseclose and McCarty's (2001, p. 114) conclusion from
their data: "Although there may be benefits to 'sunshine laws' and other measures

The problem is that closed-door, nontransparent interactions come with serious democratic hazards. We discuss three: the general normative presumption for transparency, deriving perhaps from a "right to know"; the problems that closed doors pose for accountability; and the practical problems that closed doors pose for trust in society. We then suggest several criteria for judging when nonpublic, closed-door meetings may be consistent with democratic norms.

The general presumption in favor of transparency in democracies stems from the fundamental role of a citizen in "ruling." To make good collective decisions, the citizen must be informed. Citizens therefore may have a "right to know" all the available information that could inform their decision.[68] Yet the question remains open as to which kinds of knowledge are necessary to support citizens' rights and powers to judge their representatives and their decisions.[69] We distinguish between *transparency in process*, or public access to the details of actual interactions, and *transparency in rationale*, or public access to the reasons for the outcome.[70] If the rationale is genuine, in

---

to make negotiations open, our results show that they may actually harm efficiency." See also Jacobsson and Vifell (2003): "the more closed the forum, the more openness in the discussion" (cited in Stasavage 2004, p. 694); Checkel (2001) on deliberative persuasion being more likely in "less politicized and more insulated in-camera settings" (cited in ibid.); and Stasavage (2004, p. 673) for evidence that public posturing "can provoke a breakdown in bargaining that has a negative impact for all concerned." See also Morgenthau (1950, p. 431), who commented, "It takes only common sense derived from daily experience to realize that it is impossible to negotiate in public on anything in which parties other than the negotiators are interested" (cited in Peters 2013, p. 57). See Pedrini, Bächtiger, and Steenbergen (2013) for an in-depth study of a closed-door session in the Swiss legislature demonstrating that in this context, compared with more public sessions, political actors were engaged in high-quality reasoning and creative problem-solving activities geared toward deep agreement and minority-favoring outcomes. See Chambers (2004, p. 392) for a list of situations, such as juries, in which closed doors enhance the capacity for good deliberation.

68. See also Stiglitz (1999) and Florini (2007). The recent right-to-information campaign in India had the slogan, "The right to know is the right to live"; see Singh (2007), referenced from Peters (2013).

69. See Thompson (1999), especially the section on "How much should the veil be lifted?"

70. For the distinction, see Mansbridge et al. (2010); see also Gutmann and Thompson (2012, pp. 59–60).

many cases it is all that citizens need to know to be informed, allowing the process itself to remain behind closed doors. The practical problem is that the rationale may not be genuine and often the only way that citizens can find out is to have access to the process.

The problems that closed doors pose for accountability track those posed by the right to know. Traditionally, the concept of accountability meant "giving an account"—that is, giving the reasons for one's actions. In a principal-agent relationship, in which a principal has contracted with or has otherwise relied on an agent to act in the principal's interest, the agent should be able to give an account of any seeming deviation from those interests. More recently, accountability has come to mean the combination of monitoring and sanctioning, and monitoring requires transparency for the events monitored. In representative democratic government, far more transparency in process is expected today than at the founding of the United States, when delegates at the Federal Convention debated whether to require that roll-call votes be made public. In the early years of the republic, closed-door sessions of Congress were frequent.[71] Stasavage (2004, p. 671) reports, "There is clear evidence from the United States and the U.K. that demands for transparency appeared during periods of heightened fears that representatives were biased. In strong contrast, during periods where fears of bias were less present, the public was more accepting of closed-door sessions."

The most serious source of bias is the undue influence of powerful groups, combined with the fear that any concessions to such groups will be obscured in the rationale later made public. The instrumental use of transparency in process to identify and subsequently prevent such influence must depend on the degree to which special interests have undue influence and the degree to which transparency in process would reveal it. The considerable influence, for example, of financial interests in the United States today often takes the form of

---

71. For the debates in the convention on public access to the representatives' votes, see Madison Debates, August 10, 1787, http://avalon.law.yale.edu/18th _century/debates_810.asp. We thank Gregory Koger for this reference. All of the assemblies in the U.S. states in the colonial period met in secret, and not until 1794 did the Senate vote to open its debates to the public. In 1689, 1738, and 1771, the House of Commons debated whether to drop its long-standing ban on publishing its proceedings (Stasavage 2004, pp. 685–86).

persuading key actors that the health of the economy depends on continuing support for or deregulation of such interests. Transparency in process would reveal those actors making those arguments; however, under the circumstances we specify, so would transparency in rationale.

The most normatively troubling set of issues and policy negotiations that benefit from secrecy are those that are deeply controversial, divisive, or generally involve some difficult and perhaps unpopular trade-offs. For example, the conflicts played out in the Council of the EU, which still operates more like a forum for international negotiation than a legislature in a democratic polity, usually concern national interests at the sector level rather than general political ideas.[72] The link between the negotiators in the Council and their constituents is based on geography and nationality more than political ideology. Open debates in the Council would not demonstrate conflict between, for example, liberals and conservatives, but rather between Germans and Greeks or between Poles and Italians. An important reason why the Council has refrained from having these open debates is the fear that such debates, conducted in terms of *we* and *they*, would be divisive and would reduce rather than increase the perceived legitimacy of the EU in the view of Europeans. Ulbert and Risse (2005) have thus suggested that for public discussions to have the greatest constructive influence, some degree of impartiality among the public is necessary. When these conditions do not hold, as when nationalism prevails, they believe there are good reasons for negotiations to be held behind closed doors. They argue that if the Council were to become more like a legislature over time, and both members and citizens were to come to think of themselves at least in part as representing the whole union or as citizens of that union, negotiations could become more public.[73]

The problem with respect to democratic norms is that citizens want not only their interests to be represented but also their voices and, to some degree, their selves. If they are in fact nationalistic or hold positions on issues that are more extreme than those of the median voter, they want those perspectives represented. The most politically active

72. Thomson (2011).

73. Ulbert and Risse (2005, p. 359).

want their perspectives not only represented but also fought for *within the process itself.* Transparency in process allows these kinds of citizens to monitor their representatives to prevent them from compromising their principles. Transparency in rationale is not sufficient to this end. Transparency in rationale also usually will not meet the desire to have one's voice reflected in the process unless that rationale also explicitly presents the strongest or most strongly expressed arguments on all sides. In these circumstances, regardless of the normative good or bad of holding extreme positions, closed-door processes have the normative cost of undermining citizens' powers to monitor the process and hear their voices expressed in arguments.

In addition to the democratic goods of the right to know and accountability, transparency in process has recently been advanced as a means to shore up citizen trust in government. Yet in practice transparency may not have this effect. Several studies find no effects of transparency on either trust or procedure acceptance.[74] In one recent study, transparency in process did not produce increments of perceived legitimacy significantly greater than transparency in rationale. The authors conclude that "a relatively modest reform focusing on transparency in rationale—such as a reason-giving requirement—may contribute to similar degrees of added legitimacy as more far-reaching transparency in process measures. Decision makers may improve the legitimacy of the procedure by simply outlining carefully afterward the reasons for the decisions taken behind closed doors."[75]

Given the normative problems posed by the right to know and accountability, we suggest here four circumstances under which the closed-door sessions that facilitate deliberative negotiation are more likely to be democratically acceptable.

First, it would be best if citizens themselves have the opportunity to deliberate about and agree to negotiation privacy. Such a "second-order" or "meta" agreement would then legitimize negotiating behind closed doors.[76] This condition usually can be met in the case of deci-

74. See Grimmelikhuijsen (2012), De Fine Licht (2011), and De Fine Licht et al. (2014). See also Bauhr and Grimes (2014) for a correlational study.

75. De Fine Licht et al. (2014, citation omitted).

76. For "second-order publicity," see Gutmann and Thompson (1996, p. 105) and Thompson (1999); for "meta-transparency," see Neumann and Simma

sions about military operations and some other decisions affecting national security or the market (for example, the deliberations of the U.S. Federal Reserve), but it is difficult to meet in the case of ordinary legislation. The more controversial the law, the more citizens want to know about the process that produced it. When citizens do not understand the reasons for closed-door sessions and when the natural tendency is to want all available information, the requirement of citizen agreement is difficult to meet. In a democracy, to the extent that a majority of citizens opposes nontransparent processes, they are to that degree illegitimate.

Some proxies for actual agreement can support decisions by representatives to institute closed-door negotiations. In the presence of an active and informed media and active opposition parties, tacit consent in the form of acquiescence to existing nontransparent institutions might be taken as agreement. Retrospective ratification of the results also might be considered a form of agreement to the process.[77]

Yet tacit and retrospective forms of agreement have their normative problems, particularly within low-trust, highly polarized contexts. One possible solution might be to have the records of confidential meetings made public at a later date. This solution may work well for institutions such as the U.S. Federal Reserve ("the Fed"), where access to the pros and cons of possible decisions as they were being made would, if made public, cause considerable market instability. As in the establishment of privacy in national security matters, this reason for privacy is unrelated to the quality of deliberation.[78] Because the public has an interest in long-term accountability and post facto

(2013). Both terms refer to making transparent the reasons for and scope of any intransparency.

77. See Gutmann and Thompson (1996, pp. 115–17) on ratification as "a form of retrospective accountability for the process as well as for the results," responding to their own conclusion that secrecy is "not justified merely if it promotes deliberation on the merits of public policy; citizens and their accountable representatives must also be able to deliberate about whether it does so." Chambers (2004) has argued that mere ratification does not involve citizens meaningfully enough in the deliberation to count as justification for a closed-door process.

78. For the distinction between the "intrinsic" reason for privacy that relates to the quality of deliberation and other reasons, such as those for secrecy in the Fed and military security, see Peters (2013).

transparency, in August 2012—under pressure for greater publicity—the Fed began publishing unaudited quarterly reports. Also in response to a 2011 lawsuit, the Fed now must disclose the names of firms that it bailed out during the financial crisis of 2008.

Situations in which publicity harms the quality of deliberation have a different structure: negotiators need to worry about unguarded, expressive, informal speaking and trial proposals that later might be taken in the strategic contexts of public debate as betraying principles or selling out constituents. Because public records last indefinitely, negotiators may need commitments that delays in ex post transparency *in process* (as opposed to *rationale*) will last at least the lives of their political careers. Otherwise, negotiators are likely to treat even closed-door negotiations as if they were open-door, knowing that anything they say may be used against them later.

A second condition is warranted trust. Closed-door negotiations have the fewest normative problems when constituents have good reason to trust their representatives to act on their behalf. In a political system that suffers from widespread public cynicism—itself in part the result of unjustified nontransparency in, for example, campaign financing—individual representatives will have to work especially hard to gain the trust of constituents. Some representatives, however, are in fact trustworthy. Their constituents can believe with warrant that their representative is "like" them or can have other reasons, such as the representative's earned reputation, for believing that their representative will act in their interests, even behind closed doors.[79] As with long incumbencies, this warranted trust is the best normative argument for allowing closed-door negotiations. In this case, as with so many others, a society constructed around high levels of trustworthiness and the resulting high degree of social trust can be far more efficient, as well as more normatively attractive, than societies in which trust is less warranted.[80]

A third condition that can help to reconcile closed-door negotiations with democratic norms is that the relevant interests are represented fairly in the negotiation. The exclusion of the interests of

79. On the "selection model" of representation, see Fearon (1999), Besley (2006), and Mansbridge (2009).

80. Warren (1999).

affected parties in the polity from consideration, if not representation, is prima facie evidence of an illegitimate process. Moreover, as Chambers (2004, p. 397) stated, "On fundamental questions that affect the broad public, the more secret and closed is the debate, the more important it is that all possible points of view are represented."

The fourth and final but also crucial condition is that the negotiators make public after the negotiation the larger rationale for the outcome (transparency in rationale). It often should be sufficient for the democratic norms of inclusion and acceptable agreement that the rationales for proposals or agreements are public and transparent, rather than that every aspect of the process leading to agreement be transparent.[81] Issues may emerge from affected publics, be negotiated behind closed doors by representatives, and the resulting agreements presented to these same publics for deliberation and ratification without every move, concession, and trade-off of a hard-fought negotiation having to be made public. However, the questions of why this agreement is a good deal, why this solution is the right one, and what the overall public justification is for the result should be publicly argued so that constituents may discuss that rationale and possibly engage in retrospective criticism and sanctions.[82] The rationale does not have to reproduce in full the actual set of reasons that motivated the negotiators, but it should express the best and most reasonable reasons for (and against) the agreement that produces the legislation. The rationales conveyed to the citizens after the negotiation therefore must convey enough information for the public to initiate or continue informed and even passionate discussion of the issues on the basis of the most relevant evidence. Ideally, representatives should provide reasons for their actions in a two-way process, engaging with constituents or their interest-group representatives in a discussion of why they agreed to a deal or a proposed deal. Because in practice two-way communication with constituents is highly time-consuming, the publicity

81. Kant's own test was that "all actions affecting the rights of other human beings are wrong if their *maxim* is not compatible with their being made public" ([1795] 1970, p. 130; emphasis added).

82. On the importance of the information that could inform citizen deliberation "actually reaching and being received by the public," see Lindstedt and Naurin (2010).

given an issue by public debates among elected representatives or interest groups often may have to suffice.[83]

To summarize, the more the following conditions are achieved or approached, the better closed-door negotiations conform to democratic norms:

—Citizens have the opportunity to deliberate about the rationales for closed-door negotiations.

—Citizens have, with warrant, high trust in their representatives.

—The interests of the members of the polity who are affected (or potentially affected) by the outcomes are fairly represented in the negotiation.

—Negotiators are subsequently transparent in their rationales for a decision, providing enough information, reasoning, and publicity that citizens can engage in informed debate and judgment.

Side Payments

Negotiation theorists often give the name *logrolling* to the trades made via side payments in partially integrative negotiations.[84] That name, taken from legislative negotiation, has an appropriately negative normative connotation in common parlance, although not in the negotiation literature or even in some political science. *Logrolling* refers in the first instance to vote trading, in which one legislator promises another to vote for that one's project if the other legislator votes for the first one's project. Members can trade either costly projects or costly tax reductions. Much logrolling involves "pork barrel" projects that benefit primarily a particular legislator's constituents or a portion of them. This kind of trading would not be necessary if either project could get a majority on its own. Each component of the

---

83. See Naurin (2013) for the distinction between "transparency" (that is, making information available) and "publicity" (that is, making the public aware of the information). In the best conditions, a "two-step" process (Lazarsfeld, Berelson, and Gaudet 1944, pp. 151ff.), in which public sources make information available and more informed individuals publicize the relevant parts, would bring relevant information in an understandable form to the public.

84. "Logrolling is the act of making mutually beneficial trade-offs between the resources under consideration" (Thompson and Hrebec 1996, p. 398).

logroll typically will benefit only a relatively small group, at the expense of the taxpayers as a whole. In such cases, the normative problem is that the benefits go to only some members of the population ("intense benefits") but are paid by all ("diffuse costs").[85] The outcome is inefficient and, arguably, against the general good. As Pennock wrote in 1970, logrolling regarding pork barrel projects "tends to result in overspending and it is discriminatory."[86] The problem from the perspective of democratic norms is that those affected—the broader public—are excluded from the decisionmaking. Legislators may reasonably calculate that they could not justify logrolls to the majority of those affected by them. On average, it is unlikely that matters requiring logrolling will be in the public interest, at least in the first instance.

Not all trading is logrolling in this sense. Trades may reflect differing intensities of preference on an issue, which provide opportunities for normatively unobjectionable trades in which low values are traded for high values, enabling partially integrative agreements that represent improvements on the status quo for all interested parties. However, even when the trading involves logrolling over pork barrel items, the question as to whether trading is on balance good or bad often depends on the kinds of items and the kinds of trades. In one kind of case, a local project may be in the common good—the expansion of an airport that serves as a national transportation hub, for example—but collective-action problems prevent members from voting for it. That is, no representative outside that district may be willing to commit his or her constituents to pay the costs of a project that would benefit them only in a diffuse or indirect way, especially if it appears that they can free ride on costs borne by other jurisdictions. In another kind of case, the institutional structure of a polity creates veto points that, to be surmounted to achieve democratic action, require side payments to those critically located at the veto points. In such cases, even though each side payment lacks a democratic justification, together they may be necessary to achieve broader goods. In this more difficult case, we need to judge which levels of rent-seeking required by the institutional design of checks and balances must be collectively

85. Gutmann and Thompson (2012, pp. 15–16).

86. Pennock (1970, p. 714).

borne to achieve a greater good. Similarly, we must balance the harms of expending public funds on projects that would not be voted by a majority without the logroll against the goods of enhancing mutual cooperation in ways that the health of the polity as a whole may require. Such judgments will be contingent on the circumstances.

Although there is much to be said against side payments normatively—logrolling legislators simply may be well-positioned rent-seekers for their constituents, for example—every textbook on negotiation recommends expanding the issue area in negotiation to include side payments of various sorts. Only through such an expansion can parties whose reservation stances otherwise do not create a zone of possible agreement find packages that will benefit everyone. The opposition to side payments arises primarily because they come at a cost to the taxpayer without the scrutiny—legislative or judicial— necessary to ascertain that they are in fact justified as part of agreements that improve on the status quo.[87] Side payments also may end up rendering a policy incoherent or ineffective with respect to its originally conceived purpose when the cost of the side payments spreads resources too thinly or the requirements of the side payments gut the logic of the policy or remove its teeth. Examples include features of the U.S. federal tax code that benefit special interests without any clear public benefit, and the banning of government price negotiation in the Medicare drug benefit.

We need more work on the norms of side payments; however, at present, we can say tentatively that the more the following conditions are achieved or approached, the better sidepayments conform to democratic norms:

—The side payments are transparent.

—The side payments survive cost-benefit scrutiny on the allocation itself; that is, there must be an overall benefit to the collectivity served as measured against the cost of providing that benefit.

—The rationale of the benefit provided by the side payment is justifiable to those affected (for example, taxpayers) who were not involved in the trade.

—The side payments are needed to negotiate an agreement.

87. Cf. the British system of members' Private Bills.

—The side payments are elements of a fair compromise or partially integrative agreement.

Conclusion

Democracy is, first and foremost, about the rule of the people. Yet the American political system was designed, first and foremost, to avoid tyranny, largely through the institutional device of separated powers. In consequence, the system empowers multiple actors to prevent collective action even when most of the people prefer a collective act and most would benefit. To the extent that the American political system empowers the people to rule through its most representative branch, Congress, it does so because the people's elected representatives *negotiate* across their many potential veto points with the aim of reaching agreement. To succeed in this goal, they must negotiate in ways that enable them together to discover and forge common interests, overlapping interests, convergent interests, and fair agreements. That is, they need to engage in *deliberative negotiation*.

Our goal in this chapter has been to develop the concept of deliberative negotiation, mindful not only of the harms of deadlock to democracy but also of the great extent to which the U.S. political system and many others depend on this class of agreement-seeking procedures to produce democratic action. We have clarified the concept with this context in mind. We also sought to identify features of institutions that support deliberative negotiation. We have focused on three of these—repeated interactions, closed-door interactions, and side payments—largely because they raise important normative issues in a democracy. We recognize that our application of the ideals of democracy to the question of negotiation comes at a relatively early stage of work on these issues and look forward to the contributions of future scholars.

Note: This chapter was written primarily by Mark Warren and Jane Mansbridge, drawing on the ideas and words of the other members of the Normative Working Group of the APSA Presidential Task Force on Negotiating Agreement in Politics: André Bächtiger, Maxwell A. Cameron, Simone Chambers, John Ferejohn, Alan Jacobs, Jack Knight, Daniel Naurin, Melissa Schwartzberg, Yael Tamir, Dennis

Thompson, and Melissa Williams. Members suggested many points and citations that appear here, improved the structure of the chapter, and drafted pieces of text. Daniel Naurin made particularly important contributions to table 5-1. Although each scholar would, if writing independently, put things in his or her own way, the chapter represents a direction of thought the members collectively endorse. We thank the University of British Columbia's Centre for the Study of Democratic Institutions for hosting and funding the workshop at which these ideas were expressed and discussed.

References

Albin, Cecilia. 2001. *Justice and Fairness in International Negotiation*. Cambridge University Press.

Applbaum, Arthur. 1998. *Ethics for Adversaries: The Morality of Roles in Public and Professional Life*. Princeton University Press.

Bachrach, Peter, and Morton S. Baratz. 1962. "Two Faces of Power." *American Political Science Review* 56 (4): 947–52.

———. 1963. "Decisions and Nondecisions: An Analytical Framework." *American Political Science Review* 57 (3): 632–42.

Bauhr, Monika, and Marcia Grimes. 2014. "Indignation or Resignation: The Implications of Transparency for Societal Accountability." *Governance: An International Journal of Policy, Administration, and Institutions* 27 (2): 291–320.

Beckmann, Neal W. 1977. *Negotiations: Principles and Techniques*. Lexington, MA: Lexington Books.

Beitz, Charles R. 1989. *Political Equality: An Essay in Democratic Theory*. Princeton University Press.

Besley, Timothy. 2006. *Principled Agents? The Political Economy of Good Government*. Oxford University Press.

Burnam, Jeffry. 2010. "The President and the Environment: A Reinterpretation of Neustadt's Theory of Presidential Leadership." *Congress & the Presidency* 37 (3): 302–22.

Burns, James MacGregor. 1963. *The Deadlock of Democracy*. Englewood Cliffs, NJ: Prentice Hall.

Carr, Albert Z. 1968. "Is Business Bluffing Ethical?" *Harvard Business Review*, January–February, 143–53.

Chambers, Simone. 2003. "Deliberative Democratic Theory." *Annual Review of Political Science* 6:307–26.

———. 2004. "Behind Closed Doors: Publicity, Secrecy, and the Quality of Deliberation." *Journal of Political Philosophy* 12 (4): 389–410.

———. 2009. "Rhetoric and the Public Sphere: Has Deliberative Democracy Abandoned Mass Democracy?" *Political Theory* 37 (3): 323–50.

Checkel, Jeffrey T. 2001. "Why Comply? Social Learning and European Identity Change." *International Organization* 55 (3): 553–88.

Cohen, Joshua. 1989. "Deliberation and Democratic Legitimacy." In *The Good Polity*, ed. Alan Hamlin and Philip Pettit. Oxford: Blackwell.

Cohen, Micah. 2013. "Popular Governors, and Prospects for 2016." *New York Times*, May 28. http://fivethirtyeight.blogs.nytimes.com/2013/05/28/popular-governors-and-prospects-for-2016/?_r=0.

De Fine Licht, Jenny. 2011. "Do We Really Want to Know? The Potentially Negative Effect of Transparency in Decision Making on Perceived Legitimacy." *Scandinavian Political Studies* 34 (3): 183–201.

De Fine Licht, Jenny, Daniel Naurin, Peter Esaiasson, and Mikael Gilljam. 2104. "Does Transparency Generate Legitimacy? An Experimental Study of Procedure Acceptance of Open- and Closed-Door Decision-Making." *Governance: An International Journal of Policy, Administration, and Institutions* 27 (1): 111–34.

Dryzek, John. 2000. *Deliberative Democracy and Beyond: Liberals, Critics, Contestations*. Oxford University Press.

Ehrenhalt, Alan. 1982. "Special Report: The Individualist Senate." *Congressional Quarterly* (September 4): 2175–82.

Elster, Jon. 1986. "The Market and the Forum: Three Varieties of Political Theory." In *Foundations of Social Choice Theory*, ed. Jon Elster. Cambridge University Press.

———. 1995. "Strategic Uses of Argument." In *Barriers to Conflict Resolution*, ed. Kenneth Arrow, Robert H. Mnookin, Lee Ross, Amos Tversky, and Robert Wilson. New York: W. W. Norton.

———. 1998. "Deliberation and Constitution Making." In *Deliberative Democracy*, ed. Jon Elster. Cambridge University Press.

———. 2000. "Arguing and Bargaining in Two Constituent Assemblies." *University of Pennsylvania Journal of Constitutional Law* 2:345–421.

Fearon, James D. 1999. "Electoral Accountability and the Control of Politicians: Selecting Good Types versus Sanctioning Poor Performance." In *Democracy, Accountability, and Representation*, ed. Adam Przeworski, Susan C. Stokes, and Bernard Manin. Cambridge University Press.

Fisher, Roger, William Ury, and Bruce Patton. 1991. *Getting to Yes: Negotiating Agreement without Giving In*. Boston: Houghton Mifflin.

Fishkin, James. 2005. "Defending Deliberation." *Critical Review of International Social and Political Philosophy* 8:71–78.

Florini, Ann. 2007. "Conclusions." In *The Right to Know: Transparency for an Open World*, ed. Ann Florini. Columbia University Press.

Follett, Mary Parker. [1925] 1942. "Constructive Conflict." In *Dynamic Administration: The Collected Papers of Mary Parker Follett*, ed. H. C. Metcalf and L. Urwick. New York: Harper.

Fumurescu, Alin. 2013. *Compromise: A Political and Philosophical History*. Cambridge University Press.

Fung, Archon. 2013. "The Principle of Affected Interests: An Interpretation and Defense." In *Representation: Elections and Beyond*, ed. Jack H. Nagel and Rogers M. Smith. University of Pennsylvania Press.

Goodin, Robert E. 2007. "Enfranchising All Affected Interests, and Its Alternatives." *Philosophy and Public Affairs* 35 (1): 40–68.

———. 2008. *Innovating Democracy: Democratic Theory and Practice after the Deliberative Turn*. Oxford University Press.

Grimmelikhuijsen, Stephan G. 2012. *Transparency and Trust: An Experimental Study of Online Disclosure and Trust in Government*. Utrecht University Press.

Groseclose, Tim, and Nolan McCarty. 2001. "The Politics of Blame: Bargaining before an Audience." *American Journal of Political Science* 45 (1): 100–19.

Gutmann, Amy, and Dennis Thompson. 1996. *Democracy and Disagreement*. Harvard University Press.

———. 2004. *Why Deliberative Democracy?* Princeton University Press.

————. 2012. *The Spirit of Compromise: Why Governing Demands It and Campaigning Undermines It*. Princeton University Press.

Habermas, Jürgen. [1962] 1989. *Structural Transformation of the Public Sphere: An Inquiry into a Category of Bourgeois Society*. Trans. Thomas Berger. MIT Press.

————. [1981] 1984, 1987. *The Theory of Communicative Action*, vols. 1 and 2. Trans. Thomas McCarthy. MIT Press.

————. [1992] 1996. *Between Facts and Norms*. Trans. William Rehg. MIT Press.

Hacker, Jacob, and Paul Pierson. 2010. *Winner-Take-All Politics: How Washington Made the Rich Richer—and Turned Its Back on the Middle Class*. New York: Simon and Schuster.

Jacobsson, Kerstin, and Asa Vifell. 2003. "Integration by Deliberation? On the Role of Committees in the Open Method of Coordination." Unpublished manuscript, State Center for Organized Research (SCORE), Stockholm, Sweden.

Kant, Immanuel. [1781] 1998. *Critique of Pure Reason*, ed. P. Guyer and A. Wood. Cambridge University Press.

————. [1795] 1970. "Perpetual Peace." In *Kant's Political Writings*, ed. Hans Reiss. Cambridge University Press.

King, Anthony. 1997. *Running Scared: Why America's Politicians Campaign Too Much and Govern Too Little*. New York: Simon and Schuster.

Knight, Jack, and James Johnson. 1994. "Aggregation and Deliberation: On the Possibility of Democratic Legitimacy." *Political Theory* 22 (2): 277–96.

————. 2011. *The Priority of Democracy: Political Consequences of Pragmatism*. New York: Sage.

Lax, David A., and James K. Sebenius. 1986. *The Manager as Negotiator*. New York: Free Press.

Lazarsfeld, Paul Felix, Bernard Berelson, and Hazel Gaudet. 1944. *The People's Choice: How the Voter Makes Up His Mind in a Presidential Campaign*. Columbia University Press.

Lessig, Lawrence. 2012. *Republic, Lost: How Money Corrupts Congress—and a Plan to Stop It*. New York: Twelve.

Lewis, Jeffrey. 1998. "Is the 'Hard Bargaining' Image of the Council Misleading? The Committee of Permanent Representatives and the

Local Elections Directive." *Journal of Common Market Studies* 36 (4): 479–504.

Lindstedt, Catharina, and Daniel Naurin. 2010. "Transparency Is Not Enough: Making Transparency Effective in Reducing Corruption." *International Political Science Review* 31 (3): 301–22.

List, Christian, Robert C. Luskin, James S. Fishkin, and Ian McLean. 2013. "Deliberation, Single-Peakedness, and the Possibility of Meaningful Democracy. Evidence from Deliberative Polls." *Journal of Politics* 75 (1): 80–95.

Manin, Bernard. 2005. "Democratic Deliberation: Why We Should Promote Debate Rather Than Discussion." Paper delivered at the Program in Ethics and Public Affairs Seminar, Princeton University, Princeton, NJ.

Mansbridge, Jane. 2009. "The 'Selection Model' of Political Representation." *The Journal of Political Philosophy* 17 (4): 369–98.

———. 2011. "On the Importance of Getting Things Done." *P.S.: Political Science and Politics* 45:1–8.

Mansbridge, Jane, with James Bohman, Simone Chambers, David Estlund, Andreas Føllesdal, Archon Fung, Cristina Lafont, Bernard Manin, and José Luis Martí. 2010. "The Place of Self-Interest and the Role of Power in Deliberative Democracy." *Journal of Political Philosophy* 18 (1): 64–100.

Menkel-Meadow, Carrie, and Michael Wheeler. 2004. *What's Fair: Ethics for Negotiators*. San Francisco: Jossey-Bass.

Morgenthau, Hans. 1950. *Politics among Nations*. New York: Alfred A. Knopf.

Mussolini, Benito. [1932] 1935. "The Doctrine of Fascism." In *Fascism: Doctrine and Institutions*. Rome: Ardita Publishers, pp. 7–42.

Nagel, Jack. 1975. *A Descriptive Analysis of Power*. Yale University Press.

Naurin, Daniel. 2007a. "Backstage Behavior? Lobbyists in Public and Private Settings in Sweden and the European Union." *Comparative Politics* 39 (2): 209–28.

———. 2007b. *Deliberation behind Closed Doors: Transparency and Lobbying in the European Union*. Colchester, UK: ECPR Press.

———. 2013. "Why Publishing Even More Documents Will Not Make the Council a Fully Transparent Legislature." Paper presented at the conference on "Transparency and Access to the Records and

Archives of the EU Institutions," Historical Archives of the European Union, Florence, January 25.

Neumann, Thore, and Bruno Simma. 2013. "Transparency in International Adjudication." In *Transparency in International Law*, ed. Andrea Bianchi and Anne Peters. Cambridge University Press.

Newport, Frank. 2013. "Congressional Approval Sinks to Record Low." Princeton, NJ: Gallup Organization. Press release of November 13, 2013. www.gallup.com/poll/165809/congressional-approval-sinks-record-low.aspx?version=print.

Ober, Josiah. 2008. "The Original Meaning of 'Democracy': Capacity to Do Things, Not Majority Rule." *Constellations* 15 (1): 3–9.

Odell, John S. 2012. "Negotiation and Bargaining." In *Handbook of International Relations*, ed. Walter Carlsnaes, Thomas Risse, and Beth A. Simmons. London: Sage.

Ornstein, Norman, and Thomas Mann. 2000. *The Permanent Campaign and Its Future*. Washington, DC: American Enterprise Institute.

Pedrini, Seraina, André Bächtiger, and Marco R. Steenbergen. 2013. "Deliberative Inclusion of Minorities: Patterns of Reciprocity among Linguistic Groups in Switzerland." *European Political Science Review* 5:483–512.

Pennock, J. Roland. 1970. "The 'Pork Barrel' and Majority Rule." *Journal of Politics* 32:709–16.

Peters, Anne. 2013. "Towards Transparency as a Global Norm." In *Transparency in International Law*, ed. Andrea Bianchi and Anne Peters. Cambridge University Press.

Pruitt, Dean G. 1983. "Achieving Integrative Agreements." In *Negotiating in Organizations*, ed. Max H. Bazerman and Roy J. LeWicki. Beverly Hills, CA: Sage.

Przeworski, Adam. 1998. "Deliberation and Ideological Domination." In *Deliberative Democracy*, ed. Jon Elster. Cambridge University Press.

Putnam, Robert D. 1988. "Diplomacy and Domestic Politics: The Logic of Two-Level Games." *International Organization* 42 (3): 427–60.

Rae, Douglas W. 1975. "The Limits of Consensual Decision." *American Political Science Review* 69 (4): 1270–94.

Raiffa, Howard. 1982. *The Art and Science of Negotiation*. Harvard University Press.

Rawls, John. 1971. *A Theory of Justice*. Harvard University Press.

———. 2001. *Justice as Fairness: A Restatement*. Harvard University Press.

Richardson, Henry S. 2002. *Democratic Autonomy: Public Reasoning about the Ends of Policy*. Oxford University Press.

Schumpeter, Joseph A. [1942] 1962. *Capitalism, Socialism and Democracy*. New York: Harper and Row.

Schwartzberg, Melissa. 2013. *Counting the Many*. Cambridge University Press.

Shapiro, Ian. 2003. *The State of Democratic Theory*. Princeton University Press.

Sherif, Muzafer, O. J. Harvey, B. Jack White, William R. Hood, Carolyn W. Sherif. 1961. *Intergroup Conflict and Cooperation: The Robbers Cave Experiment*. Norman, OK: University Book Exchange.

Singh, Shekar. 2007. "India: Grassroots Initiatives." In *The Right to Know: Transparency for an Open World*, ed. Ann Florini. Columbia University Press.

Stasavage, David. 2004. "Open-Door or Closed-Door? Transparency in Domestic and International Bargaining." *International Organization* 58 (4): 667–703.

Steiner, Jürg, André Bächtiger, Markus Spörndli, and Marco R. Steenbergen. 2004. *Deliberative Politics in Action: Analysing Parliamentary Discourse*. Cambridge University Press.

Stiglitz, Joseph. 1999. "On Liberty, the Right to Know, and Public Discourse: The Role of Transparency in Public Life." In *Globalizing Rights, The Oxford Amnesty Lectures 1999*, ed. Matthew Gibney. Oxford University Press.

Stokes, Susan. 1998. "Pathologies of Deliberation." In *Deliberative Democracy*, ed. Jon Elster. Cambridge University Press.

Sunstein, Cass R. 1988. "Beyond the Republican Revival." *Yale Law Journal* 97 (8): 1539–90.

Thompson, Dennis F. 1995. *Ethics in Congress: From Individual to Institutional Corruption*. Brookings Institution Press.

———. 1999. "Democratic Secrecy." *Political Science Quarterly* 114 (2): 184–85.

———. 2002. *Just Elections: Creating a Fair Electoral Process in the United States*. University of Chicago Press.

Thompson, Leigh, and Dennis Hrebec. 1996. "Lose-Lose Agreements in Interdependent Decision Making." *Psychological Bulletin* 120 (3): 396–409.

Thomson, Robert. 2011. *Resolving Controversy in the European Union: Legislative Decision-Making before and after Enlargement.* Cambridge University Press.

Ulbert, Cornelia, and Thomas Risse. 2005. "Deliberately Changing the Discourse: What Does Make Arguing Effective?" *Acta Politica* 40:351–67.

United States Constitutional Convention. 1937. *The Records of the Federal Convention of 1787*, ed. Max Ferrand. 3 vols. Yale University Press.

Van Parijs, Philippe. 2012. "What Makes a Good Compromise?" *Government and Opposition* 47 (3): 466–80.

Wallace, Helen. 2002. "The Council: An Institutional Chameleon." *Governance* 15 (3): 325–344.

Walton, Richard E., and Robert B. McKersie. 1965. *A Behavioral Theory of Labor Negotiations.* Ithaca, NY: Cornell University Press.

Warren, Mark E. 1999. "Democratic Theory and Trust." In *Democracy and Trust*, ed. Mark E. Warren. New York: Cambridge University Press, pp. 310–45.

Waxman, Henry, with Joshua Green. 2009. *The Waxman Report: How Congress Really Works.* New York: Twelve.

Wetlaufer, Gerald B. 1996. "The Limits of Integrative Bargaining." *Georgetown Law Journal* 85 (2): 369–94.

White, James J. 1980. "Machiavelli and the Bar: Ethical Limitations on Lying in Negotiation." *American Bar Foundation Research Journal* 4:926–38.

Young, Iris Marion. 2000. *Inclusion and Democracy.* Oxford University Press.

Part III

INSTITUTIONS
AND RULES
OF COLLECTIVE
POLITICAL
ENGAGEMENT

CHAPTER SIX

Conditions for Successful Negotiation

Lessons from Europe

CATHIE JO MARTIN

The American legislative process today seems incapable of solving a variety of vexing collective problems, which often require the payment of short- and medium-term costs for long-term gains. We are burdening our children with a lifetime of public debt because we cannot meet our current collective financial obligations. We face a future of water in all the wrong places, with likely shortages of potable drinking water even while rising seas destroy our coastal communities. Our education system is largely failing the 25 percent of America's children who live in poverty, yet a shortage of skilled workers continues to bedevil employers.

Our contemporary legislative failures to negotiate policy solutions present something of a mystery, when compared with past congressional performance and the practices of other advanced democracies. Although our separated powers doctrine undoubtedly contributes to constraining congressional action, many countries with severe institutional hurdles to easy majoritarian rule still produce political deals. This chapter explores how political actors in other countries find the means to engage in deliberative negotiations that produce agreements on collectively beneficial policy solutions and, thereby, explains the enormous disconnects between foreign and domestic experiences, and past and present practices in the United States. We briefly review obstacles to deliberative negotiation and the production of collective goods, such as negotiation myopia and distributional conflicts. We then consider how rules and institutions for collective political engagement—that is, the practices governing how people come together to negotiate political deals—help overcome these obstacles and shape actors' incentives for cooperation. We analyze particularly the positive effects on negotiation of a careful incorporation of technical expertise, repeated interactions, penalty defaults, and relative autonomy in private meetings. These distinctive rules of collective engagement not only help parties reach agreement but also, when combined with broadening the scope of representation, can have positive impacts on patterns of democratic struggle.

Some countries rely more extensively on cooperation, compromise, and negotiating to agreement in their daily practice of politics because their political institutions incorporate these rules of collective engagement as a matter of course. For example, proportional electoral systems with multiple parties produce greater incentives for cooperation than winner-take-all, majoritarian systems because coalitions of parties to form governments require negotiation and cooperation. The macro-corporatist organization of societal interests also fosters cooperative capacities more than pluralist systems of interest intermediation do because macro-corporatism routinely brings together business and labor groups to deliberate policy problems (Martin and Swank 2008, 2012). Thus, these countries have greater *needs* for cooperation that make them organize and greater *capacities* for deliberative negotiations to meet these needs (Lijphart 2012).

Even countries that lack coordinating institutions may adopt rules of collective engagement that are conducive to negotiation; and this adoption may alter the logic of how interests come together to solve their political problems, to engage in deliberative negotiations, and to produce compromises that previously seemed beyond their capacities. Although countries develop certain characteristic styles of collective decisionmaking with varying potential for successful negotiation, these styles are far from immutable because institutional effects are neither completely deterministic nor constant. Deliberative negotiation may become more possible with the adoption of certain rules of engagement, just as stalemate periodically may develop even when countries normally rely on high levels of deliberative negotiation. This is why policymaking processes sometimes surprise us, and these rules of engagement may offer inspiration for expanding the political openings for negotiated reforms.

Negotiation is not the cure-all for all conflicts: distributive battles and conflicting interests may drive an immutable wedge between parties, destroying any zone of possible agreement. Significant redistribution to redress fundamental inequities is unlikely to appeal to elites who benefited from the unequal distribution of resources. The class injustices that fueled the French Revolution were unlikely to have been negotiated away. Another problem with negotiation as a decision-making mechanism is that negotiating partners may hold strongly opposing beliefs, competing conceptions of equality and justice, and different cognitive assessments of problems and viable solutions. Battles over the right to an abortion reflect fundamentally different worldviews about issues ranging from the origins of life to the appropriate role of women in the workforce. These deeply held ideological convictions may be more difficult to negotiate than less value-laden, economic claims.[1]

Politics is at least a two-level game and sometimes a three-level game (see chapter 5), with representatives first negotiating with one another and then with their own multiple constituencies. In this process, the legislators might well endorse agreements that benefit their core constituents while leaving less powerful groups "out in the cold" (Page and Jacobs 2009). Certainly, any set of institutions that promotes deliberative negotiation must also build in safeguards against its abuses. Yet the negotiating practices of representatives also may have a positive impact on collective social identities: citizens who discern their representatives as engaging in deliberative negotiations may become more trusting of government and better able to perceive their commonalities of interest. As chapter 5 discusses, thoughtful action based on public support tends to produce legitimacy. Thus, our work is driven by a normative ambition: to use our knowledge about

1. See Luker (1984). See also the discussion of abortion in chapter 5 in this report.

the impacts of institutions and procedural rules on negotiation to improve politics in the real world.

Negotiation Myopia and Problems of Collective Action

Deliberative negotiations within government are both necessary and difficult to achieve because of the nature of collective (or free-access) goods, which offer benefits to individuals that are not related to their contribution to the costs of the goods (Ostrom 1990). When collective goods impose concentrated costs on a subset of producer interests but offer only diffuse benefits to citizens, those issues are often subject to political capture by those producer interests (Lowi 1964). Policies with strong distributive consequences are thus more difficult to pass than policies in which the zero-sum character of the distribution is more muted. The problems of producing a collective good become magnified when the good in question will not materialize until sometime in the future. Whereas it is relatively easy to pass legislation when one realizes the benefits of a collective good in the short term but pays for those goods in the long term, other issues such as pension reform require short- or medium-term contributions for long-term gains and are more difficult to address (Jacobs 2011).

Deliberative negotiations also are constrained because the human brain falls prey to several forms of *negotiation myopia*, a constellation of nearsighted cognitive, psychological, and strategic mistakes that stand in the way of achieving agreement (see chapter 4 for a detailed discussion of these forms of myopia). The forms of myopia that seduce us into suboptimal deals fall into several categories, related to our *perspective* of self in relation to other, the *scope* of our goals, and our capacities to grasp longer and more complex periods of *time*. One type of myopia, *self-serving bias*, distorts our *perspective* of self in relation to others and stems from our tendency to interpret events from a vantage that places us in a good light, relies on our own selective memories, and holds our beliefs to be objective truths. This impulse is exacerbated by *information asymmetry* and the difficulties of *perspective taking*. This myopic self-focus may blind us to the perspectives of others, some of which may point to action benefiting a larger group of interests, often at minor discomfort to ourselves.

A second type of myopia narrows the *scope* of our goals; for example, a *fixed-pie bias* makes us focus on claiming value rather than creating value and worry more about the *redistributive allocation of benefits* rather than the expansion of the desired outcome. In a classic sibling-rivalry problem, the zero-sum competition for benefits leads the parties to forget that together they may bring in new issues, "expand the pie," maximize shared interests, and jointly achieve more of their desired ends. Scholars demonstrate in laboratory settings that most people express an irrational *loss aversion*: that is, even when the expected gain is greater than a possible loss, participants are unwilling to risk losing ground. The impulse for *reactive devaluation* also leads people to mistake their interests in negotiation and make faulty inferences about the motives of the other party. When offered a unilateral deal, they tend to discount it and try to bargain up, and a concession offered frequently is valued less than a concession withheld.

Third, we may suffer from a *time* myopia that diminishes our capacities for long-term thinking, our material incentives for "saving for a rainy day," and our abilities to consider second- and third-order effects. Public-policy costs and benefits often are structured to exacerbate the problem because few want to make short-term investments in exchange for risky, long-term rewards (Jacobs 2011, p. 52). Time myopia may reinforce the aversion of producer groups to bearing short-term costs (concentrated on them) for long-term collective gain, and producer groups often have disproportionate influence in legislative processes.

Rules of Engagement and Deliberative Negotiation

When the problems of reaching a political settlement are caused by negotiation myopia, the adoption of certain collective rules of engagement may influence the preferences of political actors and facilitate deliberative negotiation (see chapter 5).[2] Particularly important are the

---

2. Deliberative negotiation is characterized by mutual justification, respect, and the search for fair terms of interaction and outcomes. Such negotiations, parts of which are grounded in a mutual search for the common good, often enable participants to solve creatively a problem with an integrative (or partially integrative) solution, in which both sides gain something of what they actually want, or create a fair compromise. See also Mansbridge (2010).

use of *nonpartisan third-party experts* (often in the form of fact-finding bodies), *repeated interactions* among negotiators, *penalty defaults*, and *private meetings* for deliberations (balanced with some transparency to ensure democratic accountability).[3]

First, procedural rules and norms that include a strong role for *nonpartisan third-party experts* may contribute to deliberative negotiation because the creation of an authoritative body of expertise and evidence can discipline political debate and push it in a deliberative direction. Countries' "knowledge regimes" may include the use of fact-finding bodies, peer review, and performance benchmarking against agreed indicators, and these tools can define problems and solutions in more neutral, mutually acceptable terms (Blyth 2002; Campbell and Pedersen, 2014; Schmidt 2009). These bodies may be particularly helpful in moving the negotiating partners beyond the ideological definition of issues along left-right cleavages.

The Italian pension reform in 1995 constitutes an instance in which the introduction of new rules of engagement—including the introduction of greater technical expertise and the threat of state action in response to nonaction by labor—altered the negotiation processes between the state and societal actors and made possible a value-adding policy reform. Italian politics is often marked by significant distributive conflicts due to its corrupt and "particularistic" parties, which attract constituents with narrowly focused material payments, and its weak industrial relations organizations. The costly, unequal, and Byzantine Italian pensions were one of the most problem-ridden systems in Europe, yet the Italian pension reform implemented a set of painful changes and structural innovations that ameliorated many of the long-term problems of the pension system. Crucially, government reformers made these changes with the full support of and participation by the unions, which offered significant input to the design of the reforms (Baccaro 2002).

A new technocratic government was able to pass the expansive pension reform by setting up a dialogue with labor in which technical

3. Chapter 5 expands on the uses of these institutions and also on their normative pros and cons. It argues, for example, that *transparency in rationale* (giving reasons for a policy) can often do the same positive work as *transparency in process* (allowing audiences into the negotiating room) without the negative effects on deliberative negotiation.

expertise was the object of exchange. In 1994, the Berlusconi-led government attempted to impose unilateral pension cuts, but the prime minister did not appear to be a trustworthy negotiating partner and the reforms were met with a general strike by protesting workers. Berlusconi was forced to resign; however, the new government under the leadership of Lamberto Dini offered a more trustworthy negotiating partner and acted as a catalyst to organize institutional change. Dini began a dialogue with labor and, initially, business to launch the pension reform, and he consulted with unions to develop fast-track reform mechanisms. The reforms were not expected to be popular because they tightened the links between contributions and benefits in a way that mimicked a funded plan and made early retirement more difficult. In the negotiations with labor, technical expertise played a major role. Union leaders took a tentative reform plan to assemblies of workers within plants and engaged in extensive explanation of the technical-rational needs for pension reform. When given an opportunity to take a more proactive role, the unions struggled to overcome internal divisions, adopted new processes of open deliberation, and set limits on amendments to the reform proposal. Great efforts were made to explain the pension issues to the rank and file, and workers were given the right to vote in a referendum on the pension reform, which augmented the democratic legitimacy of the reform (Baccaro 2002, pp. 419–22).

A second rule for collective engagement that is conducive to deliberative negotiation is to bring together participants in *repeated interactions*. Repeated interactions among parties may be built into institutions for long-term processes of cooperation; these help build collective understandings, make parties aware of one another's perspectives, encourage a longer time perspective, and create trust sufficient to support risky but collectively beneficial choices. Such repeated interactions also promote honesty in communication and other trustworthy behaviors because the participants anticipate punishment for dishonesty at future meetings.

Policymaking within the European Union (EU) offers a compelling example of the use of repeated interactions to improve negotiating capacities because governance and regulation have expanded through a recursive process of framework rule making and revision. Framework goals are set at the EU level, and individual units are allowed considerable discretion in developing and implementing the programs to achieve these goals; however, lower-level decisionmakers also participate in reviewing, rethinking, and renegotiating practices. Thus, revision happens without central steering, and these governance processes allow for the extension of regulation into new issue areas and across the vastly different institutional terrains found among the national members. Participants develop commonly agreed-on metrics or indicators for measuring progress toward joint objectives; however, various permutations are possible, implementation is decentralized, participants routinely compare their governing experiences, and actors converge on those that best serve their purposes. The ongoing adjustment through a process of deliberation, monitoring, and peer review of alternative experiences fosters the emergence of a multiplicity of political best practices. Lacking the standard command-and-control, top-down regulatory processes, this process of "experimentalist governance" also offers the necessary flexibility to respond to the rapid changes and uncertainty characteristic of twenty-first-century life (Sabel and Zeitlin 2010).[4] The "recursive processes" of decisionmaking in experimentalist governance led to a high level of consensus in European food-safety policies as repeated episodes of deliberation helped build consensus about common interests among actors in the foodstuffs sector as well as mechanisms for meeting challenges to those interests (Joerges and Neyer 1997, p. 609).

4. Moravcsik suggests that the EU has an easier political mandate because many issues are preapproved by members' domestic legislatures and the supranational deliberations may proceed on a faster track. Countries delegate a small subset of issues to the EU, which often excludes questions of redistribution and enjoys the near-unanimous approval of member countries' heads of state. Moreover, the issues of the EU are selected because they are linked to the common interests of the member states and, above all, the internal market, whereas more contentious issues such as fiscal policy and redistributive policy are left largely to the member states (Moravcsik 2005). Sabel and Zeitlin, however, suggest that many policy areas are potentially quite contentious—for example, environment, energy, telecommunications, finance, and data privacy. Moreover, distributive agenda items within the EU almost always have redistributive elements— agricultural regulations and subsidies, for example—and many of the pressing concerns of the EU are rooted in cultural conflicts (for example, immigration) that inspire strong emotional responses.

Third, the provision by external agents of *penalty defaults*—which include deadlines, threats of exclusion from the table, and other action-forcing rules (that is, external conditionalities)—also may facilitate positive negotiation processes and outcomes. These defaults may work against the use of deceptive strategies and may be structured to distribute costs over the medium term for long-run social benefits. Penalty defaults could simply produce a minimally utility enhancing deal; for example, actors might impose long-term costs for short-term benefits, thereby benefiting all participants at the table but harming future generations and others not represented in the negotiations. Yet these defaults also might be structured to motivate processes and decisions that are more other regarding, pie expanding, and long term. Penalty defaults are not always successful. For example, the January 2013 "fiscal cliff" in the U.S. Congress represented a classic effort to force negotiating partners to come to a negotiated pact; these efforts fell apart primarily because the negotiators' allegiance to their partisan allies and the strategic benefits of their position trumped their desire to negotiate solutions. Pressing in the other direction, bodies such as the European Commission can use their invitational discretion to punish noncooperative behavior, although actors also can "forum-shop" to avoid the effects of that sanction (Carpenter 2001; Woll 2008).

The threat of the consequences of nonaction worked in favor of an integrative solution in the Canadian pension reform negotiated in the mid-1990s. Under the law, two-thirds of the provinces representing two-thirds of Canada's population would have to agree to any reform, and the provinces had widely differing preferences over pension policy. Whereas Ontario was most interested in keeping payroll taxes as low as possible, Quebec and other provinces could be expected to fight to maintain benefits at current levels. Although stalemate appeared likely, the costs of inaction were exceedingly high: if nothing were done, Canada's aging population would automatically force either a near tripling of tax rates in the next few decades or deep cuts in benefits. Because all provinces viewed this default outcome as unacceptable, they were willing to accept a creative integrative solution: a reform that immediately doubled the payroll tax and modestly trimmed benefits to build up a fund that would be professionally invested in private markets. The earnings from the fund, in turn, would stabilize both tax and benefit rates over the long run. Although this costly reform was not any stakeholder's first choice, the unacceptable costs of inaction helped create agreement on an intertemporal solution that would expand the long-term pie (Jacobs 2008).

Fourth, deliberative negotiation may be aided by procedural rules and norms that use *closed-door private meetings* to offer protection from the media, give negotiators more leeway to communicate freely, and enable participants to respond more positively to the communications of others. Closed-door protection from media glare and lobbyist pressures allows legislators to trade public posturing for private deliberation, especially when the patterns of deliberation allow for social-learning feedback. Although transparency often is defended as guaranteeing political legitimacy, it is not always the case. For example, gridlock in U.S. Congress has been exacerbated by the "sunshine laws," that opened up committee deliberation to the public but also to lobbyists and other special interests. Adding openness in this instance has not increased legitimacy.

At the same time, transparency has many democratic virtues. There is a tension between the privacy needed to promote deliberative negotiation and the openness needed for some forms of accountability (see chapter 5). Transparency in certain respects is essential to "dynamic accountability" because it greatly enhances the capacities of expert participants to make superior judgment calls, to explain political decisions to the public, and to build support for these pacts over the long term (Sabel and Zeitlin 2010). Moreover, although elite decisionmaking may produce greater efficiency, it also may contribute to a deficit of legitimacy when power shifts to undemocratic institutions, such as the European Commission (Medrano 2003). The EU provides an example of trade-offs among procedures to enhance successful negotiations. Certain macro institutions make negotiations structurally somewhat easier because privacy is more readily assured on a number of levels. For example, informal "trialogues" rely heavily on privacy, when the Council, European Parliament, and Commission come together behind closed doors to engage in informal deliberations in advance of formal political decisionmaking (Reh 2012).

Cross-National Differences in the Needs
and Capacities for Negotiation

Advanced industrial democracies face broadly similar challenges; however, countries diverge significantly in their capacities to negotiate major, sustainable social and economic reforms. Some countries have stronger political institutional needs, as well as capacities for cooperation and consensual negotiation, than other countries do. We suggest that rules of engagement are embedded in countries' political institutions and contribute to their characteristic governing styles. This section explores the impacts of political institutions on capacities for deliberative negotiation and identifies clusters of national models according to their institutional needs and capacities for negotiation. These insights locate the United States in comparative perspective and explain why countries periodically act against type when they adopt rules of engagement that deviate from their "politics as usual."

Various political systems have different *needs* for consensual negotiation owing to the size of the majorities that are necessary to pass legislation and the choices about whose interests should rule. Governments in Europe have gravitated toward two models. Some countries adopt the Westminster model, in which democratic polity is driven by the will of the majority of the people through majoritarian rule. Other countries adopt the consensus model, in which efforts are made to incorporate as many people as possible into a governing coalition. The choice of majoritarian rule versus consensual rule reflects the constitutional design of government and the number of "veto points," which constitute the points at which actors have formal authority to block legislative change. Consensus countries have a high number of veto points (due to the horizontal or vertical dispersion of power within government) and require the inclusion of a larger proportion of societal interests in the governing coalition. Majoritarian countries of the Westminster type have a lower number of veto points; concentrate governmental authority in a strong, centralized executive controlled by a single body; and may pass legislation with simple majorities (Lipjhart 2012).

For example, a presidential system with its separated powers has more veto points than a parliamentary system because in the latter, the executive is chosen by and comes from the same party as the parliament. Parliamentary systems constrain conflict between the executive and legislative branches, and parliamentary leaders have recourse to "deadlock-breaking devices" (that is, votes of no confidence and new elections), which make it more difficult for special interests to capture the policymaking process. In presidential systems, the legislature and the president are elected independently (often bringing different parties to office) and they have separated but overlapping powers, motivating actors in each branch to guard jealously their institutional prerogatives (Cox and McCubbins 1997; Linz 1990; Shugart and Carey 1992; Stepan and Skach 1993, pp. 18, 3).

Federal systems of government also have more veto points than unitary systems do because formal authority is shared by actors at diverse levels (Bednar et. al. 1996). Compared with the majoritarian governance model, federalism creates a "joint-decision trap" that may stop governmental action. Government leaders at subnational levels have incentives to block policy reforms that have overall advantageous but regionally uneven impacts, or to lobby for policies with sharply drawn winners and losers. In contrast, majoritarian, unitary governance must reconcile the needs of a broader spectrum of citizens and create more universalistic policy initiatives (Scharpf 1988).

Proponents of the majoritarian Westminster model believe that governments with a higher number of veto points will be confronted with greater obstacles to policy reforms and that negotiation is a second-best alternative to straightforward majority rule (Cutler 1980). Proponents of the consensus model point to its positive impacts on democratic governance by forcing parties to learn to negotiate, increasing the number of enduring policy compromises and ultimately enhancing the stability of governing systems. In this argument, placing many veto points in the system privileges the public interest by reducing the chances that any special-interest measure will make it through the battery of obstacles (Cox and McCubbins 1997, pp. 5–6; Goodin 1996; Tsebelis 1995).

We suggest that consensus-model countries not only have greater *needs* for negotiation; they also have stronger *capacities* for negotiation because their governing institutions incorporate rules of engagement that suppress negotiation myopia. Two institutions in particular endow consensus-model countries with greater capacities for deliberative negotiation: proportional party systems and macrocorporatist institutions for interest intermediation.

First, multiparty systems with proportional-representation electoral rules foster greater incentives and capacities for cooperation than two-party systems with majoritarian rule do. Multiparty systems with proportional electoral rules have a much higher coverage of specific groups than two-party systems; therefore, significant class interests—for example, employers, workers, and farmers—are likely to belong to a single party. Party identities are based on ideological party platforms and reflect attention on common goals. They encourage repeated interactions among their active members because they are dedicated to the interests of their core constituents, do not poach voters from other parties, and do not constantly change their positions to compete for the median voter. These parties also foster cooperation within their membership because they can make credible commitments to follow through on long-term policy promises that serve as mandates for action.

Proportional systems also include greater incentives for cooperation among competing parties because coalition governments are the norm in multiparty systems. Countries with proportional representation utilize expert commissions of diverse interests to develop multipartisan policy solutions and incorporate repeated interactions among parties within successive coalition governments. The need to form a coalition to govern constitutes a mandate for action. Because parties frequently cooperate through successive electoral cycles, public-policy outcomes tend to be more stable and enduring than in majoritarian, two-party systems (Boix 2003; Cusack, Iversen, and Soskice 2007; Kitschelt 1999).[5]

In contrast, catchall parties in two-party systems integrate varied constituency groups under the partisan umbrella, and the major parties vie for the median voter; consequently, their platforms frequently fluctuate and members feel less confidence in their political representation. In two-party systems, even parties that fulfill promises to their members may be voted out of office in the next election, and all gains

5. We note, however, that in presidential (as opposed to parliamentary) proportional systems such as those found in many Latin American countries, parties can more easily engage in deadlock strategies (Cox and McCubbins 1997). Bellamy (2012) pointed out that a party's core constituents may view cooperation with competing parties as disloyal. Yet it is possible that negotiations grounded in a mutual search for value-creating outcomes might be viewed more favorably than shallow bargaining.

may be lost in a system with little continuity across governments (Downs [1957] 2001). Moreover, in contrast to the "programmatic" parties found in multiparty systems, "particularistic" parties in majoritarian systems are more likely to distribute policy benefits for patronage reasons; this process fragments benefits and erodes the legitimacy of social policies (Lynch 2006).

Second, consensus-model countries have developed stronger societal organizations for industrial relations and interest-group representation than majoritarian countries: "pluralist" interest-group and industrial relations systems tend to be found in majoritarian countries, whereas "corporatist" systems are found in consensus-model countries. The rules of engagement found in consensus-model systems for industrial relations and interest-group representation tend to diminish negotiation myopia and enhance the capacities for deliberative negotiation. These robust societal vehicles offer citizens input into policymaking, help overcome the many veto points in these systems, and provide the political will for reform. The ideal types of pluralist and corporatist systems differ in the nature of the groups representing the core economic actors, the role of these groups in policymaking, and the capacities of these groups for coordination and deliberative negotiation.[6]

Corporatist industrial relations systems organizing business and labor interests in consensus-model countries are functionally specific (that is, each group represents one segment of the economy), are hier-

---

6. This bimodal view of nations—those with and without high levels of coordination—masks the fact that coordination can occur at various levels of society. Coordination can transpire through largely private relations between industry-level associations and unions or can entail a strong role for government in sustaining collective bargaining and interest intermediation through tripartite policymaking channels (Martin and Thelen 2007; Martin and Swank 2012; see also Hicks and Kenworthy 1998). Thus, we have elsewhere identified a third type of industrial-relations system, "sectoral cooperation," which entails coordination among firms and workers at a more intermediate level. This may include cooperation across enterprises that is less national in focus and that evolves without direct, ongoing state participation (Martin and Swank 2012). This form of coordination includes tightly coordinated connections among purchasers and suppliers, cooperation among competing firms within the same industrial sector for training or for research and development, long-term relations between firms and investors, teamwork-based production at the firm level, and intrafirm departments working in multidivisional project teams.

archical (that is, lower-level groups are members of a centralized peak association), and are given the formal authority to represent their members in policymaking processes. The encompassing groups convene a broad range of interests, construct collective identities among their members, and aggregate interests at a more universal level. The groups have cognitive impacts on their members' preferences because they educate their members about political problems and their solutions, and more encompassing organizations tend to draw their members' attention to broader, longer-term collective benefits. Encompassing organizations also reinforce norms of trust and social partnership. Peak associations negotiate public policy in collective-bargaining forums and in tripartite commissions set up under the auspices of ministries; consequently, many more political decisions are made in nonlegislative channels than in the United States, where policies are typically made by Congress. In corporatist systems, strong stakeholders give coherence to policymaking and add to the society's capacities to overcome party fragmentation; moreover, firms and workers are bound to the decisions negotiated by their groups (Crouch 1993; Hicks and Kenworthy 1998; Katzenstein 1985; Martin and Swank 2004; Rothstein 2000; Streeck 1992, pp. 265–84; Visser and Hemerijck 1997; Wilensky 1976).

In pluralist systems (for example, the United States), firms and workers belong to multiple groups, the groups are narrow in scope and overlap in function, and no single centralized peak association aggregates the broad interests of members. These pluralist interest groups tend to concentrate on the particularistic self-interests of their members, and both employers and workers are more divided than in countries with encompassing associations to aggregate interests.[7] General Motors may belong to the Automobile Manufacturers' Association, the National Association of Manufacturers, and the Chamber

7. This is not to say that business interests are a priori less diverse in countries with a high level of corporate organization; indeed, significant material cleavages divide employers in all advanced, industrialized countries that are related to the firm's size, labor intensity of the production process, exposure to foreign trade, skill level of the workers, and so forth (Gourevitch 1978; Kurth 1979). But the aggregation at a higher level allows participants to find common ground more easily, for example, in accepting wage or income restraints to achieve price stability or to create policies for skills-upgrading, human capital development, and solidarity (Martin 2000; Streeck 1992; Visser and Hemerijck 1997).

of Commerce, and although the auto association has a more limited focus than the other two, all three of these groups do more or less the same thing. Thus, pluralist groups tend to compete with one another for members, are highly risk adverse, and have a limited capacity to foster cooperation (Martin 2000).

Repeated interactions in the ongoing policy discussions among labor, business, and government bureaucrats foster a shared understanding of policy problems and commonly agreed-on perceptions of technical solutions. Because these forums are outside of the legislative process, they enjoy greater privacy; moreover, the threat of legislative action contingent on the breakdown of negotiations among the social partners constitutes a penalty default with an incentive for action. Repeated corporatist patterns of interaction create a positive-sum game for business and labor in tripartite or collective-bargaining settings: because the groups foster a long-term perspective and guarantee compliance, each side is more willing to take positions that will benefit the broader economy. Interests that are organized in a more encompassing manner are also more likely to demand long-term policy solutions because it is more difficult for any single group to redistribute resources from other segments of society, and encompassing organizations internalize long-run social problems. If the encompassing interest groups are concerned that the long-term costs of not resolving a problem are sufficiently high, they may generate the political will necessary for imposing short-term sacrifices to invest in longterm solutions for society. As a result of many of these mechanisms, countries with encompassing employers' associations have higher levels of spending on the welfare state, more positive views toward government, and a greater willingness of citizens and interest groups to accept negotiated bargains favoring longer-term, pie-expanding solutions (Jacobs 2008; Martin and Swank 2004, 2012).

The two institutions of political parties and societal organization highlighted herein are related because different patterns of party competition influenced the emergence of corporatist and pluralist systems of industrial relations at the dawn of the twentieth century. Employers across industrialized countries sought similar national industrialdevelopment policies, labor-market coordination, and the right to selfregulation to compete more successfully in international markets and to manage growing industrial unrest. However, politicians in two-party and multiparty systems had different views about allowing stakeholders in business and labor to negotiate public policies. Fearful of growing democratization, conservative party leaders in countries with multiple parties helped create strong, encompassing industrial relations institutions with expansive powers of self-regulation because the leaders feared that labor and farmer parties might form parliamentary coalitions against them. They reasoned that their business constituents could secure more favorable policy outcomes in direct negotiations with workers than through legislative processes. In time, the resulting high levels of labor-market coordination inspired stronger motives for successful negotiation between business and labor. The mandates for action coming from the social partners also strengthened the politicians' incentives for successful negotiation. In contrast, politicians in two-party systems jealously held on to their prerogatives over policymaking because they anticipated ongoing electoral contention. As a consequence, employers and workers in two-party systems such as the United States had much less access to policymaking negotiations than their European counterparts did, and their willingness to support risky, longer-term, pie-expanding negotiations decreased accordingly (Martin and Swank 2008, 2012).

Institutional features of government create country clusters with somewhat distinctive approaches to reaching political agreements. For example, Lijphart (2012) identified ten separate dimensions that differentiate consensus and majoritarian models. We deviate slightly from his rubric and suggest four clusters within the universe of democratic polities that vary on two axes:

1. Whether countries have proportional, multiparty systems or majoritarian, two-party systems
2. Whether countries have unitary or federal governments

Table 6-1 illustrates these four clusters.

In the following discussion, we suggest that each country cluster has a characteristic mode of democratic decisionmaking and negotiation. Moreover, we demonstrate how the adoption of somewhat different rules of engagement allows these countries to deviate from their standard approaches to policymaking and, in some cases, to engage in deliberative negotiation. These meso-institutional procedural rules

Table 6-1. *Two Axes*

	Winner-take-all electoral rules	*Proportional electoral rules*
Unitary Government	Cluster 1: Centralized Majoritarian Model U.K. (prime minister)	Cluster 2: Centralized Consensus Model Nordic countries Netherlands
Federal Government	Cluster 4: Decentralized Majoritarian Model U.S. (presidential) Canada (prime minister)	Cluster 3: Decentralized Consensus Model Germany

influence the institutional impacts on processes of negotiation and alter the macro-institutional story of cross-national variation.

Cluster 1: The Centralized Majoritarian Model

The first cluster contains countries with majoritarian electoral institutions and unitary governance. It is best represented by the United Kingdom—at least, before Tony Blair took actions to decentralize policymaking authority. This cluster contains the fewest number of veto points, and many political scientists celebrate the Westminster system as the most capable of forming a government (Cutler 1980). We might expect to find the most limited use of deliberative negotiation in these countries because centralized, majoritarian parties may simply take unilateral action.

Yet the capacities to arrive at policy decisions do not necessarily include the negotiation of enduring agreements, and critics of this model suggest that whereas centralized authority may produce rapid outcomes, the solutions must be not only rapid but also short term and therefore may suffer in both political legitimacy and staying power. Concentrated authority allows for thinner societal coalitions, ironically, and the ease of passage may diminish the legitimacy of the outcome. Majoritarian catchall parties also bring together varied constituencies, compete for the median voter, have fluctuating platforms, and inspire less confidence among their constituents (Boix 2003; Cusack, Iversen, and Soskice 2007; Kitschelt 1999). Moreover, in countries with few veto points, authority is concentrated in the hands of a few actors, such as the prime minister and his or her cabinet, and these actors may use their concentrated authority to benefit the social groups with whom they have the strongest linkages. Thus, reducing the number of veto points does not necessarily insulate politicians from social pressures; rather, centralization may reward a somewhat different set of pressures. Yet centralized authority may be useful in policy arenas in which direct losses must be imposed on everyone to provide goods to future generations.

Despite the capacity for imposing top-down solutions in such systems, one still finds examples of (at least thin) negotiation in this quadrant, in that the implementation of reform may require the participation of a broad set of social actors, and negotiation may be a mechanism for building support for compliance. For example, with its centralized government and mixed use of both proportional and winner-take-all voting, France frequently engages in top-down majoritarian rule. Yet, in 1993, the French state was compelled to negotiate with labor to reform the pension system. French workers are weakly organized and do not have a history of corporatist negotiations; however, they were too strong electorally to be ignored during the pension debate. In this instance, the French state sought to create a more consensual policymaking process by repeatedly meeting with labor leaders in nonconfrontational settings and by building in labor demands in its draft proposal (Natali and Rhodes 2004).

Irish efforts to construct quasi-corporatist relations among the social partners provide an example of how a majoritarian country might adopt repeated interactions to alter the negotiating framework. In the 1980s, Ireland developed rather loose institutions for social partnership, what Hardiman (2006) called "flexible network governance," to govern more effectively the welfare state, industrial relations, and demands on human-capital growth prompted by expanding international competition. These structures were voluntary, overlapping, and fluid; in these ways, they differed from the formal structures for interest intermediation found in the macro-corporatist countries. Yet these arrangements, taking their inspiration from across the North Sea, set up repeated interactions among participants across time and policy areas to use "competitive corporatism" to enhance international economic advantage and expand human-capital investment (Hardiman 2006). For some time, these networks fostered a shared understanding of policy problems and priorities, and they built support for governmental legislative proposals. At their most influential, these networks helped people become aware of their joint interests and brought diverse agendas into alignment. However, even in their heyday, their ultimate impact on pay and related nonwage benefits outcomes remained disappointing, and the system essentially disintegrated after the 2008 global financial crisis (Hardiman 2010).

Cluster 2: The Centralized Consensus Model

A second cluster of countries combines proportional, multiparty systems with unitary governing institutions and is epitomized by the Nordic countries.[8] Although the unitary distribution of power might accord political leaders the capacity to impose decisions, the proportional-representation electoral systems produce many parties, and (except in Sweden) one party rarely gains a sufficient majority to rule alone. These systems need coalitions, and coalition governments need extensive consensual negotiations. Fortunately, these countries also have strong *capacities* for producing national accords that extend across the economy. Their capacities derive to some extent from the incorporation of rules of engagement that nurture deliberative negotiation.

An expansive role for technical experts constitutes a staple of policymaking in consensual regimes: these countries routinely set up special commissions to investigate social and economic problems, and these commissions often pave the way for pie-expanding, long-term, and other-regarding policy reforms. In the Netherlands, a 1989 expert report on women's employment served to awaken the country to the desperate need for expanded child-care facilities. It did so by

8. Although countries with unitary, proportional government institutions have greater incentives to engage in consensual negotiations, this tendency breaks down when internal party rules and norms create particularistic rather than programmatic multiparty systems. Thus, the culture of the political parties reflects both the electoral rules and the institutional rules unifying the diverse parts of the party (Sorauf 1972). For example, Italian parties operate according to a clientelist rather than programmatic logic, which produces fragmented social and labor-market policies (Lynch 2006). There also is a danger in proportional systems that partners in coalition governments may have marginal political interests that swing the ideological content to the extremes; conservative religious parties have played this role in Israel.

consolidating evidence that previously had not been presented so succinctly and thereby changing the popular perception of the issue (Morgan 2006).

The countries in this quadrant also make use of repeated interactions and private meetings in both their party and industrial relations systems. The parties in the coalition governments broker deals through successive electoral cycles, and these repeated interactions build the trust needed to develop longer-term, value-creating solutions. Unitary governing structures prevent significant variations at the local level and enable rulers to broker deals that extend across the economic and political regions. The highly coordinated, corporatist industrial relations systems in these countries contribute to their superior capacities for negotiation because the peak employers' associations and unions develop collective policy preferences among their members. When organized into strong encompassing organizations, individual managers or workers from diverse sectors can identify with those in other sectors, set a priority on shared concerns, and possibly take action.

The case of Danish active labor-market policy shows how repeated interactions in private forums foster consensual policymaking, as the various parties and social partners all participated in negotiations leading to the far-reaching reforms. Denmark had high rates of unemployment before other core European countries did. The government proposed labor-market and social reforms that would diverge radically from past policies by tightening and shortening the eligibility for receiving passive income supports and, at the same time, greatly expanding workforce training for the long-term unemployed. Although the reforms were motivated by ideas on the left and the right—particularly in their neoliberal restrictions on assistance and social-democratic investments in human capital—these happened with the full support of both unions and employers' associations (Martin and Swank 2012).

The reform process incorporated rules of engagement that contribute to deliberative negotiation. Core ideas underlying the reforms were developed by two blue-ribbon committees (that is, the Zeuthen Commission for labor policy and the Social Commission for public assistance), and representatives from the peak business and labor associations regularly participated in these private forums for policymaking. The bulk of the committees' recommendations were incorporated into subsequent law. Danish employers also recognized that negotiation-inspiring rules of engagement brought them to favorable impressions of the reforms. Employers credited their own regular participation in corporatist employers' associations for helping them engage with the active social programs. These forums provided information on the ways that training of the unemployed could aid in workforce development, and the managers recognized that their representative employers' associations worked extensively to produce a realistic program that would serve the pragmatic interests of firms in its implementation (Martin and Swank 2012).[9]

Cluster 3: The Decentralized Consensus Model

A third cluster of countries combines proportional electoral systems with a federal distribution of governmental power. These countries should have the greatest number of veto points and the highest *need* for negotiation to overcome the many competing locations of policy authority. Countries in the decentralized-consensus model also have adopted rules of engagement that nurture *capacities* for cooperation and coordination. Their proportional parties and coordinated industrial relations systems bring diverse actors together in repeated interactions, which build shared conceptions of policy problems and solutions.

The main difference between centralized and decentralized consensus-model countries is that nations with decentralized governmental power tend to produce fewer national-level economic and social pacts that extend across the economy. In Germany, for example, the principle of "subsidiarity" requires that policy decisions be made at the lowest level of government, creating regional disparities. Moreover, peak industrial relations organizations are weaker in these federal countries. The extensive, corporatist labor-market coopera-

---

9. These insights into employers' positions on the program came from a study of 107 randomly selected firms in Great Britain and Denmark. Membership in a Danish corporatist employers' association was a significant determinant of a firm's participation in the voluntary, state-directed active labor-market programs for the long-term unemployed; however, membership in a pluralist employers' association in Great Britain did nothing to enhance firms' support for the welfare state (Martin 2004).

tion between business and labor tends to happen at the sectoral level and often without significant engagement with government; consequently, workers' economic fortunes are more varied in these countries than in Scandinavia (Busemeyer and Trampusch 2011; Höpner 2006; Martin and Thelen 2007; Palier 2010).

Yet the decentralization found in federal systems may also enhance opportunities for negotiation, albeit at a lower level of government. Decentralizing governmental functions to lower-level units allows political decisions to fit better with people's preferences, which may enhance the acceptance of longer-term, pie-expanding policy choices (Qian and Weingast 1997). Federalism also allows for lower units to act as laboratories of learning, and these experiments may be subsequently picked up at the national level (Maioni 1998; Sabel and Zeitlin 2010). In Germany, local experiments often have "trickled up" to national solutions because proportionality demands a high level of negotiation among diverse parties, and the Länder (local governments) have considerable influence in national politics. Finally, although the decentralization of authority may make it more difficult to obtain national-level agreements, the agreements that do develop tend to be more enduring because they reflect more faithfully the concerns of lower-level actors.

The German long-term-care reforms provide an excellent example of how federalism may drive innovative policy solutions, particularly when issues that are difficult to resolve at the central level can be resolved at the subnational level. The German Länder are directly represented in national deliberations and enjoy a de facto veto power over legislation; in the case of long-term care, this arrangement solved a burning social issue. When German people could not afford long-term care, they went on social assistance that was funded by the Länder in a cost-sharing scheme with the national government. The Länder felt squeezed by the financial crisis of long-term care and lobbied the national government for a legislative solution at that level. In this way they became proxy representatives for the unorganized interests of future beneficiaries of the policy (Campbell and Morgan 2005). In a similar experience, the Spanish healthcare system passed because regional leaders were allowed to implement the reforms according to their own local preferences (Lynch 2006).

Cluster 4: The Decentralized Majoritarian Model

The final cluster of countries combines two-party, majoritarian rule (which reduces the need for negotiation) with federalism (which fragments political authority). In the United States, which figures in this cluster, the logic of majoritarian-party dominance is diminished by the separation of executive and legislative powers. Divided government under a presidential system with a bicameral legislature creates a greater need to negotiate; however, because the individual units may be controlled with majority rule, the structure encourages the emergence of individual and separate centers of power, institutional warfare, gridlock, dual government policies, and unilateral action. The many veto points decrease policy coherence by forcing politicians to accommodate a wider array of preferences, to use pork barrel spending to attract diverse constituents, and to cater to minority interests, thereby undermining a coherent policymaking process (Cox and McCubbins 1997; Linz 1990). The recent U.S. government shutdown illustrates perfectly the dynamics producing stalemate within this cluster of countries.

In the Westminster systems found in cluster 1, party discipline is a virtue because it allows political leaders to "gather their troops" in a united campaign to deliver their promised policy agenda. Yet, in cluster 4, party discipline can exacerbate the potential for stalemate because it strengthens the capacity of individual centers of power to engage in institutional warfare. The case of the United States illustrates the point. When political parties in the United States were more diverse and less disciplined, they also included a greater share of legislators in the center of the ideological spectrum. The overlaps between the parties expanded the space for both "horse-trading" and deliberative negotiation among legislators. Congress was then a more integrated, consensus-oriented institution, in which legislators developed "internal careers" in the House or Senate that were guided by seniority and reputation. But the high levels of negotiation that these patterns made possible broke down when the internal careers and institutional norms were challenged by the opening of committees and other parts of the institution to public scrutiny in the 1970s (Polsby 1980) and by the growing polarization and internal coherence of the parties (see chapter 2).

In this quadrant, federalism has had mixed impacts on the polities' capacities for deliberative negotiation. Under Canadian federalism, the provinces are loosely held together by the national polity and have significant autonomy in experimenting with policy innovations in areas such as pensions and healthcare (Maioni 1998). Policymaking at the state level has also provided a solution to national incapacities in the United States; however, this fragmentation of political authority has also, at times, prompted a competition among subunits for business and a "race to the bottom" to avoid overly taxing and regulating potential investors (Elazar 1972).

Countries in this quadrant also have weakly organized pluralist industrial relations and interest organizations. The United States, for example, has a great need for societal capacities of consensual politics to overcome the many veto points associated with a presidential system and federalism, but it has a low capacity among social groups to aid in building support for reforms (Martin 2000).

Introducing different rules of engagement can make a difference in countries that are not otherwise institutionally equipped for consensual negotiations. Even in the United States, for example, legislators and private actors have been able to engage in higher levels of negotiation under some circumstances. American legislators have frequently turned to penalty defaults because the multiple veto points in the system construct such high barriers to successful negotiation (although as recent events demonstrate, these defaults are not always successful). After the "sunshine laws" opened up committees and other venues to public observance, U.S. legislators sought to reintroduce into the legislative process private meetings with repeated interactions among party leaders, and these efforts produced some crucial deals. In 1983, when legislators sought to make the social security system solvent, they faced a choice of cutting payouts to future retirees or investing in the accumulation of a fund that would help defray long-run pension costs. The Democrats and their labor allies wanted to solve the problem with an influx of cash from outside revenue sources, whereas the Republicans and their business allies sought to cut benefits and freeze payroll taxes. However, neither the left (in control of the House) nor the right (in control of the Senate and White House) had a sufficient concentration of institutional power to impose a solution on their fellow negotiators. Moreover, neither party wanted to accept the blame for inaction. The desire to escape blame motivated both parties to adopt a "circle-the-wagons" strategy and produce a bipartisan deal. Negotiating in secret, both sides accepted an immediate sharp increase in payroll taxes and cut in benefits in order to guarantee the longer-term solvency of the system (Jacobs 2008, p. 205; Weaver 1987).

Conclusion

This chapter explores the impacts of rules of engagement on negotiation processes. Countries have distinctive styles of governance that reflect their institutions for aggregating citizen preferences and some governmental institutions are associated with a greater need and capacity for negotiation. Countries with concentrated political authority in two-party systems with unitary government may rely more easily on simple majoritarian political rules and have a more limited need for political negotiation because reforms may be imposed from the top down. In contrast, consensus-oriented countries with proportional electoral rules tend to form broader multiparty coalitions in support of policy reforms, include a stronger role for social partners in policy formation, and are more likely to use consensual negotiation to arrive at political resolutions.

Institutions in consensus-model countries incorporate several rules of collective political engagement that overcome negotiation myopia and inspire successful negotiation. The use of *nonpartisan third-party experts* to establish a common understanding of policy problems and solutions helps negotiating participants overcome suspicions about the motives of other actors and build a shared perception of the task at hand. *Repeated interactions* among negotiating partners help diminish opportunities for deception and build trust, shared perception, and commitment to the negotiating process. The use of *penalty defaults* strengthens the resolve of actors to find solutions because the consequential alternative is likely to be worse for all. *Private meetings* help diminish the ability of other forces to "hijack" negotiations for illegitimate gains, although this privacy must be balanced by transparency in holding legislators accountable for their actions.

Negotiation is certainly not a ubiquitous palliative to political conflict. Deep material, ideological, ethnic, and cultural interests may lead actors to have strongly—perhaps intractably—divergent ambitions; in these instances, negotiation may become a waste of time at best or an opportunity for strategic subterfuge at worst. In other instances, negotiations that include many actors may prevent the enactment of important policies. For example, to achieve significant redistribution, a coalition of the middle and lower classes might wish to exclude the wealthy from the negotiations (Iversen 2005). International negotiations suggest several instances in which, at least early in the negotiation process, some affected parties are excluded (chapter 6, p. 349). Such negotiation practices do not meet the ideal of the inclusion of the affected parties on fair terms (chapter 5), but they may be practically necessary at certain points to bring about outcomes that benefit most parties and even, occasionally, the excluded themselves.

Economic constraints have great effects on opportunities for successful negotiations; pie-expanding social reforms are more possible when budgets are tight. Thus, efforts to advance greater cooperation in industrial relations in Ireland seemed much less promising in the punishing aftermath of the global financial crisis (Hardiman 2010). Agents must have the support of their principals, and the congeniality of the negotiating table does not always translate to the world beyond.

The goals of negotiation are also multidimensional, and institutions and procedural rules may facilitate some aspects of negotiation but not others. Pie-expanding negotiation techniques may benefit current stakeholders but may damage long-term prosperity because the needs of current parties in the negotiation may differ enormously from those of the next generation. Measures with broad coalitional support often are highly visible; yet quiet policies with lower stakes may slip more easily under the radar screen of political conflict. The impacts of manipulating meso-level rules may be limited by entrenched expectations and practices associated with political culture.

Americans, like citizens of all countries, want security, cooperation, and community; however, we have marshaled evidence that the institutional design of our political system works against these goods. Thus, the overarching aim of this chapter is to identify some of the processes of negotiation that allow other countries and supranational entities to avoid the deadlock and stalemate that characterizes American politics today and to better understand the institutions and procedural arrangements that facilitate these processes for successful negotiation.

Note: This chapter grew out of thoughtful discussion with the American Political Science Association task force on European politics, which included John Ferejohn, Torben Iversen, Alan Jacobs, Julia Lynch, Andrew Moravcsik, Kimberly Morgan, Christine Reh, and Cornelia Woll. I also wish to thank Jane Mansbridge, Daniel Carpenter, Richard Deeg, Fredrik Engelstad, Chase Foster, Peter Hall, Alexander Hertel-Fernandez, Christine Trampusch, Jonathan Zeitlin, and participants in seminars at the Council for European Studies, Harvard University Center for European Studies, Oslo University, and Society for the Advancement of Socio-Economics.

References

Baccaro, Lucio. 2002. "Negotiating the Italian Pension Reform with the Unions: Lessons for Corporatist Theory." *Industrial and Labor Relations Review* 55 (3): 413–31.

Bednar, Jenna, John Ferejohn, and Geoffrey Garrett. 1996. "The Politics of European Federalism." *International Review of Law and Economics* 16: 279–94.

Bellamy, Richard. 2012. "Democracy, Compromise and the Representation Paradox: Coalition Government and Political Integrity." *Governance and Opposition, "Politics as Compromise: Special Issue"* 47 (3): 275–95.

Blyth, Mark. 2002. *Great Transformations: Economic Ideas and Institutional Change in the Twentieth Century.* Cambridge University Press.

Boix, Carles. 2003. *Democracy and Redistribution.* Cambridge University Press.

Busemeyer, Marius, and Christine Trampusch. 2011. "Review Article: Comparative Political Science and the Study of Education." *British Journal of Political Science* 41:413–43.

Campbell, Andrea Louise, and Kimberly J. Morgan. 2005. "Federalism and the Politics of Old-Age Care in Germany and the United States." *Comparative Political Studies* 38 (8): 887–914.

Campbell, John, and Ove Kaj Pedersen. 2014. *The National Origins of Policy Ideas: Knowledge Regimes in the United States, France, Germany, and Denmark.* Princeton University Press.

Carpenter, Daniel P. 2001. *The Forging of Bureaucratic Autonomy: Reputations, Networks, and Policy Innovation in Executive Agencies, 1862–1928.* Princeton University Press.

Cox, Gary W., and Mathew D. McCubbins. 1997. "Structure and Economic Policy: The Institutional Determinants of Policy Outcomes." Social Science Research Network. http://ssrn.com/ abstract =1009999.

Crouch, Colin. 1993. *Industrial Relations and European State Traditions.* Oxford University Press.

Cusack, Thomas R., Torben Iversen, and David Soskice. 2007. "Economic Interests and the Origins of Electoral Systems." *American Political Science Review* 101 (3): 373–91.

Cutler, Lloyd. 1980. "To Form a Government." *Foreign Affairs* 59 (1): 126–43.

Downs, Anthony. [1957] 2001. "An Economic Theory of Democracy." In *Democracy: A Reader*, ed. Ricardo Blaug and John Schwarzmantel. Columbia University Press.

Elazar, Daniel. 1972. *American Federalism: A View from the States.* New York: Crowell.

Goodin, Robert E. 1996. "Institutionalizing the Public Interest: The Defense of Deadlock and Beyond." *American Political Science Review* 90 (2): 331–43.

Gourevitch, Peter. 1978. "The Second Image Reversed: The International Sources of Domestic Politics." *International Organization* 32 (4): 881–912.

Hardiman, Niamh. 2006. "Politics and Social Partnership: Flexible Network Governance." *Economic and Social Review* 37 (3): 343–74.

———. 2010. "Bringing Domestic Institutions Back into an Understanding of Ireland's Economic Crisis." *Irish Studies in International Affairs* 21:73–89.

Hicks, Alexander, and Lane Kenworthy. 1998. "Cooperation and Political Economic Performance in Affluent Democratic Capitalism 1." *American Journal of Sociology* 103 (6): 1631–72.

Höpner, Martin. 2006. "What Is Organized Capitalism: The Two Dimensions of Nonliberal Capitalism." Presented at Workshop on Institutional Emergence, Stability and Change, Copenhagen, June 1–2.

Iversen, Torben. 2005. *Capitalism, Democracy and Welfare*. Cambridge University Press.

Jacobs, Alan M. 2008. "The Politics of When: Redistribution, Investment, and Policymaking for the Long Term." *British Journal of Political Science* 38 (2): 193–220.

———. 2011. *Governing for the Long Term: Democracy and the Politics of Investment*. Cambridge University Press.

Joerges, Christian, and Jurgen Neyer. 1997. "Transforming Strategic Interaction into Deliberative Problem-Solving: European Comitology in the Foodstuffs Sector." *Journal of European Public Policy* 4 (4): 609–25.

Katzenstein, Peter J. 1985. *Small States in World Markets: Industrial Policy in Europe*. Cornell University Press.

Kitschelt, Herbert, ed. 1999. *Post-Communist Party Systems: Competition, Representation, and Inter-Party Cooperation*. Cambridge University Press.

Kurth, James R. 1979. "The Political Consequences of the Product Cycle: Industrial History and Political Outcomes." *International Organization* 33:1–34.

Lijphart, Arend. 2012. *Patterns of Democracy: Government Forms and Performance in Thirty-Six Countries*. 2nd ed. Yale University Press.

Linz, Juan J. 1990. "The Perils of Presidentialism." *Journal of Democracy* 1:51–69.

Lowi, Theodore J. 1964. "American Business, Public Policy, Case Studies, and Political Theory." *World Politics* 16 (4): 677–715.

Luker, Kristin. 1984. *Abortion and the Politics of Motherhood*. Vol. 3. University of California Press.

Lynch, Julia. 2006. *Age in the Welfare State: The Origins of Social Spending on Pensioners, Workers and Children*. Cambridge University Press.

Maioni, Antonia. 1998. *Parting at the Crossroads: The Emergence of Health Insurance in the United States and Canada*. Princeton University Press.

Mansbridge, Jane. 2010. "Beyond the Tragedy of the Commons." *Symposium in Perspectives in Politics* 8 (2): 590–93.

Martin, Cathie Jo. 2000. *Stuck in Neutral: Business and the Politics of Human Capital Investment Policy*. Princeton University Press.

———. 2004. "Reinventing Welfare Regimes." *World Politics* 57 (1): 39–69.

Martin, Cathie Jo, and Duane Swank. 2004. "Does the Organization of Capital Matter?" *American Political Science Review* 98 (4): 593–611.

———. 2008. "The Political Origins of Coordinated Capitalism." *American Political Science Review* (May): 181–98

———. 2012. *The Political Construction of Business Interests: Coordination, Growth, and Equality.* Cambridge University Press.

Martin, Cathie Jo, and Kathleen Thelen. 2007. "The State and Coordinated Capitalism: Contributions of the Public Sector to Social Solidarity in Postindustrial Societies." *World Politics* 60:1–36.

Medrano, Juan Diez. 2003. *Framing Europe: Attitudes to European Integration in Germany, Spain, and the United Kingdom.* Princeton University Press.

Moravcsik, Andrew. 2005. "The European Constitutional Compromise and the Neofunctionalist Legacy." *Journal of European Public Policy* 12 (2): 349–86.

Morgan, Kimberly. 2006. *Working Mothers and the Welfare State: Religion and the Politics of Work-Family Policies in Western Europe and the United States.* Stanford University Press.

Natali, David, and Martin Rhodes. 2004. "Trade-Offs and Veto Players: Reforming Pensions in France and Italy." *French Politics* 2 (1): 1–23.

Ostrom, Elinor. 1990. *Governing the Commons: The Evolution of Institutions for Collective Action.* Cambridge University Press.

Page, Benjamin I., and Lawrence R. Jacobs. 2009. *Class War? What Americans Really Think about Economic Inequality.* University of Chicago Press.

Palier, Bruno, ed. 2010. *A Long Goodbye to Bismarck? The Politics of Welfare Reforms in Continental Europe.* Amsterdam University Press.

Polsby, Nelson W. 1980. *Community Power and Political Theory.* Yale University Press.

Qian, Yingyi, and Barry Weingast. 1997. "Federalism as a Commitment to Preserving Market Incentives." *Journal of Economic Perspectives* 11 (4): 83–92.

Reh, Christine. 2012. "European Integration as Compromise." *Government and Opposition* 47 (3): 414–40.

Rothstein, Bo. 2000. "Trust, Social Dilemmas and Collective Memories." *Journal of Theoretical Politics* 12 (4): 477–501.

Sabel, Charles F., and Jonathan Zeitlin. 2010. "Learning from Difference: The New Architecture of Experimentalist Governance in the EU." *Experimentalist Governance in the European Union.* Oxford University Press.

Scharpf, Fritz. 1988. "The Joint-Decision Trap: Lessons from German Federalism and European Integration." *Public Administration* 66 (3): 239–78.

Schmidt, Vivien A. 2009. "Putting the Political Back into Political Economy by Bringing the State Back in Yet Again." *World Politics* 61 (3): 516–46.

Shugart, Matthew Soberg, and John M. Carey. 1992. *Presidents and Assemblies: Constitutional Design and Electoral Dynamics.* Cambridge University Press.

Sorauf, Frank. 1972. *Party Politics in America.* Boston: Little, Brown.

Stepan, Alfred, and Cindy Skach. 1993. "Constitutional Frameworks and Democratic Consolidation: Parliamentarianism versus Presidentialism." *World Politics* 46 (1): 1–22.

Streeck, Wolfgang. 1992. *Social Institutions and Economic Performance: Studies of Industrial Relations in Advanced Capitalist Economies.* London: Sage.

Tsebelis, George. 1995. "Decision Making in Political Systems: Veto Players in Presidentialism, Parliamentarism, Multicameralism, and Multipartyism." *British Journal of Political Science* 25:289–326.

Visser, Jelle, and Anton Hemerijck. 1997. *A Dutch Miracle: Job Growth, Welfare Reform and Corporatism in the Netherlands.* Amsterdam University Press.

Weaver, R. Kent. 1987. *The Politics of Blame Avoidance.* Brookings Institution Press.

Wilensky, Harold L. 1976. *The "New Corporatism": Centralization and the Welfare State.* London: Sage.

Woll, Cornelia. 2008. *Firm Interests: How Governments Shape Business Lobbying on Global Trade.* Cornell University Press.

———. 2012. "The Brash and the Soft-Spoken: Lobbying Styles in a Transatlantic Comparison." *Interest Groups and Advocacy* 1 (2): 193–204.

CHAPTER SEVEN

Negotiating Agreements in International Relations

JOHN S. ODELL AND DUSTIN TINGLEY

International relations is the only field in political science to address the practice of negotiation systematically and with a full arsenal of methodologies. Over the past sixty-five years, it has developed a body of recognized findings. This chapter synthesizes the key insights and findings from the research on negotiating international agreements, underlines the importance of negotiation to the field of international relations, and suggests specific paths for future research. It also provides templates for the study of domestic political negotiation. As democratic parliaments around the world struggle to create institutions that facilitate successful negotiation, they can learn from what has been already established in the study of international negotiation.

We conceptualize negotiation as a process in which actors take steps to agree on an outcome, and all the actors seek to make that outcome as good as possible from their own perspectives. Some actors' perspectives may include making the outcome as good as possible for their community or a common institution.[1] The agreements that derive

---

1. We follow the negotiation literature that treats the terms *negotiation* and *bargaining* as synonyms. The broad literature lacks consensus on the meanings

from negotiation may be explicit or tacit. We assume that differing preferences will be present in all cases of negotiation and will always present obstacles to agreement. For instance, any joint gains created in the course of a deal will need to be allocated between the parties to that deal, so that even "value-creating" moments can generate conflict.[2] We do not assume that influence and coercion are absent from negotiation by definition, that parties always negotiate in good faith, or that negotiated agreements are all "win-win" relative to the status quo.

This chapter does, however, concentrate on a subset of situations in which the parties see some prospect for mutual gain, consistent with the focus of this volume. Chapter 4, "Negotiation Myopia," defines a political negotiation as successful when it meets two criteria, reworded here as follows:

1. At a minimum, parties reach a mutual-gain deal (one that would benefit the set of parties as a whole and many if not all of them individually) when such a deal is feasible.
2. A negotiation that does reach such a deal is more successful to the degree that it exhausts the potential for enhancing the parties' utilities.

Some negotiations discover and realize greater gains than others, sometimes even creatively producing an integrative solution that costs neither party anything at all (Follett [1929] 1995). Negotiations are also more successful, we add, to the extent that they are efficient by reducing process costs and to the extent that both the process and the deal are just (Albin 2001).[3] Thus, the negotiations addressed here

---

of these central concepts. Some studies, including chapter 5, "Deliberative Negotiation," in this book, instead use *bargaining* as a subtype of *negotiation*, referring to an exclusively distributive haggling process and contrasting bargaining with problem-solving negotiation (Elgström and Jönsson 2000). As an alternative, some prefer to use *bargaining* as the most encompassing category and restrict *negotiation* to mean diplomats at a table making explicit verbal offers to one another.

2. Here, *gain* and *value* include intangibles; they do not mean only tangible values that can be expressed in numbers.

3. For a discussion of justice in negotiation, see also chapter 5.

involve both *integrative* questions (How can the size of the pie be maximized?) and *distributive* questions (How much of the gain and the cost does each participant get?). This chapter identifies key obstacles that can impede agreements in such situations and documents the responses that have helped make agreements more likely and more successful. But this chapter does not give priority to the many ways in which one party can gain at the expense of others or defend against the others' claims and threats. Much research on international relations has illuminated deterrence, coercion, and value claiming. Were it not for the focus of this book on successful agreements, this chapter would have more to say about distributive bargaining. This chapter also concentrates on negotiations that involve explicit communications and explicit agreements, which may be linked with potentially tacit bargaining. It does not concentrate on exclusively tacit bargaining, which international relations research has analyzed at length.

Another caveat: it is not always morally appropriate to privilege agreement over disagreement. Agreement among the members of one set of parties may involve losses for others not included in the negotiation. The agreement among Austria, Prussia, and Russia to partition Poland in the eighteenth century was not better than disagreement from the Polish perspective. Agreement between a set of countries to lower their tariff barriers in a free-trade area may harm exports from countries not included in the deal. It may harm some citizens and help others within the countries making the agreement. The harm suffered by excluded parties and others may be justifiable, unjust, or even illegal. For the purposes of this analysis, we will assume that in the cases we discuss here most and sometimes almost all the players prefer eventual agreement to disagreement. Actors favoring disagreement in a given case may wish to use the insights uncovered in the research reported here to exacerbate rather than reduce the obstacles it identifies, both before and during negotiation.[4]

4. Finally, while negotiation and bargaining studies have established considerable knowledge, this multidisciplinary field also has many gaps—in empirical support as well as theoretical linkage. Many of its parts originate in disciplines other than political science—including psychology, law, economics, and business. It lacks a single, integrated grand theory that has been shown to be valid in a wide range of issue areas, regions, and periods (Kydd 2010; Odell 2013;

This chapter, then, will first identify recurring conditions that have impeded or facilitated agreement, and next will document actions by states and their negotiators that have responded effectively to those conditions in many diverse cases.

Conditions, Positive and Negative

Key factors in the conditions surrounding a potential agreement can either block or enable that agreement and influence its terms. Conflicting preferences are the most obvious barriers to agreement. Many responses documented in the literature and in the following section are addressed to them. The conceptual zone of possible agreement is bounded by the parties' *reservation values* (also called *security points* and *resistance points*), which can be understood as the minimum deal each party would accept. These limiting values are determined by the parties' best alternatives to a negotiated agreement (BATNA) with the other party. If an offer is worse than a party's best outside option, the party will not accept that deal. All deals that fall within a positive zone of agreement are theoretically possible negotiation outcomes. Reservation values and zones of agreement are difficult to measure in historical international cases but are nonetheless powerful analytical tools.[5] Many negotiating moves are directed at attempting to influence how parties perceive their alternatives to a negotiated agreement, for the sake of both creating joint gains and claiming shares.

This section on the positive and negative conditions that negotiators face emphasizes barriers to agreement. It has three major parts. The first two, on information and commitment, and on cognition and culture, introduce factors that can operate at the level of the individual negotiator, and the third, on the setting of negotiation, discusses

---

Walter 2013). Thus there is great need for additional research, and an appendix to this chapter identifies many opportunities.

5. Reservation values may be hard to decipher, even for the negotiating partners themselves. One veteran negotiator of complex legal issues in the World Trade Organization (WTO) declared flatly: "Most negotiators don't know their own bottom lines" (Odell, confidential interview, Florence, Italy, July 3, 2004). Many ambassadors from developing countries have only vague instructions on this point, including the technical issues of what alternatives to a negotiated agreement might exist.

factors that are mostly beyond the control of the negotiators in the short term. We do not assume that these factors operate exclusively at the individual or situational levels.

The first part of this section, on information and commitment, discusses concepts associated with the rationalist or rational-choice tradition in international relations theory. Although we could take the state as the unit of analysis, we will analyze these issues at the level of the individual negotiator. We root negotiations in their individual microfoundations because decisions, such as decisions to reveal, withhold, or distort information, or decisions about the likelihood of future enforcement, must ultimately pass through individual minds, either directly or by transmission through other actors. The second part of the section, on cognition and culture, discusses concepts more associated with the psychological and sociocultural branches of negotiation analysis. These include the role of different types of biases. Presenting these two traditions in separate parts of this analysis is not meant to imply that researchers must choose one or the other. Many researchers productively blend insights from the rationalist and the psychological branches (for example, Hafner-Burton et al. 2014; Mintz 2007; Ostrom 1998) and more could do so. The third part of this section, on the setting, addresses concepts associated with various aspects of the settings in which negotiation happens, including the distribution of power and the institutional environment, including both domestic and international institutions.

Information and Commitment: The Rationalist View

The rational choice tradition has contributed important insights about the effects of information and commitment in international bargaining.

Information

Information is central to any negotiation.[6] It affects negotiation both nonstrategically, as simple information about the way the world works,

---

6. By *information*, we mean facts that are commonly understood worldwide. Facts are also interpreted, and different individuals, cultures, states, and non-state groups see them through different lenses. We introduce a discussion of these lenses and influences in subsequent sections.

and strategically, as a resource that parties may have greater or lesser incentives to share. When a shortage of information is a barrier to agreement (Kydd 2012), adding information can be a remedy. Conversely, withholding certain information from some participants or observers can enable agreements.

In many situations, all parties to a negotiation share simple non-strategic uncertainty about many features of the world in which the negotiation takes place.[7] This uncertainty includes the possible effects of alternative deals and what will happen if no deal is reached. For example, in a complex situation such as the multilateral talks on possible regulation of the world's chlorofluorocarbon (CFC) emissions, when governments began discussing the ozone hole question in 1985, scientists were not certain that Earth's ozone layer was in fact being depleted or that CFC emissions were a cause. Such uncertainty could have obscured any zone of agreement. In this case, governments nevertheless found ways to negotiate an initial agreement to curb CFC emissions as early as 1987 (Benedick 1991).

One of the most fundamental obstacles to success in negotiation is that negotiators often do not know, in the absence of actual negotiations, whether any mutual gain deal is feasible. The zone of agreement is not fully specified ex ante. In addition, none of the parties know how their home governments will respond to rival proposals and whether domestic coalitions will form to support or block each proposal. If the negotiating parties were to wait until they had complete information on all these elements, no complex negotiations would ever occur. In practice, parties often form expectations. They can decide to make their expectations public in an effort to persuade other parties or keep those expectations private for strategic reasons. These choices open up the strategic domain of negotiation.

When parties have private information, such as information about their expectations, they may strategically reveal, withhold, or distort that information. Parties that have different preferences and face distributive issues have incentives to exaggerate their bargaining strengths and conceal their weaknesses (including how they per-

7. Uncertainty could be structural, in the Knightian (Knight 1921) sense that it is impossible to form probabilistic expectations over well-defined outcomes, or it could be that known probabilities are assigned to every outcome.

ceive the alternatives to agreement and the internal pressures they may face to reject the concessions of the other party). They may also have incentives to conceal elements of their strengths (Walter 2013). Thus a clever negotiator may relentlessly but falsely disparage a proposal she knows is above her reservation value in the hope of gaining more in the final days. She may also take tough steps, such as walking away from a possible deal, simply to establish a reputation for resolve, even when she knows she would settle for less if forced to do so. In addition, negotiators may attempt in private to feed false information to a mediator.[8] Such tactics based on the strategic manipulation of information can exacerbate conflict. Deadlock is another possibility. When parties face incomplete information about the other's trustworthiness, they are likely to err on the side of caution and perhaps fail to reach an agreement.[9]

COMMITMENT

Committing to fulfill an agreement in the future is often crucial to the success of a negotiation. In chapter 2 of *The Strategy of Conflict*, Thomas Schelling (1960) focused on the credibility of the threats and promises, arguing that for these threats and promises to be effective in influencing the behavior of other parties, they must have a specific basis for credibility. They might rest on a reputation for trustworthiness, or the signal sent might be costly to the sender and thus more believable. Schelling also stressed the dynamic nature of making and keeping commitments, as the incentives for the parties change over time.

Commitment problems can impede agreement. If parties can gain in the future by reneging on a past commitment, and if no strong enforcement mechanism is provided, parties may be reluctant to enter an agreement in the first place. In international relations many proposed forms of cooperation do entail significant payoffs to defection after signing the agreement. In the absence of effective monitoring and enforcement mechanisms, such as might be provided by a world

8. Odell, personal interviews with former mediators.

9. See Kydd (2000). Rathbun (2011) developed an alternative approach to trust in international relations that differs from these information-based rationalist accounts. Psychologists add that distrust also can be due to stereotyped thinking and biased information processing.

government, uncertainty about enforcement often arises in inter-state agreements (Koremenos, Lipson, and Snidal 2001).[10] A different view suggests that if all know that enforcement will be strict, the potential deal will be more valuable, and so parties will bargain harder over the terms, which also could delay or prevent agreement (Fearon 1998).[11]

The expectation of power shifts over time can also generate commitment problems. If one party is expected to grow stronger over time and hence may not have incentives to keep the agreement in the future, the credibility of its commitments to that agreement can be compromised (Fearon 1995; Powell 2006; Tingley 2011). This problem is especially acute in negotiations to end civil wars, where agreement means that the rebel parties must give up their armies and their control over territory, making them and the people they represent vulnerable to exploitation by the government during the transition and later (Walter 2013). A longer-term commitment problem can occur when an agreement will shift the balance of power decisively from one side to the other. In an agreement to replace an autocracy with a democracy, for example, the institutional change could enable the new democratic majority to abuse former elites (Przeworski 1991).

Cognition and Culture: A Psychological and Sociocultural Perspective

Additional barriers to, and possible enablers of, agreement are found in the way the human mind operates and in properties of political cultures.

---

10. The early neoliberal tradition of international relations typically separated bargaining/negotiating from enforcing and focused on enforcement (Axelrod and Keohane 1986). Commitment problems differ across issue areas. For example, in the area of human rights, commitment problems are particularly acute because of the limited ability to monitor outcomes and the difficulty in making reciprocity effective (Simmons 2009, p. 123). For similar points about differences across issue areas and their impacts on monitoring and enforcement, see Copelovitch and Putnam (2014) and Mitchell and Keilbach (2001).

11. Such enforcement considerations are central to the rationalist tradition, although often not conceptualized at the individual level.

COGNITION

Issues of cognition and cognitive bias play a considerable role in negotiation[12] Because each party to a possible agreement has private information and incentives to conceal or distort that information, each negotiator must make inferences before the negotiation begins about how compatible the different sides' preferences are. Those inferences are often faulty. Much experimental evidence shows that "fixed-pie bias" leads many negotiators to assume that "what is good for them must be bad for us."[13] Negotiators with this assumption do not then expect or look for opportunities to make both sides better off. Research also shows that this assumption is resistant to change. It is still observed after efforts to warn negotiators of its existence, after negotiators learn though negotiating experience, and even after feedback about the other party's interests (Thompson 2001, p. 66). In a meta-analysis of two-party negotiations, Thompson and Hrebec (1996) found that negotiators failed to identify true instances of compatible interests 46 percent of the time, on average. Even after multiple rounds of talks and some learning, they still settled for suboptimal agreements 20 percent of the time.

This obstacle has been documented among professionals in business (Lax and Sebenius 2006, p. 80) as well as in politics and international relations. During one dispute between a police union and a city administration, for example, the union wanted to dismiss the popular police commissioner. The mayor, who had appointed the chief, privately had the same preference because the chief had become an administrative nightmare. Yet, influenced by a fixed-pie bias, neither probed the other for this information (Lax and Sebenius 1986, pp. 107–08). The 1965–75 war between North Vietnam and the United States provides a particularly tragic example. After the war was over, during

---

12. Of the large literature on the effects of cognitive bias in negotiation, we develop only a sample, noting, however, that the effects, now studied primarily in North America, may differ in other cultures. See chapter 4 for more depth on these points. In addition to work on cognition, there is also a rich literature on affective influences on decisionmaking, also touched upon in chapter 4.

13. Some research has also questioned the universality of the fixed-pie bias. The great bulk of early research was conducted with North American subjects. Greek subjects manifest less of this bias, and East Asians tend to show different biases (Morris and Gelfand 2004).

the 1990s, representatives of the two countries—including some who had participated in wartime decisions—studied formerly secret documents, then met. After discussion, they concluded that several of the negotiation initiatives of that period could have succeeded had it not been for repeated inaccurate beliefs about the other by one or both sides (McNamara, Blight, and Brigham 1999, pp. 223–24). Lack of trust and fixed-pie bias contributed to each side's failure to draw out the other to explore possible areas of compromise and trading.

Framing can also change negotiators' perceptions of alternatives and either enable or impede agreement. Even introducing a simple reference point, such as telling people to think like a "seller" or a "buyer," changes behavior. One study using senior business leaders showed that even experts with long experience and identical information overvalue an item if framed as a seller and undervalue it if framed as a buyer (Lax and Sebenius 2006, p. 80).

Each negotiator is a partisan, and a partisan frame can have similar effects. In experiments that give all subjects the same information, subjects framed as partisans—compared with neutral subjects—significantly overestimate the value of their own outside options (Lax and Sebenius 1986); underestimate the degree to which the other side's objectives are compatible with theirs (Bazerman et al. 1995); and use a self-serving definition of fairness, believing their own views to be impartial (Babcock and Loewenstein 1997). Partisan bias therefore narrows the zone of agreement from what would exist on objective grounds. Partisan biases may be especially forceful in international negotiations, where considerations of sovereignty, nationalism, and religion often exacerbate material conflicts of interest.

To illustrate, in 1977 Jorge Díaz Serrano, head of the state oil firm Petróleos Mexicanos (PEMEX), negotiated for Mexico with the United States for approval of PEMEX's plan to export newly discovered natural gas to the United States through a proposed pipeline from the south. Mexico had a gas surplus and the United States was having shortages, so investment bankers considered this a "golden deal" and expected easy agreement. The price of the gas, however, was a critical distributive issue. Mexico's team reasoned that a fair price was the Organization of the Petroleum Exporting Countries (OPEC) world oil price converted to its gas equivalent. As they cognitively anchored on the OPEC price, these partisans misjudged the other side's outside option: the United States could import gas from Canada at a lower price. Canada was the salient reference point in Washington's thinking. Mexico's team's self-serving OPEC reference point led their negotiators to demand a price above the true zone of agreement. Although this offer could have been a starting point in a value-creating negotiation, Díaz Serrano refused to fall back, evidently dismissing as a bluff the U.S. arguments that it could not come up to Mexico's price. The United States was not bluffing, and it had an equally self-serving reference point. The talks thus ended in partisan acrimony with no deal, leaving serious "money on the table" (Vietor 1982).

It has long been known that individuals make decisions differently depending on whether those decisions are framed as being in the domain of gains or losses. Such findings have important implications for international relations (McDermott 2001). When negotiators in experiments have their experience framed with instructions to "minimize your losses," they use strategies, such as making threats, which run a higher risk of breakdown. They reach significantly fewer agreements than negotiators who have identical interests and information but are instructed to "maximize your gains" (Bazerman and Neale 1992, chap. 5). The same dynamic appeared in a matched pair of U.S. bilateral trade negotiations, where negotiators who perceived themselves in the domain of losses engaged in more risky and aggressive strategies (Elms 2006).[14]

Education and professional experience do not necessarily eliminate these cognitive biases. According to Rabin (1998, p. 32), "Experts who have rich models of the system in question" are particularly susceptible to overconfidence in judgments and confirmatory bias. Learning from experience often reinforces rather than offsetting biases (Babcock and Loewenstein 1997). A study of international trade officials in a WTO course in Geneva confirmed some of the laboratory findings (Dupont, Beverelli, and Pézard 2006). Although they were experts in the field, they too showed signs of self-serving bias and made tactical decisions by relying on rules of thumb rather than responding to new information derived from others' moves.

14. Chapter 4 discusses other forms of framing.

CULTURE

Much of the voluminous experimental research on culture in negotiation compares cases in which two persons of one nationality negotiate with each other to cases in which two persons from another nationality negotiate with each other. The most studied dimensions of culture are the "individualistic" and "collectivistic" orientations, long thought to be mutually exclusive. Recent work indicates that both can occur in the same culture. Indeed, the same negotiator can act individualistically in some conditions and collectively in others (Weiss 2006). Brett et al. (1998), while finding that some cultures achieve greater joint gains than others, also found that the key cultural variables are not individualism-collectivism but instead the ability to deal with multiple issues simultaneously, the motivation to continue working to improve an initial deal, and the value the culture places on information sharing.

Regarding cross-cultural negotiations, an American and a Japanese achieve significantly smaller joint gains when negotiating with one another, on average, than when either negotiates with a partner from the same culture (Brett et al. 1998). Asian cultures place a higher value on establishing personal relationships of respect and trust between negotiators and business partners than Western cultures do (see, for example, Miles 2000). Thus a request to "put it in writing" may be taken as a sign of disrespect that damages the relationship. Asian negotiators traditionally prefer informal arrangements to highly legalized agreements with precise, binding obligations and enforcement measures (Kahler 2000).

The influence of culture also interacts with other conditions and settings. Kahler (2000) points out that when Asia-Pacific countries have judged a more legalized institution to be most effective for their current objectives, they have adopted it (for example, the WTO and institutions developed during the 1998 financial crisis). In another example, a survey of Chinese and U.S. managers of international joint ventures in China found that U.S. managers were more likely than Chinese managers to favor negotiation approaches called "forcing" (using management authority or expertise to make a decision) and "legalism" (citing the provisions of the joint-venture agreement to resolve a problem). However, once engaged in a joint venture where each firm had made an institutional commitment to the local enterprise, both

Chinese and U.S. managers said their most preferred negotiation approach was "problem solving." In addition, in both cultures, the managers who were more committed to the relationship were less likely to favor legalism and more likely to favor problem solving. This conditioning effect was stronger among the Chinese because they place a higher value on the relationship (Lin and Miller 2003).

The Setting

Negotiation outcomes depend not only on these individual properties but also on elements of the negotiator's setting. In many cases these dimensions are fixed and not subject to the negotiator's influence during the short term.

THE POWER DISTRIBUTION

A major part of the setting is the distribution of power across the negotiating parties. Political science lacks consensus on a definition of this central concept. Before 1950, power in international relations meant the distribution of *resources*, material and symbolic, that can be used to achieve influence and effects. Some researchers argue that in negotiations, the distribution of outcomes derives relatively directly from the distribution of power in this first sense (Krasner 1991; Steinberg 2002; Telhami 1990). In the 1950s, an alternative *relational* meaning became popular, with power meaning the capacity of A to cause, at least in part, some change in the behavior of B (Baldwin 2013). Recently Barnett and Duval (2005, p. 3) have offered a third definition, with *power* meaning "the production, in and through social relations, of effects that shape the capacities of actors to determine their circumstances and fate."

Bargaining and negotiation analysts conceptualize power by comparing the parties' best alternatives to negotiated agreement in the particular situation. The party with a better alternative to a negotiated agreement than the other, in that particular situation and time, will have the advantage in the distributional part of the negotiation.

In general, having greater resources facilitates better alternatives for that party and therefore a greater distributional share of the joint outcome. Yet this is not always the case. A state may have many power assets but have committed some of those assets to other objectives. A state with many assets may claim a smaller share because its obligations under an international institution prevent it from claiming more and it values this institution. In some cases, weaker parties have been able to use deadlock to generate costs to the stronger party that were greater than the costs of the concession they demanded (for example, Wriggins 1976). How parties perceive their alternatives at a given time also sometimes can be shaped by argument and framing, not just the material assets of the parties.

Despite the lack of consensus on the meaning of power, most scholars agree that the power distribution, in some sense, is relevant for the distributions of benefits and costs embodied in negotiated agreements. We are less clear on the effects of power structures on the likelihood of coming to agreement. Our appendix on needs for further research returns to this question.

INTERNATIONAL INSTITUTIONS

The presence of an international institution can shape negotiations and either facilitate or hinder their success by providing information to members and encouraging issue linkages, such as when cooperating to impose economic sanctions (Keohane 1984; Martin 1992). Shared norms differ across organizations, and an organization's norms empower certain actors as legitimate in the negotiation, rule certain arguments out of order, and determine which discursive strategy will be effective (Deitelhoff and Müller 2005; Ulbert and Risse 2005). For example, in the European Union (EU), day-to-day internal negotiations are usually dominated by problem-solving integrative behavior. The trend is toward institutionalizing this behavior. Yet conflictual distributive behavior also occurs in some circumstances (Elgström and Jönsson 2000; Niemann 2006). In contrast to the EU, United Nations (UN) rules and norms governing environmental talks discourage integrative behavior and encourage distributive behavior (Susskind 1994).

International institutions are themselves products of negotiations. An institution's structure and purpose can be influenced by the previous institutional experiences of the negotiating parties (Copelovitch and Putnam 2014). Once an institution is established, negotiation often continues about its shape and structure (Spector and Zartman 2003). We may therefore think of international institutions as products of negotiation, recurring influences on negotiations, and, as discussed later, possible remedies for obstacles to successful negotiation.

DOMESTIC INSTITUTIONS AND POLITICS

Domestic institutions and politics, including regime type, are also key aspects of the international negotiator's context. Leaders of autocratic states, for example, are less constrained than leaders of democracies by domestic opposition in what they can accept. At first glance, this would seem to be an advantage in negotiation. Yet this relative freedom may make an autocracy's threats and promises less credible. Autocrats may be freer to renege on an agreement because they will have less need to fear attacks from domestic rivals for doing so. It is perhaps because of this difference in credibility that autocracies are less likely than democracies to reach agreements that avoid or shorten wars (Lipson 2003; Schultz 1999). Past research has also found that autocracies are less likely than democracies to engage in peaceful conflict resolution before escalating their positions (Dixon 1993), but recent research provides a more nuanced view (Leeds 1999). It has begun to unpack institutional variation among autocracies and trace the influence of this variation on interstate behavior (Weeks 2008). It has also shown that institutional decision rules have predictable effects, with unanimity rules favoring the status quo and majority voting favoring change (Jupille 1999).

Developing countries, particularly the least developed, often lack sufficient domestic institutional capacity to negotiate effectively on technical issues. WTO negotiations are a case in point. By the late 1990s, developing countries were becoming more vocal and active in WTO talks, but many had little of the expertise on trade law and economics needed to understand and defend their interests. Many also assign their ambassadors in Geneva to several international organizations simultaneously, and some give those ambassadors little support or attention in their home capitals. Not infrequently, after trade negotiators have been trained, their governments transfer this scarce talent to nontrade functions (Odell, personal interviews with ambassadors and IO officials, Geneva).

Many international and EU negotiations are deeply entangled in internal politics within the negotiating states, and these politics can change while institutions remain constant. Although leaders often have influence over their home politics, the home politics also can act as an exogenous influence on negotiations. Even in autocracies, internal opposition can limit a party's negotiating position and the agreements that it can ratify (Milner 1997; Putnam 1988). Especially in highly salient cases, such as peace talks among Israel, the Palestinian Authority, and the United States, domestic voices have a significant effect in all three countries. Leaders and negotiators must consider these voices. In high- and middle-income countries, businesses spend substantial resources on organizations that monitor their home governments and intervene with them in international negotiations over financial, trade, and environmental issues. For example, negotiators from two states might favor a linkage between two issues, agreeing that the linkage would create gain for both nations, but then face barriers when domestic organized special interests lobby vigorously to block concessions on "their" issues.

Occasionally, a domestic or transnational campaign has been decisive in launching an interstate negotiation (for example, the UN ban on land mines) or stopping a negotiation that governments had begun (for instance, the Organization for Economic Cooperation and Development [OECD] Multilateral Agreement on Investment). Sometimes governments have negotiated and initialed an agreement but then failed to achieve ratification at home, as in the International Trade Organization (1948), the European Defense Community (1952), and the EU constitution (2005).

Facilitating Successful Negotiations

Research shows that remedies for the barriers discussed in the preceding section have been found and applied successfully in many diverse cases. In this section we present examples of what practical negotiators have done to deal with these barriers and produce mutual-gain deals for the signatories, at least relative to the status quo. Following the overall structure of this book, we do not emphasize explaining the distribution of gains within agreements and we underrepresent failed negotiations. This format limited to examples also underrepresents formal work, comparative empirical studies, and case studies designed to contribute to theory development.

Table 7-1 lists the barriers mentioned in the last section and pairs each with potential responses, chosen for illustrative purposes. The

Table 7-1. *Barriers to Agreement and Successful Responses*

Barrier	Successful Responses
Conflicting preferences on an issue or issues	During a confidential diagnostic phase, explored potential parties
	Postponed details, agreed first on a formula
	Linked issues with opposite distributional effects
	Reframed the issue space itself
Shared uncertainty	During a diagnostic phase, parties studied the problem jointly or commissioned neutral third parties
	Created specialized negotiating bodies
Unknown private information on preferences	Tacit "tit for tat" in communication
	Revealed and requested private information
Commitments lack credibility	Established compliance mechanisms
	Post-agreement compliance bargaining
Partisan and national biases that narrow the perceived zone of agreement	"Tit for tat" to reward other parties for cooperative moves, to undermine hostility due to biases
	Reframed issues
	Appointed a mediator
Cultural difference	Informal Track II and workshops
	Revealed and requested private information

listed response should not be interpreted as the only factor to affect the barrier with which it is paired, and the problem listed was not necessarily the response's only target. Nor do all the responses listed in the section below appear in the table. The table only illustrates the links between certain identified barriers and the responses that negotiators have developed in specific cases over time to achieve successful negotiation despite these barriers.

Rather than follow the analytical order of the previous section, this section is organized in a dynamic order to track more closely the different stages in the practice experienced by international negotiators. A standard framework divides the process conceptually into four phases: diagnosis, formula, detail, and ratification (Hampson and Hart 1995; Zartman and Berman 1982); here we do not discuss ratification separately. Some of the steps described are moves at the negotiating table, and others are moves that take place away from the table. Throughout the section each response is linked to a previously discussed concept. We adopt this dynamic order because steps taken early in a negotiation can shape the path followed later. Another reason is to bring together research lines that have developed separately. We believe that many political science international relations scholars know relatively little about how practical negotiations occur or how negotiation scholars have conceptualized this process. Likewise, much of the negotiation literature has engaged less with recent developments in political science than would be valuable. We hope this way of linking related literatures will stimulate productive new thinking.

We assume that negotiators facing conflicting preferences always attempt to persuade their counterparts to change their minds when explicit communication is possible. Research also shows that far more than simple persuasion is involved in observed successes. Naturally this research has not found any recipe for success that is guaranteed to work in every situation. Indeed, some possible responses are inherently in tension with one another. Nor has the research identified many contingent propositions, specifying the conditions under which certain responses are more and less effective. In addition, few of the studies discussed below provide definitive support for the causal relationships they suggest. Our appendix will suggest future analytical and empirical work that could push this literature forward.

Diagnosis and Other Preparation

Parties contemplating a possible negotiation face a broad range of uncertainties, shared and strategic, as well as possible distrust and biased information processing. To deal with these problems without taking high risks, the parties often begin with a modest diagnostic or preparatory or prenegotiation phase. At first, a party may not be certain that negotiation is the best available move; no agreement might be preferable. Parties often are uncertain about how others would respond to a proposal for formal talks and do not want to make a public offer that will be rejected. In this phase, parties explore cautiously whether a mutual-gain deal could be negotiated (Stein 1989). An initial diagnosis may be revised throughout the negotiation.

During the diagnostic stage, the parties consider which setup for the prospective negotiation, if any, would be best for success. Which parties should be included and excluded? Which issues should be added or subtracted (Lax and Sebenius 2006)? Which international regime, if any, should be selected as the legal context? Should domestic skeptics be added to the delegation to help with ratification? In 1944, U.S. Treasury Secretary Henry Morgenthau included an isolationist midwestern banker on the delegation to Bretton Woods. After this isolationist experienced the arguments and processed the costs and benefits in the negotiation, he eventually supported the campaign for ratification of the historic agreement to create the International Monetary Fund and World Bank, doing so over the opposition of the American Bankers' Association (Eckes 1975). Choosing an appropriate *representative from the opposition* can facilitate information transmission and credibility when ex ante the representative would have been expected to oppose the deal (Calvert 1985).

In this early stage planners often *explore potential parties* and have sometimes *excluded parties with extreme preferences*, at least until after an initial smaller agreement has been implemented. Arguably, the 1993 Arusha Agreement over Rwanda could not have been attained with the inclusion of the Akazu (that is, the future génocidaires), as the mediators had wanted (Jones 2001). The decision whether to include "spoilers" depends on the degree or type of spoilers and their ability to upset an agreement if excluded compared with their ability to prevent an agreement if included (Calvert 1985; Leeds 1999). This point comes with important caveats. Many international organizations negotiate under a consensus or unanimity rule, so that no party can be excluded. An agreement's value will also diminish with the size and number of parties excluded.

In all cases, an early diagnostic question is whether the parties (once identified) face a positive zone of agreement or bargaining range. When attempting to settle a war in particular, an early question for a prospective negotiator or mediator is whether all parties to the conflict believe that they have reached a painful stalemate that is unlikely to change, or some believe they still can win by fighting. In some cases, in which this subjective appreciation of the situation was absent and there was no clear positive zone of agreement, mediators have taken steps to influence the parties' perceptions in ways that opened a positive subjective bargaining range. Such steps are sometimes termed "making the situation ripe" for a negotiation to begin. Examples include U.S. Secretary of State Henry Kissinger with Golda Meir in 1974 in the Sinai withdrawal negotiations and U.S. Assistant Secretary of State Chester Crocker in 1986 with South Africa and Angola (Zartman 2000).

When severe distrust has prevailed between warring groups or societies, especially in protracted conflicts, *informal transnational links* have reduced distrust, improved relationships, and permitted more flexible information processing and the formulating of new ideas. *"Track II" contacts* (for example, between academic scholars and retired government officials) and problem-solving workshops (often mediated by an international party not directly involved in the conflict) exemplify these informal links. The early stages have also allowed time for the *preparation of cadres of individuals* ready to conduct productive negotiations when conditions were propitious (Kelman 1996), even when the governments' reservation values do not change in the short term.

With strongly opposing preferences and severe distrust, such as between Mao's China and the United States during the Cold War, explicit communication is unlikely to be believed. In such cases, a *tacit "tit for tat" communicative strategy* has signaled openness to at least a tacit agreement to limit hostile acts and has enabled learning about the other's openness to negotiation, while protecting against exploitation (Axelrod 1984; Schelling 1960). In this strategy, one party initiates a cooperative move, then rewards the other for a cooperative response and punishes it for a hostile response. This strategy has sometimes finessed the challenges of uncertainty, distrust, bias, and cultural differences. Tacit tit for tat also has been embedded in a nonviolent bargaining strategy that includes explicit communication and aims for explicit agreement. The PRC's invitation to the U.S. Ping-Pong team to visit Beijing in 1969 was a move in a tacit negotiation that ended with an explicit China–U.S. agreement in 1972. In 2012, the Muslim Brotherhood in Egypt and the Supreme Council of the Armed Forces carried out repeated and successful occasions of tacit bargaining throughout the transition that resulted in the Brotherhood's Mohamed Morsi taking office as president.

In many successful cases of explicit bargaining, the preparatory and sometimes later phases are kept *confidential*. The parties have withheld information from their constituents and outside players at least temporarily. Electorally motivated leaders may fear that domestic constituencies will mobilize to prevent concessions and that domestic rivals will use the controversy against them for short-term gain before longer-term gains from negotiation can be developed. In 1950, the founders of the European Community thus finessed internal opposition temporarily by denying information to constituents until a provisional deal containing value for their countries could be announced. When national law requires a subsequent transparent ratification phase open to public participation, constituents have an opportunity to amend or reject the outcome of the negotiation, conferring legitimacy on the result. Knowing that ratification will be required gives the negotiator an incentive to resist a deal that could not be ratified.[15]

With some trust but substantive uncertainty, parties have engaged in *joint study and research*, collecting and discussing information to improve the knowledge base, either in parallel with sharing or in fully joint activity, without yet committing to seek a deeper agreement. When in 1982 governments that were parties to the General Agreement on Tariffs and Trade (GATT) began parallel research on what would happen if they reduced barriers to trade in services, they lacked adequate information to know their own interests. After learning and subsequent negotiation over details, they signed a multilateral services deal in 1993 (Paemen and Bensch 1995).

Parties have sometimes invited *neutral third parties* such as international agencies and research universities to serve as trusted fact-finders and provide better technical information (as in the law of the sea talks; Antrim and Sebenius 1992). This step not only improves the information base; it also adds third parties that in the course of the negotiation may be able to evaluate information more credibly in a manner that most consider unbiased.

When some nations have lacked sufficient institutional capacity to participate meaningfully, *technical assistance* from wealthier parties and international organizations has improved those capacities and hence the scope of the eventual agreement. In trade negotiations, the donor states, the United Nations Conference on Trade and

---

15. Secrecy also rules out some steps that could increase the likelihood and magnitude of gains, such as campaigns to generate public support.

Development, WTO, and the development banks pursued such a program after 2000.

In some cases, states have responded to the substantive and collective action problems listed earlier not with ad hoc agreements but by attempting to negotiate the creation of a *new standing international organization* or a new pact based on an established one. Young (1994) analyzes negotiations to create created environmental organizations. Singh (2008) shows how the recent diffusion in the global power structure has affected negotiations over institutions for the global information economy.

Negotiating a Formula

A second phase begins with the agreement to negotiate toward an explicit deal. In some cases, when delegations began by trying immediately to reach agreement on specific details at issue, they faced too much shared uncertainty about the problem to know exactly how to proceed. In other cases, with plentiful information about the problem but conflicting initial preferences, distrust, and strong constituency pressures, negotiators have opened with exaggerated demands for concessions on the distributive issues. They then have defended their positions against others' demands, soon bogging down into deadlock and a shared sense of futility, in part owing to perceived difficulties in enforcing an agreement or expectation about future shifts in relative power.

One approach that has succeeded in these circumstances is to *postpone haggling over details until after a search for an agreed general formula* or set of principles that defines the negotiation process and the requirements of a final agreement (Zartman and Berman 1982). For a formula to play this structuring role, it must be comprehensive and viewed as equitable (Young 1989).[16] Parties with serious differences and deep distrust have sometimes been able at least to agree on such principles for talks. When agreeing on a formula helps, it does so by reducing the sense of distrust and futility that derive from con-

---

16. Caveat: more than one possible set of principles may be conceivable, and parties may attempt to claim value by advancing rival formulas geared to their distributional objectives.

flicting preferences and the experience of conflict. Examples of joint-gain successes that resulted from the formula-first process include Bretton Woods 1944; the Panama–U.S. Panama Canal Treaty 1977 (Kennedy School of Government 1979); the Law of the Sea Pact; the agreement on Namibia 1988; and the Dayton Accords ending war in Yugoslavia 1995 (Curran, Sebenius, and Watkins 2004).

The formula often sets the agenda of issues to be negotiated at least initially. Parties have sometimes moved forward by agreeing to *exclude or postpone an issue* they cared about but that would destroy a zone of agreement at the time (Sebenius 1984), such as Jerusalem in Israel-Palestine talks.

When parties have had conflicting preferences on one issue (such as whether OECD countries should continue to subsidize agriculture or whether Iran should continue its nuclear program), a standard response has been to *add another issue that has opposite distributional effects*, expecting that the two could be linked for balance and mutual gain during the later detail phase. In the 1980s, the formula for the GATT's talks in the Uruguay round deliberately included both services and agriculture as issues, in the hope that the EU and Japan could gain on services enough to "pay for" their concessions on agriculture.[17]

A key element of many formulas has been to *set a deadline* or, in a complex case, a sequence of intermediate deadlines, if natural deadlines do not present themselves (Zartman 1987). Negotiators thinking strategically of their distributive goals tend to hold back costly concessions until just before the last possible moment in order to extract gains. Setting deadlines could, in principle, reduce the negative effects of uncertainties that negotiating parties have about "how long their opponents can last." George Mitchell, whose mediation of the protracted Northern Ireland religious conflict resulted in the historic 1998 Good Friday agreement, said that persuading all parties to agree to set a deadline was a critical step in that dynamic success (Curran, Sebenius, and Watkins 2004; Mitchell 1998). Mediators' decisions to pack their bags also can provide an effective deadline, as U.S. Secretary of State Henry Kissinger did in Damascus in 1974 and as

---

17. At the formula stage, however, negotiators often have not yet discovered enough information about the issues, private preferences, and domestic political reactions to forecast well the consequences of selecting a particular set of issues.

Secretary Warren Christopher and Assistant Secretary Richard Holbrooke did at Dayton in 1994 (Holbrooke 1999).[18]

When uncertainties have been great, the issues complex, and dozens of states involved, negotiators have moved toward success by first creating a set of different subsidiary *specialized negotiating bodies*, each with its own chair, to specialize on different issues (Hampson and Hart 1995). In such institutional arrangements, each state is usually eligible to send a delegate to each specialized body, and mechanisms are provided for linking the specialized talks during and at the end of the negotiation. Existing international institutions can play an important role in setting up specialized bodies.

Negotiating Details

Once parties agree to negotiate, which may involve agreeing on a formula, the process proceeds to negotiating over details of a provisional deal—the stage that is most familiar and is sometimes mistakenly thought to be the whole of negotiation.

In situations that include the possible compatibility of some objectives and some trust but where missing and distorted information form barriers to agreement, negotiators have produced successes by *revealing selected private information* to other negotiators and asking the others to reciprocate in private discussions. These negotiators have used a "partially integrative" strategy (see chapter 5), which involves greater mutual openness with information than a purely distributive strategy allows. In 1985, U.S. Secretary of the Treasury James Baker faced an ever-expanding deficit in U.S. trade, rising protectionist pressure at home, and a rising value of the dollar abroad. He convinced President Reagan that the dollar was part of the problem and that the United States should do something to bring it down. Unilateral action in the foreign-exchange markets could have been highly disruptive. Baker revealed secretly to Japan's finance minister Noboru Takeshita that he was interested in negotiating an agreement that would lower

18. An important risk of setting deadlines is that if parties commit publicly to meet a deadline and then fail to do so, they may damage the credibility of their process more than if they had not set a deadline.

the dollar (a change in U.S. policy) and raise the yen, a move that was unpopular in Japan's export sector. Baker learned in return that Takeshita shared his concern about the protectionist-trade legislation then being submitted in Congress. Together, they timed the announcement of their agreement to ease the dollar down, joined by three European states, for maximum impact on Congress (Funabashi 1988).

Negotiation texts document many examples of professionals practicing what Malhotra and Bazerman (2007) call "investigative negotiation," which involves *requesting private information* from the other party. In October 2000, U.S. Ambassador to the UN Richard Holbrooke was dealing with a fixed-pie standoff. Congress had decided to stop paying its UN dues of nearly $1 billion by January 1, 2001, unless the other members agreed to lower the U.S. assessment from 25 percent to 22 percent. Many countries refused this demand, which would require increasing their own assessments. Holbrooke and his team then asked every single country why they could not agree. By asking, the Americans learned that many countries were actually willing to increase their dues but could not do so by January 1, 2001; their budgets for the coming fiscal year had already been set. With this formerly private information in view, Holbrooke proposed a deal acceptable to all: the United States would reduce its assessment to 22 percent by Congress's legal deadline, and other nations would increase their contributions in 2002. To cover the one-year shortfall, Holbrooke (through a side negotiation) persuaded billionaire Ted Turner to make a personal donation of $30 million (Malhotra and Bazerman 2007, pp. 49–52). This example illustrates two ways to break a deadlock besides asking for private information. Holbrooke's team saw a way to split a seemingly fixed-pie issue into two issues— contribution amounts and their timing—then link them. He also changed the game by adding a new party.

A classic remedy for conflicting preferences is to search for pairs of issues that could be linked for mutual gain. The ideal model is a pair of issues such that one party privately values issue A more than B, while the other party values B more than A, even though both parties say they want both issues. Parties or mediators explore for new information about these private priorities, and when possible propose to link issues that will give each side something it values more at the expense of something it values less. This remedy has repeatedly resolved issues that separately had low integrative potential. During the Law of the Sea talks of the 1970s, when states were locked in a fruitless debate over incompatible positions, a mediator learned that the delegations' private priorities across the issues in dispute were shifting. He made a creative proposal that linked two issues that had been independent and succeeded in dovetailing the evolving private differences (Antrim and Sebenius 1992; see also Haas 1980; Poast 2012; Tollison and Willett 1979). In the Namibia negotiations of 1980–88, the parties achieved their demands by pairing them exactly—withdrawal of 50,000 Cuban troops in exchange for withdrawal of 50,000 South African troops (Zartman 1987).[19] The presence of international organizations has facilitated such mutual-gain linkages of issues that were otherwise unrelated, as when Great Britain in 1982 accepted the EU budget in exchange for its EU partners' support for sanctions against Argentina during the Falklands/Malvinas war (Martin 1992).

Another response to deadlock has been to *add an issue with greater integrative potential*. For example, sometimes negotiating to establish a qualitative rule that establishes parties' future rights and obligations has greater potential to make both parties better off (even without linking to another issue) than negotiating over money (Walton and McKersie 1965; Winham 1986). With rules, a "veil of uncertainty" about their future application makes it less clear how much a party will lose or gain (Young 1989), which may reduce the anticipation of shifts in bargaining power that generate commitment problems. The more specialized and precise the rules are, however, the less is the uncertainty about their application and the less easily they can serve as general but vague guarantors of the future. Similarly, greater enforcement capacity can have an effect like more specific rules and even make agreement more difficult to reach, according to Fearon (1998).

Negotiators and mediators have also broken deadlocks by *reframing the issues* to one or more of the parties to change their reservation values. Mediators have provided new information and new interpretations of existing information to persuade a party that its alternative to agreement is worse or less likely than it believed it to be, or

19. Linking the wrong issues—such as adding one whose bargaining range is very small or zero—could destroy an agreement zone.

that a proposal is better than it believed. Such reframing has sometimes successfully changed reservation values, even the precisely stated values of powerful states.[20]

Another creative response to deadlock due to opposing preferences has been to *reframe the issue space* itself—to replace a familiar set of difficult issues with a fresh set. In the late 1940s, West European states subsumed the historic military conflict between France and Germany by embedding both countries in the regional European Coal and Steel Community and later the European Community. In 1998, Peru and Ecuador resolved a border dispute by focusing on development rather than on legal boundary lines. The Panama Canal formula of Panamanian ownership with U.S. security, the Mideast formula of Egyptian territory and Israeli security, Aceh self-government, and Chiapas free-determination are all instances of creative ways to frame an agreement in new terms that meet both sides' needs (Hampson and Zartman 2012).

Success is more likely and faster when negotiators can craft agreements around *salient and easily understood solutions.* Negotiations on a ban of an undesired practice or an across-the-board percentage cut (for example, the 1987 CFC agreement) are less likely to bog down in lengthy talks and yield disappointing results than negotiations that require highly complex arrangements, such as in the Law of the Sea talks (Young 1989) and recent WTO rounds. Complex arrangements require more information, such as forecasts of the consequences of particular detailed proposals. The time it takes to collect information and negotiate proposals allows the support of constituencies to dissipate as they shift to alternative courses of action and as other issues rise in public salience.

International negotiators often try to break deadlocks by taking steps to *influence the domestic politics* of their home and partner countries. In trade talks, governments have long striven to negotiate concessions for their exporters in order to induce the export groups to advocate ratification at home, thus countering domestic opposition to concessions. A negotiator sometimes decides to grant a concession that still leaves his or her side above its resistance point in order to

---

20. For example, on Western wartime negotiations with Stalin, see Iklé 1964, pp. 182–90; on military base negotiations in the 1970s, see Wriggins 1976; and on WTO negotiations between 1999 and 2001, see Odell 2009.

aid a counterpart in another state in achieving ratification in his or her country (Odell 2000; Odell and Lang 1992). In five bilateral trade episodes with Japan, when U.S. negotiators used the two tactics of participation expansion and alternative specification to expand Japan's domestic political support for agreement, they gained more than when they did not use these tactics (Schoppa 1993).

More lasting *changes in domestic political institutions* have encouraged closer convergence between constituencies and their negotiators during the negotiation process. In its 1973 trade act, the United States established sectoral business advisory committees to meet privately with trade negotiators dealing with their industries during GATT talks. In this process business representatives advised negotiators while simultaneously the negotiators could explain the constraints overseas to the business representatives. The negotiators were also able to moderate extreme constituency demands by playing one industry against another, preparing the way for ratification (Odell 2000, chap. 8; Winham 1980).

In multiparty talks, states often form coalitions opposing each other. In this situation, one remedy for deadlock has been to *create a bridging coalition* of states coming from both sides of the fault line. Such cross-cutting coalitions have facilitated agreements in talks over trade, the environment (Hampson and Hart 1995), and security.

An example is the negotiation that produced the 1991 Paris Agreement that finally ended the long civil war in Cambodia. The agreement came about after the United States was able to move peacemaking into the UN Security Council. The five permanent members, who were rivals on many issues including this war, decided to press the Cambodian parties to accept a compromise that ended the war. This approach worked in this case at this time in part because the Cambodian parties had fought to a costly stalemate. Also the Soviet Union under Gorbachev, China after the Tiananmen massacre, and Vietnam all changed their general foreign-policy preferences to place greater weight on improving relations with the United States. By talking confidentially they found they could agree on a formula of an all-faction National Council in Cambodia under UN trusteeship to organize elections and monitor a cease-fire and foreign troop withdrawal. The UN was organized and ready to facilitate talks and administer the transition, easing parties' commitment problems (Hampson and Zartman 2012).

When building a coalition in multiparty talks, the *sequence* in which the negotiator approaches potential partners probably affects the likelihood of success. The choice of a particular path (party A, then B, then C) has made a difference either by exploiting the influence relationships between partners, shaping outcome expectations, concealing information from other potential blocking coalitions, or worsening the no-deal alternatives of those remaining outside the coalition (Sebenius 1996). In an example of worsening the alternatives of those outside the coalition, U.S. Federal Reserve chairman Paul Volcker in the 1980s wanted to build an international coalition in support of new rules requiring OECD banks to hold greater capital. If one country added this requirement alone, it would impose a competitive disadvantage on its own banks. The European Commission was working on a plan, but Volcker disliked their approach. Therefore, while participating in the multilateral central bank negotiations in Basel, Volcker privately negotiated a deal with the Bank of England. The U.S. and U.K. preferences were close and together they were home to a major share of the world banking system. Next, he turned privately to Japan. Tokyo preferred to leave its banks free of this new costly requirement, but Japanese banks were expanding into the U.S. market and vulnerable to being shut out if they did not cooperate with the Fed. Facing this implicit threat, Tokyo signed up, after significant modifications. Then, with the U.S., U.K., and Japanese markets all committed to the same model, a European Commission model for European banks alone would have put European banks at a disadvantage. The previously implacable German Bundesbank then also fell into line. Volcker bootstrapped, moving progressively from the easiest to the most difficult, and thus progressively worsened the no-deal alternatives of outsiders (see Sebenius 1996 and works cited therein).

Both advocates and opponents of particular negotiated agreements, including transnational nongovernmental networks, have attempted to generate public support by *publicizing their ideas to mass media* and cooperating with like-minded environmental, human rights, labor, and business *networks* (Hampson and Hart 1995). Talks on the 1987 ozone treaty (Benedick 1991) and the UN treaty banning land mines (Price 1998) provide evidence of the effects of public engagement. In the land-mines case, nonstate norm entrepreneurs stimulated a systemic change in the relevant international norms. Transnational networks have contributed to overcoming several obstacles to success-ful negotiation. They provide state officials with information about the problem and later about possible noncompliance with an agree-ment; they reframe issues with different reference points; and they span multiple cultures, which may counter suspicions that the pro-posed agreement will impose alien norms on one's society. Nongov-ernmental organizations (NGOs) can also stop negotiations, as they helped stop a 1998 draft OECD investment agreement (Kobrin 1998).

Mediators have also helped address deadlocks due to problems of information, commitment credibility, conflicting preferences, distrust, and internal divisions (Crocker, Hampson, and Aall 2002; Kydd 2010). Mediations have contributed both to achieving peacetime multi-lateral regime agreements and to ending wars. Mediators have used a variety of tactics depending on the obstacle. When the obstacle was the inability to communicate credibly, as with the Israelis and Pales-tinians in 1993, the Norwegian mediators used the most passive tactic of facilitating communications. When parties were unable to provide ideas for a solution, as in the war in Bosnia, Richard Holbrooke played the more involved role of a mediator as a formulator in Day-ton. George Mitchell, like many with little power, used communica-tion and formulation tactics and succeeded in Northern Ireland, as have leaders in the EU and the WTO (Odell 2005; Tallberg 2010).[21] When available outcomes were not large enough to attract the parties, or a zone of agreement could not be opened with more gentle tactics, a mediator has played the most forceful role of manipulator. Kissinger in the second Sinai withdrawals (Mintz 2007), Lord Carrington in the war in Rhodesia (Rothchild 1996), and Holbrooke in Bosnia il-lustrate powerful manipulative tactics contributing to peace. In some 600 attempts at mediation during violent conflicts, the more manipu-lative strategies had a higher simple success rate than mediations lim-ited to less forceful moves did (Bercovitch 1996).

International mediators have varied in their degree of neutrality, the amount of power assets they wielded, and the strategies they chose.

---

21. The concept of formulation tactics here can include proposing a formula, as discussed earlier, but is broader, also including a variety of other process moves such as chairing the talks, suggesting procedures, and suggesting concessions that a party could make.

Whereas it is often assumed that neutrality is valuable, some research indicates instead that the more biased a mediator is toward one of the parties, the more successful is the mediation. The reasoning is that if a mediator is biased toward one of the parties, that party is more likely to believe advice from the mediator that it cannot expect greater concessions from the opposing party and should settle. A bias in favor of one party also gives the mediator greater capacity to extract concessions from that party (Kydd 2003; Savun 2008).[22]

Today, more than one mediator often is involved in trying to assist peace negotiations in any given conflict, sometimes sequentially, sometimes simultaneously. Both benefits and liabilities come with multiparty mediation (Kydd 2012).

Mediators and others have succeeded by proposing an *informal, single negotiating text* (Buzan 1981; Raiffa, Richardson, and Metcalfe 2002). The text is informal in the sense that at the moment of proposal no party has accepted it. Such an informal text typically covers all issues, chooses a single position on each issue, and attempts to achieve balance through the whole; it is not a cautious aggregation of all factions' positions. Such a relatively bold attempt to create a focal point contributes to agreement if the parties accept it as a basis for further negotiation. This move helps address several barriers. It has established a basis for common knowledge—for example, by laying out what is known or unknown about what is being negotiated. The text and the consultations leading to it have corrected self-serving biases, revealing to proponents that their proposals (omitted from the text) have gained little support. Such a text has also helped negotiators overcome domestic opposition from a special interest by omitting the position of that interest from the text. This helps the negotiator argue to his or her prime minister that a neutral mediator reports the demand is not negotiable; hence if the government insists on the minority's demand, it could lose the gains that the deal offers its majority. The obvious risk of the single text is that a party or faction will reject it even as a basis for future talks (Odell 2005), but mediators are willing to take greater risks as they get closer to a deadline

---

22. The strategic analysis of mediation remains an active area of research, with varying views on when or whether it can be effective (Fey and Ramsay 2010; Ramsay 2011).

(Odell interviews with WTO mediators). Such single negotiating texts contributed to the 1978 Camp David peace agreement between Egypt and Israel and the 2001 WTO agreement to launch the Doha round.

After parties have dug in behind public defensive positions, it is virtually impossible to break a significant deadlock by limiting talks to official meetings attended by 150 delegations and reported to all capitals. Domestic political constraints make breaking the deadlock difficult. To encourage delegations to consider changes in their public positions, some organization leaders and negotiators have held *confidential informal meetings* in which no official records are kept and reporting to capitals may not be required. They invite a small group, including leading defenders of rival positions. In these informal meetings, delegates and mediators report information to correct biases, improve their evolving diagnosis of the blockage, test reactions to integrative steps such as possible linkages, reframe the issue space, and explore inventive solutions not yet considered by any party—or any combination of these steps.[23]

When the subject of the agreement entails greater uncertainty about the future—subjects such as mutual security and monetary policy—in some cases agreement has been facilitated by designing *pacts with greater flexibility*. One form of this flexibility incorporates shorter duration plus an opportunity to renegotiate in the future. Group of 7 agreements for macroeconomic coordination during the 1970s and 1980s had very short durations for this reason (Koremenos 2005). Another form of dealing with uncertainty incorporates an escape clause (Koremenos 2001; Rosendorff and Milner 2001). For example, the GATT 1947 authorized tariff increases that were inconsistent with the general rules, but only after following certain investigative procedures, only if the new barrier applied equally to all exporting countries, and only for a maximum of five years.

A common view is that bargaining success is more likely if the parties agree on a *clear-cut mechanism to ensure compliance* (Young

---

23. If no agreed process assures the many excluded a genuine opportunity to study and change what is decided in the small meeting, the many may fear being coerced into accepting a fait accompli (as some did during the WTO's disappointing 1999 Seattle ministerial), and a backlash could result (Odell 2009).

1989). States have responded to the problems of incentives for future defection and weak commitment credibility with a variety of modalities. One has been to focus the negotiation on regulating actions that are easier to police (Fortna 2003; Hampson and Hart 1995; Young 1989). In other cases, when settling a civil war as in Cambodia and Rhodesia, parties have invited into the negotiation third parties (for example, the UN, a regional organization, or a powerful state not participating in the war) that are willing on an ad hoc basis to enforce compliance using armed force, thus protecting parties that would otherwise be vulnerable to exploitation (Rothchild 1996; Walter 2013).[24] In some peacetime negotiations, states have added a standing legal-dispute-settlement provision whereby an aggrieved party can seek redress through a common institution. The most highly legalized examples today are in the EU and the WTO.[25] Other remedies include using domestic political institutions to bind governments to their international promises and requiring them to pay a domestic political cost if they deviate from a commitment in the future (Morrow 1999). These problems have also been avoided by linking the agreement to an established formal institution that a potential cheater values, or by activating domestic constituency groups that would suffer from a lack of compliance. NGOs that value the agreement have monitored and publicized compliance failures in light of international norms. States with sufficient power have issued bilateral threats or promises to influence others' compliance.

At the same time, recall the arguments that stronger enforcement prospects may lead to more resolute strategies during the negotiation and some cultures may prefer informal cooperation. Many international institutions are not fully legalized: they lack tribunals independent of the member states, and their provisions are less precise and less binding than in the EU or WTO (Goldstein et al. 2000). "Soft

24. Some have argued, however, that third-party interventions create a weak basis for long-term agreements owing to artificial short term incentives provided by the third party (Beardsley 2008).

25. If the institution is not robust to future changes in the relative power of the involved parties, it may not succeed in overcoming commitment problems during the negotiation.

law" in many varieties is more widespread than hard law in international relations (Abbott and Snidal 2000).

Post-agreement compliance bargaining among signatories often has had an important effect in practice on the behavior that is covered by "compliance." For example, the goal of even the WTO's highly legalized regime is to promote settlement of disputes directly between parties. After a state files suit against another in Geneva, the states negotiate and reach a settlement agreement before a final WTO ruling in more than half the cases. Little research has illuminated compliance bargaining as such, but some studies indicate paths (Jönsson and Tallberg 1998; Spector and Zartman 2003; Tallberg and Smith 2012).

Conclusion

This chapter has summarized research on international negotiation that identifies key barriers to agreement. It documents strategies and tactics that have succeeded in overcoming barriers and breaking deadlocks in many diverse cases. It suggests effective moves at different stages of the negotiation—from the earliest stage, in which the parties aiming at agreement might consider the pros and cons of excluding parties with extreme views from the first part of the negotiation, to a later stage that might include agreeing on a formula or basic principles before tackling specific details, and to the final stage that includes negotiating about compliance.

Social scientists in the fields of international negotiation and bargaining have made significant strides, working within different analytical and methodological traditions. Yet there are still significant gaps in our understanding. Political scientists are underrepresented in the field of negotiation and are missing opportunities to improve understanding of this ubiquitous process in international relations. We suggest four main types of research opportunities in an appendix.

Lessons from the experience of international negotiation can also inform the study of domestic political negotiation. For example, members of legislatures and executive agencies might learn from the staging of a negotiation. In the first stages, exploring what parties would best be included in the preliminary negotiation involves weighing the gains from excluding individuals with extreme ideas who might act as spoilers to any negotiation versus including them in the hope that they will learn from the process and, drawing on their hard-line reputations, be able to sell the eventual agreement to other members of their party in the legislature. In the early stages, informal processes and confidentiality are particularly crucial. Joint research and fact-finding can both build trust among the individuals and create bodies of data on which the future negotiation can rely. Neutral institutions such as the U.S. Congressional Budget Office can also provide reliable data. Later, legislators and administrators who engage in negotiation can learn from the techniques of setting deadlines, establishing specialized negotiating bodies, revealing and requesting private information, agreeing on a formula before details, adding issues with integrative potential or opposite distributional consequences, linking issues and "dovetailing" by trading on issues with high values for one party but low values for the other, reframing specific issues and the issue space, creating bridging coalitions, creating an informal negotiating text, and sequencing to provide wins for all on small issues and to build trust before proceeding to the more difficult issues.

This chapter's many findings have obvious implications for the practice of political negotiation, both international and domestic, where we see frequent important deadlocks. Additional rigorous scholarship would have great benefits for both theory and practice.

Appendix on Research Opportunities

The subject of international negotiation presents many opportunities for new research by political scientists and others. The world of international relations today is replete with negotiations. Yet political science has devoted far less attention to this ubiquitous process than to other important processes and subjects. Looking forward, we advance a selection of ideas clustered into four broad sets, addressing empirical, methodological, theoretical, and normative (or prescriptive) questions and problems, recognizing that many ideas could be placed in more than one of these categories.

Empirical Questions and Problems

While some findings from case studies have been confirmed beyond a handful of cases, many others need to be checked through cases from other issue domains, regions, and periods. Some experimental findings have been documented through the field study of international negotiation, but more confirmation outside of the laboratory is needed. Negotiation research also underrepresents the experiences of developing and postcommunist countries.

Moving from these cross-cutting gaps to more particular concerns, many problems deserve investigation. When negotiators add flexibility provisions to treaties, such as escape clauses in trade agreements, these provisions have welfare costs. However, we do not know whether and when these provisions cost more than they are worth. Likewise, what are the costs of treaty-monitoring provisions and in what circumstances, if any, are they worth the bargain? A larger question is how effective international agreements have been in mitigating the problems to which they were addressed. Although some research has estimated agreement effects, research on this major issue has been stymied by a serious methodological challenge. Effectiveness can be meaningful relative only to a counterfactual agreement not reached.

In addition, we do not fully understand the role of nonstate actors in international negotiations. Thinking about negotiation as an activity exclusively between sovereign states forecloses the study of negotiations between states and NGOs, semisovereign/autonomous regions, and nonstate actors that nevertheless hold a virtual monopoly on the use of force within a region. We might also ask why, today, are so many multilateral negotiations deadlocked at the same time? Are we at the end of an era in international organization?

Negotiations also are or will be taking place in emerging issue areas. Negotiations over territories, currently in areas like the South China Sea with competing territorial claims, are likely to remain common. However, areas including human rights practices and drug smuggling give rise not only to nonstate actors but also potentially to less studied causal dynamics such as diffusion (Kydd 2000). Other areas, such as negotiations on climate change, generate new challenges due to a range of technical uncertainties, long time horizons, and potentially massive distributional consequences both across and within states.

Methodological Questions and Problems

Research on international negotiation also faces methodological challenges. At the micro level, this subject is negotiator behavior—what negotiators or delegations do in regard to other actors, what determines their behavior, and what difference it makes. Studying international negotiator behavior is only an extension of the familiar study of political behavior.

One fundamental challenge is that international negotiations are difficult to observe directly. These negotiations are confidential and rarely allow participant observation. Much of the process, as we know from case studies, is informal and not always recorded in documents; hence, archives may be incomplete. However, social scientists have found ways to study other phenomena that are difficult to observe directly; this problem need not block productive new research.

Ultimately, every known empirical or analytical research design and technique has limitations as well as strengths. For this reason, using multiple methods (over time if not simultaneously, and by teams if not by individual researchers) offers the best chance for valid answers to our questions. Along the way, new case studies can take advantage of new and more rigorous qualitative methodology for causal analysis (for a recent introduction, see Mahoney 2010). Some past negotiation case studies have not used these methods as fully as possible, perhaps discouraging the integration of these studies into political science more widely.

Few large-n data sets on negotiation behavior have been created outside the laboratory (for example, Druckman 2001; Dür and Mateo 2010; Hopmann 1974). This too could be an opportunity for future research. Once created, these data might be used to test propositions developed with case studies or formal models. Yet creating valid data on international negotiation processes outside the laboratory involves thorny problems. Hopmann (2002), a pioneer in such efforts, has explained that he shifted to qualitative methods in part because the early quantitative measures of negotiation failed to capture essential aspects of the process, casting doubt on the value of the conclusions. These failures led policymakers to show little interest in the results. Hopmann and others have nevertheless proposed ways in which better quantitative data on the process might be created today (see Carnevale and De Dreu 2006 and *International Negotiation*, volume 7, issue 1 [2002]).

Future experimental research also presents ample opportunities. One open line of inquiry concerns the universality of the cognitive factors discussed earlier. For example, the fixed-pie bias may not generalize across cultures (Morris and Gelfand 2004). Laboratory investigation could also help us better understand the role of affective variables. What types of emotions are triggered in negotiation, how are they triggered, and what are their physiological bases? Whereas studies of emotion have appeared in the bargaining literature (Tingley, Lee, and Renshon 2013), there is less work directly addressed to international relations. Other questions, such as the efficacy of having multiple mediators, are amenable to laboratory-based investigation. Finally, the use of field experiments has grown in recent years (Gerber and Green 2012) and these experiments have begun to be used in international relations (Chilton and Tingley 2013). These designs could help in understanding negotiation.

Theoretical Questions and Problems

In addressing theoretical questions, one class of opportunities involves investigating conditions under which remedies discussed earlier are more and less effective. Although some research, not reported here, has addressed this problem, much more along this line is needed. For example, under what conditions are attempts to change reservation values more effective? Folk wisdom and scholarship often discuss using "carrots and sticks" at roughly the same time, but thinking of the target behaviorally, the two could have contradictory effects. How might the two moves or tactics interact? The present literature is inconsistent regarding when partial or small-scale agreements lead to larger ones, and when smaller agreements bleed off pressure for more resolution and undermine larger agreements. We also need cases and contexts in which new scientific information may discourage negotiated agreement as well as promote it.

Formal work could study how the order of issues discussed can affect the negotiation outcome. Formal and other research is needed to improve our knowledge of coalition formation, including the trade-off between larger-size coalitions and shifting the median preference. Formal work could go further in explaining mediation, including questions such as where the mediators obtain their information and the differences between single and multiple mediators.

Much negotiation and bargaining research has sidestepped the effects of emotions. Outside the laboratory it is difficult to find credible evidence of strong emotions in international negotiators or leaders and isolate the effects of emotions from those of other causal factors. Yet pioneers in this field have suggested some exciting possible paths for research. Neuroscientists and psychologists are moving to the view that cognition and emotion are intertwined rather than competing processes in the human mind, and that rationality itself depends on a type of prior emotional processing (McDermott 2004; Mercer 2005, 2010). Laboratory research on emotion in negotiation has been under way since the late 1980s and has become progressively more complex (Barry 2008). Some research shows that positive affect can lead to more integrative agreements. Some studies focus on the effects of negotiators' emotions on their own behavior, while others focus on the effect of negotiators' emotions on others' behavior. In an example of negotiators' emotions affecting their own behavior, Carnevale (2008) found that even mild positive affect reverses the familiar finding about loss aversion. Usually, a loss frame produces fewer concessions than a gain frame does. However, subjects exposed to a positive-affect manipulation made *more* concessions when their outcomes were framed as losses and fewer concessions when the outcomes were framed as gains, both in comparison with controls. As an example of negotiators' emotions affecting others' behavior, Kopelman and Rosette (2008) studied how cultural difference may interact with emotions. They presented videos showing U.S. negotiators displaying either positive or negative emotions to two sets of subjects from East Asia and Israel. The East Asians were more likely to accept an offer from the positive than the negative U.S. negotiator; the Israelis were equally likely to accept an offer from either.

The role of power is relatively well understood in determining the distributional outcomes of negotiation, but there is less clarity about the effect of power on whether any agreement is reached. One source of haziness is the literature's varying conceptions of power. If we think

of the power structure as piles of assets each has to play with, equality might seem more favorable to agreement than inequality, as the
weaker would avoid agreement, fearing exploitation. However, if we
conceive of power in terms of the parties' relative alternatives to agreement and of the parties as strategic thinkers, this conclusion might
not hold in general. Power asymmetry should not block agreement
when the weak party's preferences are close to those of the strong,
or when the weak party prefers not to make concessions but believes
it has a terrible alternative to agreement.

Some empirical research has addressed this question. In the special
case of civil wars, a particular asymmetry has impeded negotiated settlements. Agreement in civil wars normally means that one side, usually the rebels, must lay down its arms and cede territory to the central government. As mentioned earlier, the concentration of power in
the government's hands creates a commitment problem that explains
bargaining failures (Walter 2013). Yet a set of nine case studies representing peacetime and wartime (but not civil war) negotiations
concludes that perceived asymmetry is actually more favorable for
agreement than symmetry (Zartman and Rubin 2000), perhaps because the weaker party has ongoing reasons to please the stronger one.
This and other studies (for example, Habeeb 1988; Keohane 1971)
show that aggregate power-as-assets is not a sufficient predictor of
outcomes, partly because weaker parties can use strategies during
the process that offset their weaknesses. In some cases, paradoxically,
small size even confers some advantages (Odell 2010).

The two variables of the outcome as agreement or no deal and the
outcome as a particular distribution of gains and losses are conceptually related: the proposed distribution of a resource is part of what
an actor considers in deciding whether to accept an offer. However,
parties in principle can continue to negotiate. If there are disparities
between large and small powers, how should we think about incentives to continue negotiation? Different types of changes in power may
also have different effects. In the sphere of interstate economic negotiations, future changes in economic productivity could induce commitment problems just as shifts in military technology bear on security
negotiations. Are these two types of change in power equally problematic for negotiation, and do certain institutions provide more
buttressing than others? Finally, the role of domestic politics should

be figured more centrally into thinking about power in negotiation. A classic tension exists theoretically: leaders might use domestic politics to constrain what they can "accept" in an international negotiation, but, at the same time, the progress of international negotiations can reshape domestic politics. Hence, the source of bargaining power vis-à-vis domestic politics also remains unclear and undertheorized.

In negotiation case studies, a large underexploited opportunity is to generate a new falsifiable general proposition that could explain observed variation, which could be tested in later research, while making clear that the case study itself was not designed to test any proposition. Whereas a few have expressed this type of theoretical contribution, many have not.

Generally lacking and needed in the long term is theorizing that will show how propositions at the different levels relate to one another. As we have seen, international negotiation and bargaining research includes diverse studies sets, respectively, at the level of individuals, states, and coalitions of states as actors. For example, do particular international institutional designs encourage integrative negotiation behavior more than other designs? Is there any relation between domestic regime type and the behavior of the negotiators representing those regimes as defined in the individual-level literature? Do strategies found to facilitate agreement among states that have internal divisions have the same effects when the actors are coalitions of states whose members have divisions?

There is also great opportunity to advance further by blending elements from different analytical traditions to take advantage of cross-fertilization. For example, we might select cases in which leaders seemed not to act rationally according to rationalist theory and explain why not using cognition and culture. Lessons from case studies have been and might be used more to innovate in formal modeling. International relations constructivists writing about negotiations might build some findings from psychological negotiation studies into their own work, and other researchers might take more advantage of constructivist insights.

Finally, the lack of parsimony in the negotiation-bargaining literature is a serious weakness for some readers. Another broad challenge is to find ways to increase negotiation theory's parsimony and leverage.

If this can be accomplished without making great sacrifices of conceptual clarity, empirical validity, or utility, it would be a significant breakthrough. If actual proposals aiming for greater parsimony entail significant trade-offs, scholars may reach different judgments about the best ways to strike this balance among legitimate objectives.

Normative or Prescriptive Questions and Problems

Finally, what is the meaning of justice with reference to international negotiation, and what difference does justice make? Research on this question is in its infancy, but some basic distinctions have been blocked out. Justice can have at least two meanings. We can consider value judgments about justice or fairness as part of the parties' mental maps or preference functions, or we can consider justice instead as an external standard with which to evaluate a negotiation. A second major distinction is between judging the outcome and judging the process that produced it—that is, distributive justice versus procedural justice.

In the first sense of justice as reflective of negotiators' values, many ultimatum-bargaining experiments confirm that bargainers are concerned about the fairness of their outcomes as well as how much money they receive. Mean offers by proposers fall between 40 percent and 50 percent; 50–50 is often the mode; and responders frequently reject offers smaller than 20 percent, even though they know that their rejection entails receiving zero instead. These results are robust to many manipulations, including varying the subjects' cultures and increasing the stakes (Camerer and Thaler 1995)—even up to three times the monthly expenditure of the average Indonesian subject (Cameron 1999).

Outside the laboratory, a few negotiation studies have begun to argue that another barrier to international agreement can arise when parties adhere to different principles of justice. For instance, the difficulties negotiators have experienced in dealing with the distributive aspects of global warming show that there is little consensus in the world about the principles that should be used to assign responsibility and share costs for adaptive or preventive responses (Victor 2011). A pioneering comparative study chose two cases in which the parties held conflicting principles of justice. It found that in a case in which power was highly asymmetrical, the strong forced the weak to abandon its principle and accept the best deal it could get; in a case in which power was more symmetrical, part of the negotiation dealt with reconciling the different principles (Albin 1999). Much more research is needed to confirm and extend this line of inquiry.[26]

Turning to justice in the second sense as an external standard, a few studies aimed at helping practitioners have deployed a variety of alternative ethical standards to evaluate the ethics of various negotiation tactics, including withholding or falsifying information (Menkel-Meadow and Wheeler 2004; Reitz, Wall, and Love 1998). Chapter 5 makes a start on elaborating certain norms appropriate to negotiation. However, to our knowledge, little research has attempted to evaluate the degree of procedural justice in an international negotiation as a whole, to compare negotiations on this dimension, or to relate procedural justice to the likelihood of agreement and the duration and effectiveness of the resulting deals.

Not only negotiators but also external mediators and interveners in conflict sometimes face painful dilemmas. Consider the decisions that the British, French, and Dutch governments faced on whether to deploy their soldiers in the 1993 war in Bosnia to promote peace talks while war was under way; the decision of Dutch leaders about whether to withdraw from Srebrenica in 1995 just before its people were massacred; and the later decision of U.S. leaders about whether to bomb and kill Bosnians fighting for one side to coerce their leaders into a negotiation to end the war.

We are less aware of systematic efforts to articulate independent standards of justice or fairness for evaluating the contents of international agreements or of efforts to apply such standards uniformly to different agreements. Such efforts may not even be feasible. Advances in this area will need the expertise of political theorists and philosophers.[27]

---

26. Of course, a particular expression of a feeling of injustice could be false, merely another tactic to gain more from an agreement. A methodological challenge here is to obtain evidence of justice beliefs independent of the negotiation behavior they are to explain, as usual with arguments from ideas and beliefs. Also see Barry and Robinson (2008).

27. For background, see Beitz (1979), Kapstein (2006), and chapter 5 of this book.

These are only illustrations of the many opportunities for researchers to contribute valuable new insights to this important research program.

Note: This chapter, written primarily by John S. Odell and Dustin Tingley, draws on ideas of fellow group members: Fen Osler Hampson, Andrew H. Kydd, Brett Ashley Leeds, James K. Sebenius, Janice Gross Stein, Barbara F. Walter, and I. William Zartman. Although each scholar, if writing independently, would put things in his or her own way, the report represents a direction of thought that the members collectively endorse. Robert O. Keohane also participated in some of the task force deliberations. We are grateful to Chase Foster, Dana Higgins, and Robert Schub for excellent research assistance and to Harvard's Weatherhead Center for International and Area Studies for its vital support and hospitality.

References

Abbott, Kenneth W., and Duncan Snidal. 2000. "Hard and Soft Law in International Governance." *International Organization* 54 (3): 421–56.

Albin, Cecilia. 1999. "Justice, Fairness, and Negotiation: Theory and Reality." In *International Negotiation: Actors, Structure/Process, Values*, ed. P. Berton, H. Kimura, and I. W. Zartman. Basingstoke: Macmillan.

———. 2001. *Justice and Fairness in International Negotiation.* Cambridge University Press.

Antrim, Caitlyn Lance, and James K. Sebenius. 1992. "Formal Individual Mediation and the Negotiators' Dilemma: Tommy Koh at the Law of the Sea Conference." In *Mediation in International Relations: Multiple Approaches to Conflict Management*, ed. J. Bercovitch and J. Z. Rubin. London: Macmillan.

Axelrod, Robert. 1984. *The Evolution of Cooperation.* New York: Basic Books.

Axelrod, Robert, and Robert O. Keohane. 1986. "Achieving Cooperation under Anarchy: Strategies and Institutions." In *Cooperation under Anarchy*, ed. K. A. Oye. Princeton University Press.

Babcock, Linda, and George Loewenstein. 1997. "Explaining Bargaining Impasse: The Role of Self-Serving Biases." *Journal of Economic Perspectives* 11 (1): 109–26.

Baldwin, David. 2013. "Power and International Relations." In *Handbook of International Relations*, ed. W. Carlsnaes, T. Risse, and B. A. Simmons. Thousand Oaks, CA: Sage.

Barnett, Michael N., and Raymond Duvall. 2005. *Power in Global Governance.* Cambridge University Press.

Barry, Bruce. 2008. "Negotiator Affect: The State of the Art (and the Science)." *Group Decision and Negotiation* 17 (1): 97–105.

Barry, Bruce, and Robert J. Robinson. 2008. "Ethics in Conflict Resolution: The Ties that Bind, a Special Issue." *International Negotiation* 7 (2): 137–285.

Bazerman, Max H., Robert Gibbons, Leigh Thompson, and Kathleen L. Valley. 1995. "When and Why Do Negotiators Outperform Game Theory?" In *The Role of Nonrationality in Organizational Decision Making: Current Research into the Nature and Processes of the Informal Organization*, ed. R. Stern and J. Halpern. Cornell University, ILR Press.

Bazerman, Max H., and Margaret Ann Neale. 1992. *Negotiating Rationally.* New York: Free Press.

Beardsley, Kyle. 2008. "Agreement without Peace? International Mediation and Time Inconsistency Problems." *American Journal of Political Science* 52 (4): 723–40.

Beitz, Charles R. 1979. *Political Theory and International Relations.* Princeton University Press.

Benedick, Richard Elliot. 1991. *Ozone Diplomacy: New Directions in Safeguarding the Planet.* Harvard University Press.

Bercovitch, Jacob. 1996. "Understanding Mediation's Role in Preventive Diplomacy." *Negotiation Journal* 12 (3): 241–58.

Brett, Jeanne M., Wendi Adair, Alain Lempereur, Tetsushi Okumura, Peter Shikhirev, Catherine Tinsley, and Ann Lytle. 1998. "Culture and Joint Gains in Negotiation." *Negotiation Journal* 14:61–87.

Buzan, Barry. 1981. "Negotiating by Consensus: Developments in Technique at the United Nations Conference on the Law of the Sea." *American Journal of International Law* 75:324–48.

Calvert, Randall L. 1985. "The Value of Biased Information: A Rational Choice Model of Political Advice." *Journal of Politics* 47 (2): 530–55.

Camerer, Colin, and Richard H. Thaler. 1995. "Anomalies: Ultimatums, Dictators and Manners." *Journal of Economic Perspectives* 9 (2): 209–19.

Cameron, Lisa A. 1999. "Raising the Stakes in the Ultimatum Game: Experimental Evidence from Indonesia." *Economic Inquiry* 37 (1): 47–59.

Carnevale, Peter J. 2008. "Positive Affect and Decision Frame in Negotiation." *Group Decision and Negotiation* 17:51–63.

Carnevale, Peter J., and Carsten K. W. De Dreu. 2006. *Methods of Negotiation Research*. Boston: Martinus Nijhoff Publishers/Brill Academic.

Chilton, A., and D. Tingley. 2013. "Why the Study of International Law Needs Experiments." *Columbia Journal of Transnational Law* 52 (1): 173–238.

Copelovitch, Mark S., and Tonya L. Putnam. 2014. "Design in Context: Existing International Agreements and New Cooperation." *International Organization* 68 (2): 471–93.

Crocker, Chester A., Fen O. Hampson, and Pamela Aall. 2002. *Taming Intractable Conflicts: Mediation in the Hardest Cases*. Washington, DC: United States Institute of Peace.

Curran, Daniel, James K. Sebenius, and Michael Watkins. 2004. "Two Paths to Peace: Contrasting George Mitchell in Northern Ireland with Richard Holbrooke in Bosnia-Herzegovina." *Negotiation Journal* 20 (4): 513–37.

Deitelhoff, Nicole, and Harald Müller. 2005. "Theoretical Paradise—Empirically Lost? Arguing with Habermas." *Review of International Studies* 31 (1): 167–79.

Dixon, William J. 1993. "Democracy and the Management of International Conflict." *Journal of Conflict Resolution* 34 (1): 42–68.

Druckman, Daniel. 2001. "Turning Points in International Negotiation—A Comparative Analysis." *Journal of Conflict Resolution* 45 (4): 519–44.

Dupont, Cédric, Cosimo Beverelli, and Stéphanie Pézard. 2006. "Learning in Multilateral Trade Negotiations: Some Results from

Simulation for Developing Countries." In *Negotiating Trade: Developing Countries in the WTO and NAFTA*, ed. J. S. Odell. Cambridge University Press.

Dür, Andreas, and Gemma Mateo. 2010. "Bargaining Power and Negotiation Tactics: The Negotiations on the EU's Financial Perspective, 2007–13." *Journal of Common Market Studies* 48 (3): 557–78.

Eckes, Alfred E., Jr. 1975. *A Search for Solvency*. University of Texas Press.

Elgström, Ole, and Christer Jönsson. 2000. "Negotiation in the European Union: Bargaining or Problem-Solving?" *Journal of European Public Policy* 7 (5): 684–704.

Elms, Deborah. 2006. How Bargaining Alters Outcomes: Bilateral Trade Negotiations and Bargaining Strategies. *International Negotiation* 11 (3): 399–429.

Fearon, James D. 1995. "Rationalist Explanations for War." *International Organization* 49 (3): 379–414.

———. 1998. "Bargaining, Enforcement, and International Cooperation." *International Organization* 52 (2): 269–305.

Fey, Mark, and Kristopher W. Ramsay. 2010. "When Is Shuttle Diplomacy Worth the Commute? Information Sharing through Mediation." *World Politics* 62 (4): 529–60.

Follett, Mary Parker. [1929] 1995. "Constructive Conflict." In *Mary Parker Follett: Prophet of Management*, ed. P. Graham. Harvard Business School Press.

Fortna, Virginia Page. 2003. "Scraps of Paper? Agreements and the Durability of Peace." *International Organization* 57 (2): 337–72.

Funabashi, Yoichi. 1988. *Managing the Dollar: From the Plaza to the Louvre*. Washington, DC: Institute for International Economics.

Gerber, Alan S, and Donald P Green. 2012. *Field Experiments: Design, Analysis, and Interpretation*. New York: W. W. Norton.

Goldstein, Judith, Miles Kahler, Robert O. Keohane, and Anne-Marie Slaughter. 2000. "Introduction: Legalization and World Politics." *International Organization* 54 (3): 385–99.

Haas, Ernst B. 1980. "Why Collaborate? Issue-Linkage and International Regimes." *World Politics* 32:357–405.

Habeeb, William Mark. 1988. *Power and Tactics in International Negotiations: How Weak Nations Bargain with Strong Nations*. Johns Hopkins University Press.

Hafner-Burton, Emilie, Brad LeVeck, David Victor, and James Fowler. 2014. "Decision Maker Preferences for International Legal Cooperation." *International Organization* 68: 845–76.

Hampson, Fen Osler, and Michael Hart. 1995. *Multilateral Negotiations: Lessons from Arms Control, Trade and the Environment.* Johns Hopkins University Press.

Hampson, Fen Osler, and Bill Zartman. 2012. *The Global Power of Talk*. Boulder, CO: Paradigm.

Holbrooke, Richard. 1999. *To End a War*. New York: Modern Library.

Hopmann, P. Terrence. 1974. "Bargaining in Arms Control Negotiations: The Sea Beds Denuclearization Treaty." *International Organization* 28 (3): 313–443.

———. 2002. "Negotiating Data: Reflections on the Qualitative and Quantitative Analysis of Negotiating Processes." *International Negotiation* 7 (1): 67–85.

Iklé, Fred Charles. 1964. *How Nations Negotiate*. New York: Harper and Row.

Jones, Bruce D. 2001. *Peacemaking in Rwanda: The Dynamics of Failure*. Boulder, CO: Lynne Rienner Publishers.

Jönsson, Christer, and Jonas Tallberg. 1998. "Compliance and Post-Agreement Bargaining." *European Journal of International Relations* 4:371–408.

Jupille, Joseph. 1999. "The European Union and International Outcomes." *International Organization* 53 (2): 409–25.

Kahler, Miles. 2000. "Conclusion: The Causes and Consequences of Legalization." *International Organization* 54 (3): 661–83.

Kapstein, Ethan B. 2006. *Economic Justice in an Unfair World: Toward a Level Playing Field*. Princeton University Press.

Kelman, Herbert C. 1996. "The Interactive Problem-Solving Approach." In *Managing Global Chaos: Sources of and Responses to International Conflict*, ed. C. A. Crocker, F. O. Hampson, and P. Aall. Washington, DC: United States Institute of Peace Press.

Kennedy School of Government. 1979. *Panama Canal Treaty Negotiations, Part A and Part B*. Harvard University.

Keohane, Robert O. 1971. "The Big Influence of Small Allies." *Foreign Policy* 2:161–82.

———. 1984. *After Hegemony: Cooperation and Discord in the World Political Economy*. Princeton University Press.

Knight, Frank H. 1921. *Risk, Uncertainty and Profit*. Boston: Houghton.

Kobrin, Stephen J. 1998. "The MAI and the Clash of Globalizations." *Foreign Policy* 112:97–109.

Kopelman, Shirli, and Ashleigh Shelby Rosette. 2008. "Cultural Variation in Response to Strategic Emotions in Negotiation." *Group Decision and Negotiation* 17 (1): 65–77.

Koremenos, Barbara. 2001. "Loosening the Ties that Bind: A Learning Model of Agreement Flexibility." *International Organization* 55 (2): 289–325.

———. 2005. "Contracting around International Uncertainty." *American Political Science Review* 99 (4): 549–65.

Koremenos, Barbara, Charles Lipson, and Duncan Snidal. 2001. "The Rational Design of International Institutions." *International Organization* 55 (4): 761–99.

Krasner, Stephen D. 1991. "Global Communications and National Power: Life on the Pareto Frontier." *World Politics* 43 (3): 336–66.

Kydd, Andrew. 2000. "Trust, Reassurance, and Cooperation." *International Organization* 54 (2): 325–57.

———. 2003. "Which Side Are You On? Bias, Credibility, and Mediation." *American Journal of Political Science* 47 (4): 597–611.

———. 2010. "Rationalist Approaches to Conflict Prevention and Resolution." *Annual Review of Political Science* 13:101–21.

———. 2012. "A Failure to Communicate: Uncertainty, Information, and Unsuccessful Negotiations." In *Unfinished Business: Why International Negotiations Fail*, ed. G. O. Faure. University of Georgia Press.

Lax, David A., and James K. Sebenius. 1986. *The Manager as Negotiator: Bargaining for Cooperation and Competitive Gain*. New York: Free Press.

———. 2006. *3–D Negotiation: Powerful Tools to Change the Game in Your Most Important Negotiations*. Harvard Business School Press.

Leeds, Brett Ashley. 1999. "Domestic Political Institutions, Credible Commitments, and International Cooperation." *American Journal of Political Science* 43 (4): 979–1002.

Lin, Xiaohua, and Stephen J. Miller. 2003. "Negotiation Approaches: Direct and Indirect Effect of National Culture." *International Marketing Review* 20 (3): 286–303.

Lipson, Charles. 2003. *Reliable Partners: How Democracies Have Made a Separate Peace.* Princeton University Press.

Mahoney, James. 2010. "After KKV: The New Methodology of Qualitative Research." *World Politics* 62 (1): 120–47.

Malhotra, Deepak, and Max H. Bazerman. 2007. *Negotiation Genius.* New York: Bantam Dell.

Martin, Lisa L. 1992. *Coercive Cooperation: Explaining Multilateral Economic Sanctions.* Princeton University Press.

McDermott, Rose. 2001. *Risk-Taking in International Politics: Prospect Theory in American Foreign Policy.* University of Michigan Press.

———. 2004. "The Feeling of Rationality: The Meaning of Neuroscientific Advances for Political Science." *Perspectives on Politics* 2 (4): 691–706.

McNamara, Robert S., James Blight, and Robert Brigham. 1999. *Argument without End: In Search of Answers to the Vietnam Tragedy.* New York: Public Affairs.

Menkel-Meadow, Carrie, and Michael Wheeler, eds. 2004. *What's Fair: Ethics for Negotiators.* San Francisco, CA: Program on Negotiation and Jossey-Bass.

Mercer, Jonathan. 2005. "Rationality and Psychology in International Politics." *International Organization* 59:77–106.

———. 2010. "Emotional Beliefs." *International Organization* 64 (1): 1–32.

Miles, Michael. 2000. "Power and Relationship: Two Elements of the Chinese/Western Divide." *Journal of Comparative International Management* 3 (1): 39–54.

Milner, Helen V. 1997. *Interests, Institutions, and Information: Domestic Politics and International Relations.* Princeton University Press.

Mintz, Alex. 2007. "Why Behavioral IR?" *International Studies Review* 9 (1): 157–62.

Mitchell, George. 1998. Address at the University of Southern California, October 14.

Mitchell, Ronald B., and Patricia M. Keilbach. 2001. "Situation Structure and Institutional Design: Reciprocity, Coercion, and Exchange." *International Organization* 55 (4): 891–917.

Morris, Michael W., and Michele J. Gelfand. 2004. "Cultural Differences and Cognitive Dynamics: Expanding the Cognitive Perspective on Negotiation." In *The Handbook of Negotiation and Culture*, ed. M. J. Gelfand and J. M. Brett. Stanford University Press.

Morrow, James. 1999. "The Strategic Setting of Choices: Signaling, Commitment, and Negotiation in International Politics." In *Strategic Choice and International Relations*, ed. D. A. Lake and R. Powell. Princeton University Press.

Niemann, Arne. 2006. "Beyond Problem-Solving and Bargaining: Genuine Debate in EU External Trade Negotiations." *International Negotiation* 11 (3): 467–97.

Odell, John S. 2000. *Negotiating the World Economy*. Cornell University Press.

———. 2005. "Chairing a WTO Negotiation." *Journal of International Economic Law* 8 (2): 425–48.

———. 2009. "Breaking Deadlocks in International Institutional Negotiations: The WTO, Seattle and Doha." *International Studies Quarterly* 53 (2): 273–99.

———. 2010. "Negotiating from Weakness in International Trade Relations." *Journal of World Trade* 44 (3): 545–66.

———. 2013. "Negotiation and Bargaining." In *Handbook of International Relations*, ed. W. Carlsnaes, T. Risse, and B. A. Simmons. London: Sage.

Odell, John, and David Lang. 1992. *Korean Joggers*. Georgetown University, Institute for the Study of Diplomacy, School of Foreign Service.

Ostrom, Elinor. 1998. "A Behavioral Approach to the Rational Choice Theory of Collective Action: Presidential Address, American Political Science Association." *American Political Science Review* 92 (1): 1–22.

Paemen, Hugo, and Alexandra Bensch. 1995. *From the GATT to the WTO: The European Community in the Uruguay Round*. Leuven University Press.

Poast, Paul. 2012. "Does Issue Linkage Work? Evidence from European Alliance Negotiations, 1860 to 1945." *International Organization* 66 (2): 277–310.

Powell, Robert. 2006. "War as a Commitment Problem." *International Organization* 60 (1): 169–203.

Price, Richard. 1998. "Reversing the Gun Sights: Transnational Civil Society Targets Land Mines." *International Organization* 52: 613–44.

Przeworski, Adam. 1991. *Democracy and the Market: Political and Economic Reforms in Eastern Europe and Latin America.* Cambridge University Press.

Putnam, Robert D. 1988. "Diplomacy and Domestic Politics: The Logic of Two-Level Games." *International Organization* 42:427–60.

Rabin, Matthew. 1998. "Psychology and Economics." *Journal of Economic Literature* 36 (1): 11–46.

Raiffa, Howard, John Richardson, and David Metcalfe. 2002. *Negotiation Analysis: The Science and Art of Collaborative Decision Making.* Harvard University Press.

Ramsay, Kristopher W. 2011. "Cheap Talk Diplomacy, Voluntary Negotiations, and Variable Bargaining Power." *International Studies Quarterly* 55 (4): 1003–23.

Rathbun, Brian C. 2011. "Before Hegemony: Generalized Trust, International Cooperation and the Design of International Organizations." *International Organization* 45 (2): 243–73.

Reitz, H. Joseph, James A. Wall Jr., and Mary Sue Love. 1998. "Ethics in Negotiation: Oil and Water or Good Lubrication?" *Business Horizons* 41 (3): 5–15.

Rosendorff, B. Peter, and Helen V. Milner. 2001. "The Optimal Design of International Trade Institutions: Uncertainty and Escape." *International Organization* 55 (4): 829–57.

Rothchild, Donald. 1996. "Successful Mediation: Lord Carrington and the Rhodesian Settlement." In *Managing Global Chaos: Sources of and Responses to International Conflict,* ed. C. A. Crocker, F. O. Hampson, and P. Aall. Washington, DC: United States Institute of Peace.

Savun, Burcu. 2008. "Information, Bias, and Mediation Success." *International Studies Quarterly* 52 (1): 25–47.

Schelling, Thomas C. 1960. *The Strategy of Conflict*. Harvard University Press.

Schoppa, Leonard J. 1993. "Two-Level Games and Bargaining Outcomes: Why Gaiatsu Succeeds in Japan in Some Cases but Not Others." *International Organization* 47 (3): 353–86.

Schultz, Kenneth A. 1999. "Do Democratic Institutions Constrain or Inform? Contrasting Two Institutional Perspectives on Democracy and War." *International Organization* 53 (2): 233–66.

Sebenius, James K. 1984. *Negotiating the Law of the Sea: Lessons in the Art and Science of Reaching Agreement*. Harvard University Press.

———. 1996. "Sequencing to Build Coalitions: With Whom Should I Talk First?" In *Wise Choices: Decisions, Games, and Negotiations*, ed. R. J. Zeckhauser, R. L. Keeney, and J. K. Sebenius. Harvard Business School Press.

Simmons, Beth A. 2009. *Mobilizing for Human Rights: International Law in Domestic Politics*. Cambridge University Press.

Singh, J. P. 2008. *Negotiation and the Global Information Economy*. Cambridge University Press.

Spector, Bertram, and I. William Zartman. 2003. *Getting It Done: Post-Agreement Negotiation and International Regimes*. Washington, DC: United States Institute of Peace Press.

Stein, Janice Gross, ed. 1989. *Getting to the Table: The Processes of International Prenegotiation*. Johns Hopkins University Press.

Steinberg, Richard H. 2002. "In the Shadow of Law or Power? Consensus-Based Bargaining and Outcomes in the GATT/WTO." *International Organization* 56 (2): 339–74.

Susskind, Lawrence E. 1994. *Environmental Diplomacy: Negotiating More Effective Global Agreements*. Oxford University Press.

Tallberg, Jonas. 2010. "The Power of the Chair: Formal Leadership in International Cooperation." *International Studies Quarterly* 54:241–65.

Tallberg, Jonas, and James McCall Smith. 2012. "Dispute Settlement in World Politics: States, Supranational Prosecutors, and Compliance." *European Journal of International Relations Online*. http://ssrn.com/abstract=2181027.

Telhami, Shibley. 1990. *Power and Leadership in International Bargaining: The Path to the Camp David Accords.* Columbia University Press.

Thompson, Leigh L. 2001. *The Mind and Heart of the Negotiator.* 2nd ed. Upper Saddle River, NJ: Prentice Hall.

Thompson, Leigh, and Dennis Hrebec. 1996. "Lose-Lose Agreements in Interdependent Decision Making." *Psychological Bulletin* 120 (3): 396–409.

Tingley, Dustin H. 2011. "The Dark Side of the Future: An Experimental Test of Commitment Problems in Bargaining." *International Studies Quarterly* 55:1–24.

Tingley, D., J. Lee, and J. Renshon. 2013. "Physiological Responses to Shifting Bargaining Power: Micro-Foundations of Commitment Problems in International Politics." http://scholar.harvard.edu/dtingley/publications/term/1458.

Tollison, Robert, and Thomas D. Willett. 1979. "An Economic Theory of Mutually Advantageous Issue Linkages in International Negotiations." *International Organization* 33 (4): 425–49.

Ulbert, Cornelia, and Thomas Risse. 2005. "Deliberately Changing the Discourse: What Does Make Arguing Effective?" *Acta Politica* 40:351–67.

Victor, David G. 2011. *Global Warming Gridlock: Creating More Effective Strategies for Protecting the Planet.* Cambridge University Press.

Vietor, Richard H. K. 1982. "Mexican Natural Gas." Series of case studies for teaching. Harvard Business School.

Walter, Barbara F. 2013. "Civil Wars, Conflict Resolution, and Bargaining Theory." In *Handbook of International Relations*, ed. W. Carlsnaes, T. Risse, and B. A. Simmons. London: Sage.

Walton, Richard E., and Robert B. McKersie. 1965. *A Behavioral Theory of Labor Negotiations: An Analysis of a Social Interaction System.* New York: McGraw-Hill.

Weeks, Jessica. 2008. "Autocratic Audience Costs: Regime Type and Signaling Resolve." *International Organization* 62 (1): 35–64.

Weiss, Stephen E. 2006. "International Business Negotiation in a Globalizing World: Reflections on the Contributions and Future of a (Sub) Field." *International Negotiation* 11:287–316.

Winham, Gilbert R. 1980. "Robert Strauss, the MTN, and the Control of Faction." *Journal of World Trade Law* 14 (5): 377–97.

————. 1986. *International Trade and the Tokyo Round Negotiation*. Princeton University Press.

Wriggins, W. Howard. 1976. "Up for Auction: Malta Bargains with Great Britain, 1971." In *The 50% Solution*, ed. I. W. Zartman. Garden City, NY: Anchor Press/Doubleday.

Young, Oran R. 1989. "The Politics of International Regime Formation: Managing Natural Resources and the Environment." *International Organization* 43 (3): 349–76.

————. 1994. *International Governance: Protecting the Environment in a Stateless Society*. Cornell University Press.

Zartman, I. William. 1987. *Positive Sum: Improving North-South Negotiations*. New Brunswick, NJ: Transaction Books.

————. 2000. "Ripeness: The Hurting Stalemate and Beyond." In *International Conflict Resolution after the Cold War*, ed. P. C. Stern and D. Druckman. Washington, DC: National Academy Press.

Zartman, I. William, and Maureen R. Berman. 1982. *The Practical Negotiator*. Yale University Press.

Zartman, I. William, and Jeffrey Z. Rubin. 2000. *Power and Negotiation*. University of Michigan Press.

Contributors

MICHAEL BARBER
Brigham Young University

SARAH A. BINDER
George Washington University

CHASE FOSTER
Harvard University

FRANCES E. LEE
University of Maryland

JANE MANSBRIDGE
Harvard University

CATHIE JO MARTIN
Boston University

NOLAN MCCARTY
Princeton University

JOHN S. ODELL
University of Southern California

DUSTIN TINGLEY
Harvard University

MARK E. WARREN
University of British Columbia

Index

Private space for deliberation (cont.)
opportunities for, in Congress, 27, 107;
rationale, 3–4, 9, 14, 27, 105–07, 174–77,
208; records of proceedings held in,
182–83; as threat to democratic norms,
178–81
Problem-solving orientation, 122, 127, 243
Promises, 237
Proportional representation democracies,
8, 16–18, 210–12, 214–15
Provisional deal negotiations, in
international relations, 254–64
Psychological approaches to negotiation
analysis, 8, 235, 238–41
Public interest penalty default, 14, 18, 28
Public support for negotiating position,
259–60
Pure bargaining: defined, 12; deliberative
negotiation and, 11, 141, 165, 167–68;
democratic norms and, 167; integrative
negotiation and, 12, 158; market
transactions, 168; negative connotations,
165–66; in spectrum of agreement-
seeking procedures, 153, 155, 160–61,
165
Pure deliberation: defined, 11, 155;
deliberative negotiation and, 11, 141;
leading to informed consensus, 161;
power relations in, 150; in spectrum
of agreement-seeking procedures, 153,
155, 161, 165

Racial and ethnic differences, 51
Rational-choice tradition, 235–38
Reactive devaluation, 132, 203
Reagan administration, 16, 254–55
Reconciliation bills, 68
Recursive decisionmaking, 206
Redistricting, 3
Reframing issues and perspectives,
255–57, 265
Regional differences: in political
polarization, 40; Southern realignment
theory of political polarization, 3, 49–51
Regret aversion, 132
Repeated interactions among parties: in
consensus governments, 219–20, 224;
in corporatist system of governance,
214; in international relations, 22;
lessons from European democracies,
205–06; long incumbencies to promote,
13, 109, 173; polarization and, 64,
134–35; in private sector, 27–28;

rationale, 3–4, 9, 13, 27, 135–36,
172–74, 205–06; system of democratic
governance and, 18–19; in U.S.
Congress, 27–28, 64, 109–10,
134–35
Republican Party, 25, 28, 76, 102–03,
107, 113–14; case study of immigration
legislation gridlock, 69–72; evidence
of polarization, 39, 40; lame-duck
Congress of 2010, 75–77; Southern
realignment theory of political
polarization, 49–51. See also Partisan
politics
Reservation values, 234
Resistance points, 234
Resistance to tyranny, 143–44
Rhodesia, 260
Rove, Karl, 128
Rules of collective political engagement:
defined, 3, 12; differences across
democratic systems and nations,
14–21, 200, 209–16, 224; to facilitate
deliberative negotiation, 3, 9–10,
12–14, 200–202, 203–08; in
international relations, 4–5, 21–22;
lessons from European democracies,
203–08; to overcome negotiation
myopia, 3, 8; significance of, 12;
strategies for facilitating negotiation,
27–28; in U.S., 223–24. See also
Penalty defaults; Private space for
deliberation; Repeated interactions
among parties; Technical expertise
for policy formulation
Rwanda, 249

Sebenius, J., 122
Security points, 234
Self-interest, 168–69
Self-serving bias, 2, 10; defined, 127, 202;
effects on negotiations, 128–30, 203;
forms of, 121; strategies for reducing,
121, 130–31; susceptibility to, 127–28,
129–30
Senate, U.S.: bipartisanship in, 100–101;
causes of polarization in, 51, 54, 55,
61; debate and cloture in, 66–68;
obstructionist tactics in, 66, 67–68,
75, 113. See also Congress, U.S.
Sensenbrenner, F. James, Jr., 101
Sensenbrenner Bill, 70
Separation of powers: implications for
negotiation and governance, 3, 8,

CPSIA information can be obtained at www.ICGtesting.com
Printed in the USA
BVOW02s2306271015

423805BV00002B/2/P